ORIGINAL SIN

Also by Stanly Johny

The Comrades and the Mullahs:
China, Afghanistan and the New Asian Geopolitics
(co-written with Ananth Krishnan)

ORIGINAL SIN

ISRAEL, PALESTINE
AND THE
REVENGE
OF
OLD WEST ASIA

STANLY JOHNY

HarperCollins *Publishers* India

First published in India by HarperCollins *Publishers* 2024
4th Floor, Tower A, Building No. 10, DLF Cyber City,
DLF Phase II, Gurugram, Haryana – 122002
www.harpercollins.co.in

2 4 6 8 10 9 7 5 3 1

Copyright © Stanly Johny 2024
Author photo courtesy of Dinesh Krishnan

P-ISBN: 978-93-6213-278-9
E-ISBN: 978-93-6213-953-5

The views and opinions expressed in this book are the author's own and the facts are as reported by him, and the publishers are not in any way liable for the same.

Stanly Johny asserts the moral right
to be identified as the author of this work.

All rights reserved. No part of this publication may be reproduced, stored in a retrieval system, or transmitted, in any form or by any means, electronic, mechanical, photocopying, recording or otherwise, without the prior permission of the publishers.

Typeset in 12/16.2 Arno Pro at
HarperCollins *Publishers* India

Printed and bound at
Thomson Press (India) Ltd

This book is produced from independently certified FSC® paper
to ensure responsible forest management.

For Johny Paul Mambilly,

the man who opened a window to the world for me

Contents

Introduction — ix

1. In Search of a Homeland — 1
2. War and Un-peace — 19
3. A Passage to the West Bank — 41
4. Axis of Resistance — 60
5. The Partisan Superpower — 84
6. A Troubled Brotherhood — 105
7. 7 October 2023 — 129
8. The View from India — 153

Conclusion: The Revenge of Old West Asia — 173
Notes — 187

Introduction

IN 2018, I was in Ramallah, the de facto administrative capital of the Palestine Authority, to cover Prime Minister Narendra Modi's visit to Palestine. After Modi wrapped up his visit, I prepared to leave the city. My flight was from Tel Aviv's Ben Gurion Airport. While leaving the West Bank for Tel Aviv, my driver, a Palestinian Arab from occupied East Jerusalem, warned me about the Israeli check-points on the way. I had to call a taxi from Jerusalem to come and pick me up from Ramallah and drop me in Tel Aviv as taxi drivers in Ramallah are not allowed to go to Tel Aviv and Israeli taxis seldom come to Ramallah.

There were three check-points between Ramallah and the Tel Aviv airport. The first, in Kalandia, is the main check-point between the northern West Bank and Jerusalem. Thousands of Palestinians who live in the northern West Bank and work on the other side of 'the security wall' (which the Palestinians call the 'apartheid wall') cross this point every day. My driver greeted the soldier with a 'shalom' while he handed him his permit card. I gave my passport to the soldier with the entry permit, a separate slip of paper with my photo, passport details and the state of Israel's stamp on it that was issued by Border Control at the airport. We were asked to wait. I could see long queues of Palestinians waiting to cross the barrier. 'Free Palestine' slogans and anti-Israel graffiti were drawn on the Palestinian side of the giant wall. A while later, the soldier returned my passport and the permit, and waved us on.

From there, we entered Highway 443, which Israel had built to link Jerusalem, the holy but contested city, with Tel Aviv, Israel's commercial capital. The driver told me in broken English that the road was not open for Palestinians living in the West Bank. 'On the right is Palestine, on the left is Palestine, but this road, this is Israel,' he said, no sign of anger detected in his voice. He was able to enter the road because he lived in East Jerusalem, which had been captured by Israel in the 1967 Six-Day War and formally annexed in 1980 through the Jerusalem Law. At the exit points, the road was blocked by concrete walls or metal wires. This was what journalist Rachel Shabi had referred to as 'the apartheid road'.[1]

At the third check-point, we were stopped again. The soldier, with an automatic rifle in his hand, asked for the driver's permit and my passport. After a while, he came back and asked me why I'd gone to Ramallah. I said I had gone there to cover the Indian Prime Minister's visit. This was also written on my Israeli visa, which was stamped on my passport. The soldier did not look convinced. Another soldier asked me to get out of the car with my belongings and go to the screening room. He wasn't polite. There, three soldiers stood holding guns. I was told to take out everything from my bag, remove my belt and jacket, and walk through the screener. I handed everything to them, literally at gunpoint, including a souvenir of the Church of Nativity that I had bought in Bethlehem for my mother.

After the examination, the soldiers asked me to go to the adjacent room and wait while my bag remained in the screening room. My driver then came smiling. Again, it was just the two of us. The doors were shut. One screen was there on the wall, facing us. My passport was with them. My belongings were with them. 'Are you all right?' the driver asked me, holding his belt in one hand, still no sign of tension in his voice. 'Sorry. This is all because of me. I am an Arab from Jerusalem. Don't worry, I go through this every day,' he said, while sitting beside me on the only bench in that small room. After some twenty minutes, the door opened. One soldier returned my passport and asked me to take my stuff and leave. In the screening room, I repacked my bags and walked towards the car.

At Ben Gurion Airport, Tel Aviv, a security official stopped me again. He asked me why I'd visited Ramallah, how many days I'd stayed there, why I was travelling alone, whether this was the first time I was travelling to Israel (it wasn't) and whether I had left my bag unattended. He also walked away with my passport. After a while, another officer came only to ask me the same questions before vanishing. I waited not knowing what to do next. After some twenty minutes, an official returned my passport. 'Have a safe flight, sir,' he said, with a stiff face.

The experience was intimidating, to say the least. I had never been interrogated like that before. I wondered, if this is what a journalist from India, which has friendly ties with Israel, who went to Palestine to cover a Prime Minister's visit, faces, what would others who want to travel to Palestine experience? Or what the ordinary Palestinian, who has to pass through multiple Israel checkpoints even in Palestinian territories, must be experiencing in their daily life. Israel claims to be 'the Middle East's only democracy'. It's an ally of 'the free world'. It's protected and defended by the United States, the world's most powerful country. In the seventy-six years of its existence, the state of Israel has built itself as a powerful entity in a largely hostile region. It has multiple parties, free elections, and autonomous institutions. It has a vibrant civil society. An Israeli diplomat in Delhi told me in 2015 that the religious minorities in Israel are better off than the minorities living in any other country in the region. Despite all the progress it has made, there has been a dark reality surrounding the state of Israel—the continuing occupation of the Palestinian territories. Israeli politicians and officials are proud of the country's democratic institutions, freedoms and electoral system. But Palestinians in the West Bank, East Jerusalem and Gaza Strip, the territories that have been under the direct or indirect military occupation of Israel since 1948, are living under a different system.[2]

When I first saw the news about Hamas's 7 October, 2023 attack in Israel, in which some 1,200 people were killed, my experience at the check-point near Tel Aviv airport crossed my mind once again. I was shocked by the brutality of Hamas's attack but not surprised by the attack itself. Just a year ago, in November 2022, I was on the Gaza border, talking to Israeli Defence Forces officers. They told me how Israel, with help from advanced technologies, underground and overland barriers and manpower, managed to bring temporary calm to the border.[3] But the most obvious question I had was how the Israelis could sustain the status quo. Or how long the Palestinians would continue to live under the occupation silently. Israel had withdrawn from Gaza in 2005, but the tiny enclave of 2.3 million people, which had been controlled by Hamas since 2007, has remained under Israel's air, land and naval blockade (except the Rafah crossing in the south with Egypt). And in the West Bank and East Jerusalem, where hundreds of Palestinians were killed every year by the Israeli forces, violence became the new normal. I came back to India and wrote in *The Hindu* that an uneasy calm was prevailing in Gaza 'amid worries of the next peak'.[4]

The Hamas attack was brutal. On 8 October 2023, I talked to a journalist friend in Jerusalem who told me, 'This terror changes everything.' Six months after the attack, I visited the Jewish communities on the Gaza border which had been raided by Hamas militants and witnessed the lingering effects of the horror on the local populace. A majority of the victims were civilians, including women and children. I was asking myself the same question that many students of West Asia faced in the aftermath of 7 October—why did Hamas do this? Is it because Hamas is a Jew-hating, murderous, terrorist group that wants to destroy Israel, as Israel's leaders and right-wing intellectuals claim? Or is it because, as liberals in the West would say, Hamas hates Israel's freedoms? Can Hamas's actions be seen as insulated terror attacks, like, say, those of the Islamic State, or be placed in the ongoing Israel–Palestine conflict? Is Hamas a national liberation organization, as Palestinians and many of their supporters argue? Even if that's the case, can its violent means be justified? And can Israel and other world powers move on ignoring the original sin of West Asia, which they tried to do pre-7 October—the continuing military occupation of Palestinian territories by the Jewish state? The idea of this book was born out of my quest to find answers to these questions.

This is more of a reporter's book than a researcher's thesis. I have travelled across West Asia over the past few years for work and have interviewed dozens of serving and retired military officers, diplomats and politicians. Their words helped me connect the dots between the historical lessons I'd learnt in university libraries and the contemporary realities on the Arab and Jewish streets. In this book, I have tried to offer a close view of one of the most complicated crises of the post-war world based on my historical understanding, research and on-the-ground reporting. 'When in Rome, do as the Romans do,' an Iranian friend told me on a chilly morning in February 2022. 'If you want to understand West Asia, you should start thinking like a West Asian.'

The book is divided into nine chapters, including the conclusion. **Chapter One** explores the historical roots of the Israel–Palestine conflict, which did not break out on 7 October 2023. The state of Israel was created in May 1948 in what was then called Mandatory Palestine, which was earlier part of the Ottoman Empire and had been under British rule since the end of the First World War. Jews, fleeing persecution in Europe, had started arriving in Palestine in the late nineteenth century and building their communes. The organizing principle of the settler movement was Zionism. This chapter is written as the detailed profiles of three key figures in the Zionist movement from its origin to the creation of the state of Israel—Theodor Herzl, the Austro-Hungarian journalist who is seen as the father of modern political Zionism; Chaim Weizmann, the Russian-born biochemist who transformed the Zionist movement into a powerful organization in Europe and became the first President of the State of Israel; and David Ben-Gurion, the Zionist leader in Palestine who organized the settler Jews and led the movement to the creation of the state of Israel and became its first Prime Minister.

The creation of the state of Israel in Palestine triggered violent responses from the neighbouring Arab countries, including Egypt, Jordan and Syria. In the subsequent first Arab-Israeli war, Israel, which captured more territories of Palestine than even what the UN Partition Plan had proposed, established in undisputable terms that it was not going anywhere. This altered the regional dynamics and triggered many more wars. In 1967, by defeating its immediate Arab neighbours in six days, Israel established its military dominance across the region. But that would not stop the outbreak of another war, in 1973, between Israel, Egypt and Syria. After the 1973 war, Arabs would lose their appetite for a direct conflict with Israel over Palestine, but the rise of non-state actors such as Hezbollah, Hamas and Islamic Jihad, and Israel's occupation of Palestine and Southern Lebanon would mean that violence would continue. West Asia also witnessed multiple peace bids such as the Camp David talks, the Oslo process, the Arab Peace Initiative, the Middle East Quartet proposal and the Abraham Accords. These summits would see some positive outcomes, such as Arab-Israel reconciliation, but the Palestine question would remain unresolved. **Chapter Two** offers a broad historical view of both the wars and the peace talks that have taken place since the creation of the state of Israel and explores why peace remains elusive.

My first visit to the West Bank was in 2015. I had an Israeli visa stamped on my passport. I landed at Ben Gurion Airport, and then boarded a media van to go to the border, where I deboarded, crossed a check-point and took another vehicle on the Palestinian side. I saw first hand how the Palestinians lived under the Israeli occupation. The Palestinian Authority, the provisional administration that runs parts of the West Bank, is powerless by design and practice. Palestinian towns were encapsuled—one was separated from the other by Israeli check-points. There was palpable frustration and anger among Palestinians, both towards the Israeli occupation and their own leadership. **Chapter Three** is about the West Bank I saw and the Palestinians I met and what they said about their struggle for freedom, peace and daily existence.

Israel faced little global repudiation for its continued occupation of the Palestinian territories. Arab countries, which fought the 1948, 1956, 1967 and 1973 wars with Israel, seemed ready to turn the page of hostility and establish a more stable and predictable relationship with Israel. But Arabs were not the only major geopolitical player in West Asia besides Israel—the Islamic Republic of Iran was one too. Tehran has been building a network of resistance forces across West Asia since the 1979 revolution. And the support for the Palestinian cause has remained the central ideological theme of Iran's West Asia policy. In recent decades, when Arab countries moved towards coexistence with Israel, Iran emerged as its key rival. Iran is a strong supporter of Hamas, Islamic Jihad, Hezbollah, Houthis and Shia mobilization units. The 7 October attack heightened the Iran-Israel rivalry in the region, with a direct Iranian attack on Israel on 14 April 2024 and Israel's operations in Iran, including the killing of Hamas leader Ishmail Haniye on 30 July. **Chapter Four** tells the story of the Israel-Iran rivalry. While Israel, backed by the United States, seeks to roll back Iran's influence in the region through subversive operations inside Iran and direct war on Iran's proxies, the Islamic Republic seeks to expand its influence, from Tehran to Baghdad and Damascus to Beirut and Sana'a through its Axis of Resistance. This hot and cold war is reshaping today's West Asia.

Exit the regional power play and enter great powers. West Asia has always seen great power interest and interventions. Great Britain played a critical role in mainstreaming the Zionist demand for a homeland for the Jewish people in Palestine through the 1917 Balfour Declaration. The migration of European Jews to the east picked up when Palestine was a British colony during the interwar period. Britain's influence waned after the Second World War, but the United States would emerge as the new great power. From the 1960s, the United States and Israel would build what President John F. Kennedy called 'a special relationship', which is still going strong.[5] Today, the United States and Israel are arguably the closest two nation-states can ever get to each other. The United States, which is vocal about human rights violations across the world, continues to protect, militarily and diplomatically, the state of Israel despite its occupation of Palestine and the violent wars. After the 7 October attack, the United States continued to supply arms to Israel and pushed back international criticisms even as Israel faced allegations of genocide. When Iran launched a massive missile and drone strike towards Israel on 14 April, it was the US-led coalition that shot down most of the projectiles. The United States wants to pivot away from West Asia, but the Gaza war and the related regional crisis keep Washington pinned down in the region. Yet, it is not ready to use any meaningful pressure on Israel to bring the war to an end. Why? **Chapter Five** looks at the driving factors of the special relationship and the role the United States has historically played in the Palestine issue.

No analysis of the Israel–Palestine conflict would be complete without looking into the role of the Arabs. **Chapter Six** takes you back to the region. Before Israel occupied the Palestinian territories in 1967, the West Bank and East Jerusalem were controlled by Jordan and the Gaza Strip by Egypt. After the 1973 war, Egypt warmed up to the idea of making peace with Israel in return for the Sinai, the Egyptian peninsula which Israel had captured in 1967. In 1993, a year after the first Oslo agreement was signed, Jordan would also reach a peace treaty with Israel. By this time it was clear that the Palestine question was no longer an Arab–Israel problem.

But it remained an Israeli–Palestine problem. In 2020, the UAE first announced a normalization deal with Israel and then three more Arab countries followed. In this chapter, I look at the historical role Jordan played in the Palestine question and the larger churn in Arab–Israel relations. After the 2020 Abraham Accords, more Arab countries were seen willing to normalize ties with Israel. Saudi Arabia was particularly making progress in talks with the Israelis. But then came the 7 October attack, which turned the strategic clock of West Asia backwards.

What actually happened on 7 October? **Chapter Seven** reconstructs the events of the day from an Israeli point of view. Israel has one of the world's most advanced spy networks and surveillance tech. Netanyahu, who claimed that only he could protect Israel from its enemies, was the Prime Minister. Still, how did it happen? Based on my field trip to Jerusalem as well as Israel's border regions in the south with Gaza and the north with Lebanon, where Hezbollah has been fighting a slow-burning war since 7 October, this chapter is about the horrors of the war and its lasting implications for the region.

Now bring India into the picture. West Asia, a critical source for India's booming energy demand besides being a region that hosts millions of Indian workers, enjoys a critical position in India's foreign policy thinking. Historically, India has been a firm supporter of the Palestine cause. But since the 1990s, India has also witnessed a major turnaround in its relationship with Israel. India's West Asia policy has traditionally had three pillars—the Arab world, Iran and Israel. And India continued to maintain its balancing act between these pillars. The Hamas attack and the subsequent Israeli war on Gaza threatened to disrupt this balancing act. **Chapter Eight** looks at the changes and continuity in India's policy towards Israel–Palestine in particular and West Asia in general.

This book tells the story of Israel and Palestine as it is, through the views and experiences of the people in the region. 7 October, 2023 was a watershed moment in the Israeli–Palestine conflict, the lasting effects of which are yet to reveal themselves. As this book goes to the press, the devastating war Israel has been fighting in Gaza since the Hamas attack is still continuing with no clear end in sight. The Palestinian suffering is unimaginable, and the international community seems helpless or unwilling to do anything more than share verbal concerns. Hamas broke the status quo of the occupation without consequences on 7 October, but brought the fury of the state of Israel on the people of Palestine. At no point in the post-7 October war has Hamas looked like an organisation with a strategy. Israel appears to be belligerent, and cares little about Palestinian lives, but it doesn't seem to have an endgame. It turned Gaza into a pile of rubble, but Hamas survived. Hezbollah poses a potent challenge to Israel from southern Lebanon. The Houthis have attacked Tel Aviv using drones, a sign of what is to come. And then there is this looming hot and cold war between Israel and Iran. 'Israel wants to defeat all its enemies tomorrow. And Iran wants to make sure there are enough enemies for Israel to fight so that it would perpetually be at war in its periphery,' an Indian diplomat told me in March 2024. 'War is the reality in West Asia. Peace is just a promise.'

Stanly Johny
Chennai
October 2024

1

In Search of a Homeland

18 October 1889

THEODOR Herzl, an Austrian journalist and leader of the World Zionist Organization, and four other members of a Zionist delegation, were camping in Constantinople, the capital of the Ottoman Empire. Their mission: to get an audience with Kaiser Wilhelm II, the thirty-year-old monarch of Germany who was touring the Ottoman lands. Herzl, who had organized the world's first Zionist Congress in Basel, Switzerland, a year earlier, was seeking support from Germany for a solution to the Jewish question—the widespread, systemic discrimination Jews were facing in Europe. Weeks before travelling to Istanbul, Herzl had a meeting with Bernhard von Bülow, Germany's foreign minister, and Prince Chlodwig von Hohenlohe-Schillingsfürst, the chancellor of the German Empire. Herzl was looking for Germany's support in setting up Jewish colonies in Palestine, which was then part of the Ottoman Empire, an ally of Berlin.

Herzl, who described the meeting with great meticulousness in his diary, told the German leaders that Zionists would buy land from 'the Arabs, the Greeks—the whole mixed multitude of the Orient'. The German chancellor asked him if the plan was to establish a state in Palestine. 'We want autonomy and self-protection,' was Herzl's response.[1] He was also asked how he would fund the migration. The Zionist leader said he had tens of millions of pounds sterling at his disposal. 'The money might do the trick. With it, one can swing the matter,' said von Bülow, the foreign minister.

Back in Istanbul on 18 October, Herzl was worried whether he would get an audience with the emperor because the next day, the imperial entourage in the city would depart for Alexandria, Egypt. Herzl sent letters to von Bülow pleading for an audience, including a personal note for the Emperor, in which he explained what the Zionists wanted and what they could offer. He requested the Kaiser to take up the Zionist plan to set up settlements in Palestine with the Ottoman sultan (called the Jewish Land Society for Syria and Palestine), under Germany's protection. He promised that the Zionists could help fix the finances of the sultan's 'impoverished, bankrupt state'. He said that France and Britain, Germany's rivals in Europe, would not be happy with a German protectorate within the Ottoman territories and requested a personal audience with the emperor before he set sail from the city. Hours after the letters were sent, Herzl was summoned to the Yildiz Palace in Istanbul, where the emperor was staying.

In the meeting, the young monarch listened to Herzl's presentation, and at one point said, 'There are elements among your people [for] whom it would be quite a good thing to settle in

Palestine . . . there are usurers at work among the rural population (of Germany).' Herzl was disheartened by the emperor's comments. But he pressed on with his request. 'What should I request from the sultan when I meet him?' Wilhelm II asked the Zionist leader. 'A chartered company under German sponsorship,' Herzl said in response. 'Good, a chartered company,' said the emperor before the meeting came to an end. Herzl would meet the German emperor on two more occasions, on 28 October, at the gate of Mikveh Israel (a Jewish settlement village established in 1870 to the southeast of Jaffa on a tract of land leased from the Ottoman sultan); and then on 2 November, in Jerusalem. But for now, the Kaiser had made no promises to Herzl.[2]

Though Herzl failed to win any guarantees from the Kaiser, the meeting is seen as an important milestone in the history of Zionism. That one of the most powerful leaders of Europe met him to discuss the Jewish question turned Herzl, who until two years ago was an ordinary journalist with no political and social capital, into a leader of international Jewry. Herzl, who was an advocate of the emancipation of Jews through assimilation into European societies, changed his views in the closing years of the nineteenth century. In 1896, Herzl published 'Der Judenstaat' (The Jewish State), a pamphlet in which he argued that the political solution to the Jewish question was the creation of a separate homeland for the Jewish people. By that time, he had dropped the idea of assimilation. 'Let the sovereignty be granted us over a portion of the globe large enough to satisfy the rightful requirements of a nation; the rest we shall manage for ourselves,' the pamphlet read.[3]

Herzl was not the first Jewish leader to promote the idea of a separate homeland. The idea of returning to Palestine, which Herzl called 'our ever-memorable historic home', has historically been nurtured by Jews, especially Orthodox Jews, who had traditionally invoked the 'return to Zion (Jerusalem)' in their daily prayers. In 1862, Moses Hess, the German Jewish philosopher, wrote in *Rome and Jerusalem: A Study in Jewish Nationalism* that Jews should return to Palestine and 'redeem their soil'. Hess argued that Jews would always remainstrangers in European societies, and they should, thus, find a solution to anti-Semitism in Jewish nationalism rather than assimilation.[4] In 'Auto-Emancipation', a pamphlet written in 1882, Russian-Polish Zionist activist Leon Pinsker argued that Jews would never be equals with non-Jews in European societies and advocated for Jewish self-rule and the development of Jewish national consciousness. 'Indeed, what a pitiful figure we cut! We are not counted among the nations, neither have we a voice in their councils, even when the affairs concern us ... As men, we, too, wish to live like other men and be a nation like the others,' Pinsker wrote in the pamphlet.[5]

While these writings laid the foundation of the Zionist discourse, it was Herzl who founded a Zionist movement and gave it the organizational structure required to pursue its goal. In 'Der Judenstaat', Herzl contemplated creating a Jewish homeland in Argentina or Ottoman Palestine. Jews from Europe had started migrating to both regions. 'Shall we choose Palestine or Argentine? We shall take what's given [to] us, what's selected by Jewish public opinion,' he wrote. In the pamphlet, he also made a request to the Ottoman sultan. 'If His Majesty the Sultan were to give us Palestine, we could in return undertake to regulate the whole finances of Turkey. We should there form a portion of a rampart of Europe against Asia, an outpost of civilization as opposed to barbarism.'[6]

The socio-political conditions of Europe in the second half of the nineteenth century, especially the growing anti-Semitism, influenced these thinkers to reach the conclusion that a separate homeland, not assimilation, was the solution to the Jewish question. After the assassination of Tsar Alexander II of Russia in March 1881 by Narodnaya Volya, a revolutionary group, Jews were widely targeted in the empire as at least two of the assassins were Jewish. 'The Jews murdered our father the Tsar just as they murdered Christ,' lamented the rioters. In 1882 May, the imperial government passed the May Laws, barring Jews from settling anywhere outside their agricultural colonies and imposing other curbs on their social and economic life.[7] Thousands of Jews fled Russia to Western Europe after the crackdown, which only strengthened the anti-Semitic sentiments in Western societies. Herzl, as a journalist, witnessed the structural changes in European societies up close. In Vienna, local politicians attacked 'corrupt liberalism' and Jews for the problems Austria was facing. Anti-Semitism was on the rise in Germany, France, the Czech Republic, Serbia and other places, which had a sizeable Jewish population.

In the 1890s, Herzl was a reporter in Paris for *Neue Freie Presse*, a Vienna-based newspaper. In the French capital, he witnessed the trial and false conviction for treason of Alfred Dreyfus, a thirty-five-year-old artillery officer in the French army. Dreyfus, who was of Jewish descent, was accused of providing military secrets to the German Embassy in Paris. He was sentenced to life imprisonment and sent overseas to do his time. The Dreyfus affair became a big political controversy and an embodiment of the growing anti Semitism in Europe, which crystallized Herzl's views that Jews could not live as equal citizens in Europe. A year later, he wrote 'Der Judenstat'.

A Manifesto for Zionists

Herzl's next move was to build the organizational structures required to pursue his solution. In 1897, he founded the World

Zionist Organization at the first Zionist Congress. The Congress, held in Basel, Switzerland, had adopted the Basel Programme, a manifesto for the Zionists, which stated that 'Zionism seeks to establish a home in Palestine for the Jewish people.' To achieve this goal, the Congress also decided to promote 'the settlement of Jewish agriculturists, artisans and businessmen in Palestine; strengthen 'Jewish feelings and national consciousness' and take preparatory steps 'for obtaining the governmental approval which is necessary to the achievement of the Zionist purpose'.[8] In the pamphlet, Herzl described what he thought the solution was. In the Congress, the Zionists stated what had to be done to achieve the solution. The next step was action. Jewish migration to Palestine had already begun. Herzl set off a diplomatic push to win over the support of powerful governments in Europe for the Zionist cause. His outreach to the Germans was part of this diplomatic initiative, and the meeting with the Kaiser was a big moment for the Zionists in general and Herzl in particular.

Even though the Kaiser did not provide any guarantees to the Zionist delegation on their demands, Herzl continued his diplomatic efforts, trying to convince the Ottomans to allow concentrated Jewish settlements in Palestine that could operate with autonomy. He tried for an audience with the Ottoman sultan several times, sent letters to the sultan's court lobbying for a Charter for Jewish autonomy and offering, in return, financial assistance, including a large international loan to the imperial government guaranteed by Jewish bankers such as the Rothschilds. In July 1902, Herzl travelled to Constantinople again, hoping for an audience with the sultan. During his stay, he met a lot of Ottoman officials, including Grand Vizier Said Pasha, but the sultan refused to give him an audience. Herzl was told by cabinet ministers that the sultan would permit scattered Jewish settlements in the Empire to boost agricultural and economic development, but not in any specific region (Palestine).[9] They also said no to his request for a territorial Charter because the Ottomans knew that the creation of a new entity within imperial territories would mean the loss of more lands (the Ottomans had already lost the Balkans, and Egypt had slipped into British control). When he left Constantinople, Herzl wrote in his diary, 'Thus closes this book of my political novel.'

But Herzl was not ready to give up. As he realized that help was not forthcoming from the Germans, and the Turks had shut the door on his demands, he reached out to the British. He made different proposals to the British Colonial Secretary Joseph Chamberlain, whom he had known for years. Herzl sought British support for the creation of a Jewish homeland in Cyprus, the Sinai Peninsula or El Arish (Egypt). Chamberlain considered Herzl's proposals impractical as these regions were not directly under British control, nor were they uninhabited. In December 1902, Chamberlain started a tour of South Africa and midway he stopped in Mombasa, then part of Britain's East Africa protectorate. In 1903, after his trip to Africa, the secretary received Herzl in his London office. After fixing his monocle, Chamberlain presented his proposal with carefully chosen words. 'I have seen a land for you on my travels ... and that's Uganda. It's not on the coast, but farther inland, the climate becomes excellent even for Europeans ... and I thought to myself that would be a land for Dr Herzl.'[10] Herzl later recounted this conversation in his diary.[11]

Britain had its own reasons to support the creation of a Jewish state in East Africa (which came to be known as 'the Uganda Plan'). After the persecution of Jews in Eastern Europe, especially in Russia, the Jewish migration to the West had jumped manifold. Britain wanted to check the influx of Jews into its territories; it also thought Jews would bring money and people to East Africa, where the Empire had made huge investments in projects, including the Uganda Rail; Britain also wanted to win over the support of the international Jewry.[12] During the Sixth Zionist Congress in Basel, in 1903, Herzl unveiled the Uganda Plan. The plan would trigger heated debates in the Zionist Congress, with many arguing that it violated the spirit of the Basel Programme, which called for the creation of a Jewish state in Palestine. But Herzl's argument was that the Jewish people, who had 'a rope around their neck', should consider the proposal and take a decision based on discussions instead of rejecting it outright.

When Herzl died in July 1904, there was still no decision on the Uganda Plan. Later in the year, the World Zionist Organization would dispatch a commission to East Africa to study the proposal. But the plan had also triggered protests in East Africa by White British settlers, who set up Anti-Zionist Immigration Committees. In 1905, the Seventh Zionist Congress voted down the proposal, following which Britain withdrew the same. But for the Zionists, the British proposal itself was a phenomenal moment in their history. It was the first time a major government had supported their claim for a territorial homeland. If Herzl's meeting with Kaiser Wilhelm II provided him legitimacy as a Jewish leader and uplifted his status in world Jewry, the British support for a Jewish home in a different territory provided legitimacy to the territorial ideology of Zionism and Zionist organizations.

The Balfour Declaration

In 1904, the year Herzl died, Chaim Weizmann, a Russian-born biochemist who would later become the first President of Israel, moved to the United Kingdom from Switzerland. Weizmann, then thirty, was a regular attendee at the Zionist Congresses since the Second Congress of 1898. In the United Kingdom, he joined the chemistry department of the University of Manchester as a lecturer. His stay in Manchester, which would be his home for the next thirty years, would turn out to be crucial for Weizmann's Zionist activism. In 1905, he joined the Clayton Aniline Company, a manufacturer of dyestuffs. The company was founded by Charles Dreyfus, a biochemist-turned-entrepreneur, who was also the president of the Manchester Zionist Society. An influential local businessman and a supporter of the British Conservative Party, Dreyfus introduced Weizmann to Arthur Balfour, the then Conservative Prime Minister and an MP from East Manchester.

Balfour, as Prime Minister, was instrumental in passing the Aliens Act of 1905, which restricted the arrival of immigrants to the United Kingdom.[13] This legislation hit Jewish immigrants from Eastern Europe, who were fleeing persecution towards the West, hard. In the late nineteenth and early twentieth centuries, Britain and several other Western European countries saw tens of thousands of Jews, fleeing poverty and persecution in Eastern European countries, arriving on their shores. This triggered a political storm in the United Kingdom.[14] Balfour supported the idea of a homeland for the Jewish community, but he believed that the British plan to create a Jewish homeland in East Africa had more political support in London's political circles. In the meeting with Weizmann, which took place after Balfour resigned as Prime Minister, he asked the biochemist why the Zionists voted down the Uganda Plan. Weizmann responded with another question. 'Mr Balfour, supposing I was to offer you Paris instead of London, would you take it?'

'But Dr Weizmann, we have London,' said Balfour.

'That is true ... but we had Jerusalem when London was a marsh,' replied Weizmann.[15]

The meeting with Balfour did not produce any immediate results, but Weizmann continued to lobby for the Zionist project in Britain, while at the same time pushing for more Jewish settlements and building institutions, including the Palestine Land Development Company and the Hebrew University of Jerusalem in Ottoman Palestine. During this period, he established warm ties with Britain's political and business elites, but his demand for Britain's support for the creation of a Jewish homeland in Palestine still failed to gain momentum. Zionism would gain that momentum only after the First World War broke out.

After the war began, Britain started looking at the whole Zionist movement from a different perspective. Weizmann saw the emerging geopolitical situation in the Ottoman Empire as an opportunity to advance the Zionist cause. In Britain, he met members of the powerful Rothschild family and sought their help. James de Rothschild, son of Baron Edmond de Rothschild, told Weizmann in a meeting in November 1914 that Zionists should demand not just colonization of Palestine through settlements but the creation of a Jewish state in Palestine. He argued that 'the formation of a strong Jewish community in Palestine would be considered as a strong political asset' by London.[16] In the same month, the British Cabinet discussed Palestine for the first time, weeks after Britain entered the war. In the meeting, David Lloyd George, then chancellor of the exchequer who would soon become Prime Minister, told his colleague Herbert Samuel, a secular Jew who was sympathetic towards Zionism, that he saw the 'ultimate destiny of Palestine in becoming a Jewish state'.[17]

As the war was unfolding, Weizmann would later write: 'an opportunity offered itself to discuss the Jewish problems with

Mr C.P. Scott (editor of the *Manchester Guardian*)'. Scott, an influential figure in Manchester's liberal circles who enjoyed a close relationship with Lloyd George and Herbert Samuel, was sympathetic towards the Jewish community. He introduced Weizmann to Lloyd George, who asked the Zionist leader to meet Herbert Samuel.[18] On 10 December 1914, Samuel received Weizmann at his office. Weizmann's key demand was support for settlements and building institutions in Palestine. A state cannot be created by decree, 'but by the forces of a people and in the course of generations', he said.[19] But Samuel was more ambitious. He told Weizmann his demands were too modest. 'Big things will have to be done in Palestine.' When Weizmann asked the British leader what his ambitious plans were, he said he would rather keep them 'liquid', but added that 'Jews would have to build railways, harbours, a university, a network of schools, etc'.[20]

Within three months, Samuel circulated a memorandum titled 'The Future of Palestine' in the British Cabinet.[21] Samuel, a long-time supporter of the creation of a Jewish state in Palestine, however, believed that the time had not yet come for creating an independent state. Instead, he suggested the British Empire annexe Palestine once the war was over, and 'help the gradual growth of a considerable Jewish community, under British suzerainty, in Palestine'. Samuel argued that as a 'civilizer of the backward countries', England would be fulfilling 'yet another part of her historic part'. 'Under the Turks, Palestine has been blighted. For hundreds of years, she has produced neither men nor things useful to the world,' he wrote in the memorandum. Samuel further argued that annexation of Palestine would raise the prestige of the British Empire, help it in its war efforts, and 'win for England the lasting gratitude of the Jews throughout the world', including the 2 million Jews who resided in the United States.[22] This was the first time a

British cabinet minister put a plan in favour of the Zionist cause in the official records.

Discussions, both at the Cabinet level and between the government and the Zionists, continued. Weizmann, who by that time had become the face of the Zionist movement in Britain, was appointed as a scientific adviser in the Ministry of Munitions, which was headed by Lloyd George. In the midst of war, when Britain was under pressure for the mass production of acetone, Weizmann came up with a solution. He found a way to produce acetone by a fermentation process in a laboratory, and with help from the government, industrial scale production of acetone started. This enhanced Weizmann's reputation among the political establishment in London. Llyod George reminisces in his memoir about a conversation he had with Weizmann:

'You have rendered great service to the State, and I should like to ask the Prime Minister to recommend you to His Majesty for some honour.'

'There is nothing I want for myself.'

'But is there nothing we can do as a recognition of your valuable assistance to the country?' I asked.

'Yes, I would like you to do something for my people,' he said.

'He then explained his aspirations as to the repatriation of the Jews to the sacred land they had made famous. That was the fount and origin of the famous declaration about the National Home for Jews in Palestine,' writes Llyod George, referring to the Balfour Declaration.[23]

Llyod George's account overlooks the complex geopolitical dynamics that were at play in the early twentieth century. True, Weizmann's support for the war effort, in his individual capacity, and the respect he commanded in Britain's establishment provided him access to the top echelons of the British government. But Britain was also mindful of its own interests. In 1915–16, the war was raging on multiple fronts with no major breakthrough for either side. The Allied Powers were under enormous pressure. The United States had not joined the war yet, and Russia was going through a period of revolutionary instability with the rise of the Mensheviks and the Bolsheviks. British leaders calculated that if they supported the Zionists, they could win, as Samuel Herbert wrote in his memorandum, the support of the Jewry who could use their influence in bringing the United States into the war and persuade Russia to stay in the war. Lloyd George and Arthur Balfour had also supported the idea of dividing the Ottoman lands once the war was over. So, they thought that having a sizeable Jewish population in Palestine would help Britain's interests in West Asia. Britain could also claim moral leadership by offering a solution to the Jewish question.[24] This line of thinking emerged stronger after Lloyd George became Prime Minister and Arthur Balfour his foreign secretary in December 1916.

On 2 November 1917, after multiple rounds of talks with Zionists, during which they offered the support of the Jewish community for Britain's war efforts across geographies, Arthur Balfour issued a statement to Lord Rothschild, a leader of the British Zionist movement and an influential member of the Rothschild family, saying the British government would support 'the establishment *in Palestine* of a national home for the Jewish people'. This was the first time the British government (or any government for that matter) offered public support for the Zionist project in Palestine, in line with the Basel Declaration. The Balfour Declaration would go on to become one of the most important documents in the history of Zionism and Israel.

Road to the State

During the First World War, Britain had made different, often conflicting, geopolitical outreaches in the region to protect its interests. While British leaders were warming up to the Zionist project after the war broke out, they also reached out to the Arabs of the Ottoman Empire, seeking their support against the sultan's regime. Between July 1915 and March 1916, Lieutenant Colonel Sir Henry McMahon, the British high commissioner to Egypt (the same diplomat who drew the McMahon line between India and Tibet), exchanged a series of letters with Hussein bin Ali, the Sharif of Mecca, in which he promised that the British government would support Arab independence once the war was over. In return, the British wanted Arabs to revolt against the Ottomans. Sharif Hussein, a member of the Hashemite clan (descendants of the Prophet Mohammed) and the Emir of Mecca, claimed to represent the entire Arab population and asked the British to support the independence of a united Arab country (all the Arabic-speaking lands east of Egypt).

McMahon agreed to the call for independence but insisted that certain regions falling within the French sphere of influence (parts of today's Syria and Lebanon) would not be included.[25] While there was no agreement on the question of boundaries, Arabs, under the leadership of Sharif Hussein and his sons, Ali and Feisal, launched a massive revolt against the Ottomans in June 1916.

Simultaneously, Britain and France started secret negotiations on the dismemberment of the Ottoman Empire once the war was over. These negotiations resulted in the 1916 Sykes–Picot agreement, named after the chief negotiators from Britain and France, Sir Mark Sykes and François Georges-Picot, respectively.[26] And then they issued the Balfour Declaration offering support to the Zionists to create a national home in Palestine.

After the war, however, Britain and France took control of most of the Arab lands lying east of Egypt, in accordance with the Sykes-Picot agreement. Britain took control of most of Mesopotamia (today's Iraq) and the southern part of Ottoman Syria (Palestine and Transjordan), while France brought the rest of Ottoman Syria (today's Syria) and Lebanon under its rule. In 1923, France and Britain formalized their control of these regions through League of Nations Mandates. In Transjordan, on the eastern bank of the Jordan River, Abdullah I, the second son of Sharif Hussein of Mecca, had established an emirate in 1921, with British support.[27] Under the auspices of the British Mandate, Abdullah built an autonomous governing system in Jordan, with Amman being the centre of power. The border between Palestine and Transjordan (along the Jordan River) was agreed in the mandate document, while the northern border between Palestine and Syria (today Lebanon) was agreed between the British and the French.[28] So, Palestine emerged as a political entity between the Mediterranean Sea in the west and the Jordan River in the east, and Lebanon in the north and the Egyptian Sinai in the south, in the early 1920s under the direct authority of the British Empire. The total population of Palestine at that time was roughly 7,50,000 of which 9 per cent were Jews and the rest Arabs (including Muslims and Christians).[29]

In July 1921, when Britain formalized its colonial rule of Palestine through the League of Nations Mandate, David Ben-Gurion was a young, influential leader of the Jews in Palestine. Ben-Gurion, who would later become Israel's first Prime Minister, was born in Płońsk to Polish-Jewish parents and was influenced by Zionism at a very young age. In 1906, at age twenty, Ben-Gurion, like thousands of other East European Jews, migrated to Ottoman Palestine, where he joined Petah Tikva, the mother of Jewish agricultural settlements in the region. His goal was not only to live in the Jewish communities in Palestine, which they called their historical and spiritual homeland, but also to work towards achieving their Zionist dream. With the outbreak of the First World War, he was deported by the Ottomans. He first travelled to the United States and then to the United Kingdom, where, after the Balfour Declaration was issued, he joined the Jewish Legion of the British Army, which was sent to Palestine to fight the Ottomans. After the war, when the future of Palestine as well as the Zionist project was being discussed by the world leaders that defeated the Ottoman Empire, Ben-Gurion sensed a historic opportunity to advance the Zionist cause.

A Labour Zionist, Ben-Gurion was associated with Po'alei Zion, a Marxist-Zionist movement that was active in Eastern Europe. It had a branch in Ottoman Palestine, which was the main political vehicle of Ben-Gurion and his comrades. In the post-war Palestine, which was directly under the control of the British, Zionists got a freer hand to operate. By that time, they were clear on what they wanted. The collapse of the Ottoman Empire presented itself as an opportunity; but Jews lacked the institutions and the numbers required to achieve their goals quickly. Ben-Gurion saw three short- to medium-term challenges. They would have to: one, improve the presence of Jews in Palestine through mass immigration from

Europe; two, build political and labour institutions in Palestine that would act like the voice and political muscle of the settlers; and three, make his group the dominant voice of the Zionist movement both inside and outside Palestine.[30]

When Po'alei Zion split in February 1919 over the question of whether the movement should join the World Zionist Organization (which the left wing of the movement considered a bourgeois organization), Ben-Gurion stood by the right-wing bloc, which had taken a Jewish nationalist position. In March, Ben-Gurion and others in the right-wing bloc founded Ahdut HaAvoda, a Zionist socialist party, primarily aimed at mobilizing Jewish workers in Palestine. Ben-Gurion played a critical role in shaping the view and the charter of Aḥdut HaAvoda, which 'aspired, through organised mass immigration, to mould the life of the Jewish people in Ereẓ Israel as a commonwealth of free and equal workers living on its labour, controlling its property, and arranging its distribution of work, its economy, and its culture'.[31] A year later, Ahdut HaAvoda formed Haganah, a paramilitary wing. In the same year, the General Organization of Workers in Israel (Histadrut), a trade union centre representing Jewish workers across party platforms, was formed, and Ben-Gurion was elected its general secretary, a position which he would hold until 1935. So, by the time the British formalized their colonial hold through the mandate, the Jews of Palestine had established political, labour and military institutions in the territory.

Both Ahdut HaAvoda and Histadrut would emerge as the central political and labour movements of the Jews in Palestine in the following decade, which would make Ben-Gurion the undisputed leader of the Yishuv, the Jewish community in Palestine. In 1930, Ahdut HaAvoda would merge with Hapoel

Hatzair, another Zionist movement, to create Mapai (Workers' Party of the Land of Israel), the precursor to the modern-day Labour party. Mapai would emerge as the dominant faction of the Zionist movement, whose hold on Israeli society would continue to remain tight until the mid-1970s. By the mid-1930s, Ben-Gurion's Labour Zionism became the most powerful faction within the global Zionist movement. In 1935, he became the chairman of the Executive Committee of the Jewish Agency for Palestine, the operative branch of the World Zionist Organization. He never had to turn back.

By the end of the Second World War, the demographic, political and geopolitical landscape of Palestine had changed. Prior to the war, the British had tried to impose some restrictions on Jewish immigration, especially after the Arab–Israeli riots of the 1930s, but the arrival of settlers continued nevertheless.[32] This was also the period when Jews were going through systemic persecution with the Holocaust in Europe being organized by the Nazis and the Fascists, which triggered the mass exodus of Jewish refugees to Palestine, their 'promised land'. If Jews made up 11 per cent of Palestine's population at the beginning of Britain's Mandatory rule, by the time the Second World War came to an end in 1945, it rose to 30 per cent.[33] Britain emerged weaker from the war, and there were new great powers on the horizon. Jews, after what they went through in Europe, enjoyed international sympathy across geographies. Within Palestine, they had built political parties, labour organizations, academic institutions, agricultural cooperatives, communes and different Zionist paramilitary groups that were trained in Europe.

They became a state within the state and David Ben-Gurion was their king.

2

War and Un-peace

THE King David Hotel of Jerusalem is one of the landmark buildings of the contested city. Built with locally made pink limestone and opened in 1931 by Ezra Mosseri, a wealthy Egyptian Jewish banker, the hotel, overlooking the Old City that's holy for all three Abrahamic faiths, and Mount Zion, the highest point in Jerusalem, is a standing example of both Israel's Jewish roots and its bloody history. From its early days during the British Mandate of Palestine, the hotel has hosted royalties and other key visiting dignitaries. When King Alfonso XIII of Spain was forced to abdicate the throne in 1931, he arrived in British Palestine and took up residence at the King David Hotel. When Emperor Haile Selassie was driven out of his home country of Ethiopia by the Italians in 1936 and King George II was forced to flee Greece in 1942 after the Nazi occupation of his country, both of them took refuge in the hotel. During the Mandatory period, the British used the southern wing of the hotel for its administrative and military offices—basically, the Secretariat of the Government of Palestine and the Headquarters of the British Armed Forces in Palestine and Transjordan.

On 22 July 1946, members of Irgun, a right-wing Zionist underground militia, entered the hotel disguised as Arab workers and waiters. Their mission: plant explosives in the basement of the main building of the hotel.[1] Irgun planted the bomb in response to 'Operation Agatha', a British military raid at the office of the Jewish Agency during which they confiscated large quantities of documents implicating Haganah and Irgun, both militias, in Jewish attacks against the British. Irgun wanted to destroy those documents, which were kept at the King David. The powerful explosion led to the collapse of the western half of the southern wing. At least ninety-one people were killed and another forty-six injured.[2]

The bombing of the King David Hotel was the deadliest attack by Zionists against the British, who found it increasingly difficult to continue the rule of Palestine after the Second World War. Violence by Jewish militant organizations and between Arabs and Jews was on the rise. Britain was also struggling with its own post-war economic challenges. After the First World War, it had got the mandate to rule Palestine from the League of Nations. After the Second World War, it turned to the United Nations, saying it wanted to vacate the mandate. In 1947, the United Nations General Assembly decided to set up a Special Committee on Palestine (UNSCOP). In a report submitted to the General Assembly, UNSCOP proposed to divide Palestine into 'an independent Arab State, an independent Jewish State, and the City of Jerusalem'. The committee proposed that the city be under an international trusteeship system.[3]

The UN went ahead preparing a plan for the impending partition. The Jewish Agency immediately accepted the plan, while Arab nations opposed the partition. On 14 May 1948, the day the British Mandate expired, the Jewish People's Council gathered at the Tel Aviv Museum (today known as Independence Hall). The Jewish Agency kept the event a secret out of fear that the British would attempt to prevent it. The event was broadcast as the first transmission by the newly launched Kol Yisrael radio station. Ben-Gurion, leader of the Jewish agency, made the declaration from a podium, behind which there was a wall that had a huge portrait of Theodor Herzl, flanked by two King David stars. 'We, the members of the National Council, representing the Jewish people in Palestine and the Zionist movement of the world, met together in solemn assembly today, the day of the termination of the British Mandate for Palestine, by virtue of the natural and historic right of the Jewish and of the Resolution of the General Assembly of the United Nations, hereby proclaim the establishment of the Jewish State in Palestine, to be called Israel,' he declared from the podium.[4]

Within a few minutes, the newly declared state got the recognition of the United States. The next day, the armies of four countries— Egypt, Syria, Transjordan and Iraq—entered Palestine and clashed with the Jewish army, triggering the first Arab–Israeli war. Israeli author Amos Oz later recalled the historic day in an interview. 'That Friday morning, I saw with my eyes the British leaving the Schneller Barracks and then the Haganah' [the new Israeli Army] rushing to take over. Then, on Friday afternoon, we were told that Israel is a nation now, it has a government, but one minute after midnight we were told that Israel is being invaded by five regular Arab armies, and that there was shelling and bombardment by artillery batteries.'[5]

The Arab nations' plan was to destroy the state of Israel at its very inception. But they failed to do so. The war continued for a year and when a ceasefire was signed, Israel was controlling more territories of historic Palestine than even the UN plan offered for the Jewish state. As per the UN plan, some 55 per cent of Ottoman Palestine was to make up the Jewish state. By the time the war was over, Israel was in control of more than 75 per cent of Ottoman Palestine, including West Jerusalem. The UN plan had proposed a geographical contiguity between Gaza, which is on the Mediterranean coast, and the West Bank, which is on the western bank of the Jordan River. It's no longer there as Israel captured territories between Gaza and the West Bank. Jordan seized the West Bank and East Jerusalem and Egypt took the Gaza Strip.

For Israel, it was the 'war of independence', but for Palestinians, it was *nakba* (catastrophe). Roughly 7,50,000 Palestinians were violently displaced from their homes and lands by Zionist militias. Thousands of Palestinians were killed. Hundreds of Arab villages and towns were depopulated and destroyed, and later became part of the state of Israel.[6] For Zionists, this violent takeover of Arab lands was not an accident. Ben-Gurion, the first Prime Minister of Israel, had written in his diary on 12 July 1937: 'The compulsory transfer of the Arabs from the valleys of the proposed Jewish state could give us something which we never had ... a Galilee free from Arab population ... We must uproot from our hearts the assumption that the thing is not possible. It can be done.' On 5 October 1937, he wrote again: 'We must expel Arabs and take their places ... and, if we have to use force—not to dispossess the Arabs of the Negev and Transjordan, but to guarantee our own right to settle in those places—then we have force at our disposal.'[7] In the words of Chaim Weizmann, Israel's first President, the local Arab population in

Palestine were like 'the rocks of Judea [...] obstacles that had to be cleared on a difficult path'.⁸ So, during and after the creation of the state of Israel, what Zionist militias did was what their leaders actually wanted them to do. West Asia suddenly looked like a different region. Its map had been redrawn; hundreds of thousands of people were scattered. Arab pride and confidence was hurt. And a Jewish state was established in the heart of the Arab land.

It was only the beginning of the conflicts to come.

The Six-Day War

'The Jews are threatening war. We say to them *"ahlan wa-sahlan"* (You are welcome),' Egyptian President Gamal Abdel Nasser said on 22 May 1967, while addressing pilots at the Bir Gafgafa air base in the Sinai Peninsula.⁹ War clouds were already gathering over the West Asian skies. There were frequent conflicts between the Syrian and Israeli militaries in the demilitarized zone along their border. A week earlier, President Nasser had remilitarized the Sinai Peninsula. After Nasser's speech, Egypt and Jordan—Cold War enemies—signed a joint defence agreement. Israel read these developments as preparations for a major war ahead. On 5 June, within six days of the Jordanian–Egyptian agreement, Israel launched a surprise attack, destroying the Egyptian Air Force in a single day. King Hussein, the thirty-two-year-old monarch of Jordan, entered the war on the same day, but his troops were pushed back to the eastern part of the kingdom by the Israeli forces. The Syrians attacked Israel from its northern border but faced the same fate as the Jordanians. By the sixth day of the war, on 10 June, Israel had captured the entire Sinai Peninsula and Gaza Strip from Egypt; the West Bank and eastern Jerusalem from Jordan; and the Golan Heights from Syria.¹⁰

The UN Partition plan promised 55 per cent of historical Palestine to the Jewish state; Israel controlled some 75 per cent after the 1948 war, and now, after the 1967 war, the whole of Palestine came under Israel's control.

And it never gave the land back after this.

The war changed the region in many ways. Primarily, it broke the myth of Arab unity. Egypt, the strongest of them all, would take years to recover from the humiliation it suffered. Nasser died three years later, and with him died the idea of pan-Arabism. Second, the war reinforced Israel's military might in the region. Third, it turned Israel into an American asset in West Asia. The United States realized the true strategic potential of Israel only after the June War. Israel's easy victory over the Arab countries in six days caught the attention of President Lyndon B. Johnson at a time when American troops were fighting an increasingly tough Communist insurgency in Vietnam. The US offered diplomatic protection, advanced weapons and financial aid to Israel, and in turn the latter remained one of the pillars of American foreign policy in the region.[11]

Israel was aware of the profound changes the war had brought into regional politics and was ready to capitalize on its advantageous position. 'We have returned to our holy places ... and we shall never leave them,' thundered Gen. Moshe Dayan, defence minister, standing in front of the Western Wall, the holiest place of worship according to Judaism, in the Old City, after the war.[12] Shortly after reaching a ceasefire with the Arab countries, the Israeli Cabinet decided to annexe East Jerusalem, by extending 'the law, jurisdiction and administration of the state of Israel' to the eastern half of the city.[13] It said it would continue its military presence in the West Bank and Gaza until 'peace agreements were signed' with the Arab countries, effectively keeping the Palestinian territories under direct occupation. Promises of peace for Israel, as the decades of occupation suggest, have always been a delaying tactic.[14]

The Arab countries were in shock, and anger was simmering. They lost the whole of Palestine, including Jerusalem. They lost their own territories—Sinai and Golan. And they had been defeated in just six days. In the September 1967 Khartoum conference, the Arabs declared their famous 'Three Nos'—no peace with Israel, no recognition of Israel and no negotiations with Israel.[15] But they also realized that Israel was going to be a reality and that they needed a realistic approach to deal with the Jewish state. A month after the war, King Hussein of Jordan had sent feelers to Israel for peace. The Israeli response came in September 1968, in which it promised to return parts of the West Bank to Jordan and retain control over East Jerusalem. The monarch rejected the offer.

For Anwar Sadat, Nasser's successor in Egypt, the priority was to get Egyptian Sinai back from the Israelis. He saw Nasser's pan-Arabism rising and falling. He saw the back-to-back defeat of Arab armies by the Israelis. He knew that the state of Israel was not going anywhere. Sadat was ready to make bilateral peace, but he also knew that Israel would not return the land on its own. He wanted to shake Israel first and then push for peace.

On 6 October 1973, the Yom Kippur Day, the holiest day for Jews, Egyptian and Syrian troops launched a surprise attack in Sinai and Golan Heights.[16] Israel was ill-prepared for a war and was caught unawares. Though Israel eventually fought back against the Egyptians and the Syrians, with military support from the United States, the attack challenged the belief in Jerusalem that Israel had established credible deterrence, after its glorious 1967 victories, against its Arab neighbours. The intelligence failure to foresee such massive Egyptian troop movements plagued the Israeli military and political leadership for years. It would effectively bring the political hegemony of the Labour Party to an end, setting the stage for the rise of the right-wing Likud. It also reinforced the view that Egypt remained a potential Arab military rival. The shock of Yom Kippur, coupled with a strong line the Jimmy Carter administration of the United States was taking towards peace, prompted Israel to go for talks with Egypt.

When Carter started engaging the Palestine Liberation Organization (PLO), the Israeli government, led by right-wing leader Menachem Begin, opposed it vehemently. 'I can't ignore the various problems on the West Bank,' said President Carter, signalling a shift in the US approach. 'The continued deprivation of Palestinian rights was not only used as a primary lever against Israel, but was contrary to the basic moral and ethical principles of both our countries,' he said.[17] According to the Likud party's 1977 platform, 'between the Sea and the Jordan, there will only be Israeli sovereignty'.[18] Likud promoted Jewish settlements in occupied territories because settlements 'are the realization of the Zionist values'.

Begin was ready to talk to the Egyptians, but he did not want to address the Palestine issue. The Begin government even used the Jewish lobby in Washington to put pressure on the Carter administration and approached the Egyptians to strike a peace deal bypassing Palestinians. But Sadat knew the risks of a deal with Israel, which would definitely be unpopular in the Arab Street. He wanted something in return from the Israelis for the Palestinians. President Carter was also pushing for a resolution of 'the Palestinian problem in all aspects'. Finally, Begin, Israel's first right-wing Prime Minister, blinked. He made a counter-proposal to the Americans, which led to the Camp David Accord between Israel and Egypt, and the Framework for Peace in the Middle East.[19]

Under the agreement, Israel agreed to withdraw completely from the Sinai Peninsula. Egypt would re-establish its sovereignty. Begin also agreed to abolish Israel's military rule over the West Bank and Gaza and establish a Palestinian self-governing authority with elections, local policing and a review of all arrangements.[20] The agreement established peace between Israel and its most powerful Arab adversary. Subsequently, a full diplomatic relationship between Egypt and Israel was established. The Framework for Peace in the Middle East was not immediately implemented. But it was in this agreement that the Israelis recognized for the first time the idea of Palestinian self-rule. Begin even talked about 'Palestinian sovereignty'.[21] Sadat called it 'the first offer ever made by Israel to the Palestinians'.[22] The Framework Agreement set the agenda for the Israeli–Palestinian peace process. It served as the basis for both the Madrid Peace Conference of 1991 as well as the Oslo Accords of 1993, which actually led to the formation of a provisional government in the Palestinian territories.

From Camp David to Oslo

The Framework Agreement breathed new life into the Palestinian national movement. But in reality, it did not bring any immediate respite for the Palestinians. When the agreement was signed in 1978, the West Bank was still claimed by Jordan. The Palestinian Liberation Organization (PLO), which was founded in 1964, was operating from Lebanon. The PLO rose to prominence after Arafat, an Arab nationalist and socialist, became its chairman in 1969.

Born to Palestinian parents in Cairo, Egypt, Arafat was drawn into the Palestinian national struggle at a very young age. In 1948, he fought Jewish militias along with the Muslim Brotherhood. After the Arabs lost the war, he joined the General Union of Palestinian Students, one of the earliest Palestinian nationalist organizations operating from Egypt. In the late 1950s, he founded Fatah, a secular, nationalist militant outfit that called for the 'liberation' of the whole of Palestine.

By the late 1960s, Fatah was the most prominent organization of the PLO, which was initiated by the Arab League as an umbrella body representing Palestinian nationalism, whose main goals were 'Arab unity and the liberation of Palestine'.[23] The PLO was earlier based in Jordan but was ousted by the Jordanian authorities in a bloody crackdown in 1971 as King Hussein started seeing the Palestinian activities as a threat to stability in his fragile kingdom. From Lebanon, Arafat and his comrades continued their guerilla attacks against Israel. In November 1974, while speaking at the UN General Assembly, Arafat said the PLO wanted to establish 'one democratic Palestinian state where Jews and Muslims live in justice, equality and fraternity'. He offered both war and peace. 'I have come bearing an olive branch and a freedom fighter's gun. Do not let the olive branch fall from my hands,' he said.[24]

Israel saw the PLO's claim to the whole of Palestine as a threat. Israel attacked Lebanon in 1978 and 1982, mainly to oust the PLO from the neighbouring country. Israel also continued its military rule over the Palestinian territories amid mounting resentment among the Palestinians. This resentment blew off in 1987 after an Israeli Defence Forces' (IDF) truck collided with a civilian car, killing four Palestinians in the Jabalia refugee camp in Gaza.[25] The accident sparked widespread protests and civil disobedience movements across Gaza and the West Bank. As labour strikes, stone-throwing, boycotting of Israeli civil administrations and refusal to pay taxes spread across the territories—in what came to be known as the First Intifada—Israel found it difficult to govern the Palestinian territories.

Subsequently, Jordan gave up its claims over the West Bank, two decades after Israel captured it. 'It was [the] Intifada that really caused our decision on disengagement,' King Hussein said in 1988.[26] Jordan's decision to give up claims foreclosed the possibility of settling the question of the West Bank between Israel and Jordan. In the immediate aftermath of the 1967 war, Israel had proposed dividing the West Bank between the two countries—a proposal that Jordan had rejected. Now that Jordan had backed out, it was between the Israelis and the Palestinians. Seizing the moment, the Palestinian National Council, the legislative body of the PLO, adopted a resolution, written by poet Mahmoud Darwish, declaring independence for Palestine, which it called 'the land of the three monotheistic faiths'. On 15 November 1988, Arafat read out the declaration in Algiers, Algeria, proclaiming the birth of 'a State of Palestine in our Palestinian territory with its capital Jerusalem'.[27] Weeks later, at least 100 UN member states acknowledged the declaration of the state of Palestine.

Israel faced two major challenges at this juncture. One was the growing difficulties in governing the Palestinian territories amid continuing protests. The other was the global recognition the Palestinian leadership was drawing. In December 1988, the United States recognized the PLO. The PLO's policy was also undergoing changes. If earlier it called for 'the liberation' of the whole of historical Palestine, it was now sending signals of compromise for a deal with Israel.

After the state of Palestine was declared, the Palestinian National Council called for multilateral talks on the basis of the UN Security Council Resolution 242, which asked Israel to withdraw from all the territories it captured in the 1967 war.[28] The PNC's move was termed a 'historic compromise' (as the 1967 border would mean roughly 22 per cent of historical Palestine) and set the stage for engagement between Palestine and Israel. There was some common ground. The Palestinian leadership was ready for talks. And the Israelis wanted to calm the Palestinian territories. In early 1989, Defence Minister Yitzhak Rabin proposed autonomy for the West Bank and Gaza in return for ending the uprising. A few months later, Likud Prime Minister Yitzhak Shamir, known for his hardline views on the Palestinian question, initiated talks with the Palestinians based on the Framework Agreement of 1978.[29]

The peace bid gained momentum after Yitzhak Rabin, of Labour, became Prime Minister in 1992. Rabin, who was born in Jerusalem to Jewish parents who had immigrated from Eastern Europe, had served in the Israeli Defence Force for twenty-seven years. He was the IDF's chief of operations in the 1948 war and helped shape the Israeli military throughout the 1950s and 60s. As the chief of the general staff, Rabin oversaw Israel's victories in 1967. In 1992, Rabin campaigned against Shamir mainly on the peace platform. Rabin's approach was that the continued occupation of Palestinian territories was not sustainable. As a soldier and then defence minister, he also saw the costs of the war Israel had fought in the past and the permanence of troubles in Palestine that were accentuated by the intifada. He saw that the world was changing, with the birth of new republics in Eastern Europe and Central Asia and the rise of the US as the sole superpower of the world. He wanted global recognition for Israel and peace at home but the terms had to be favourable for Israel's long-term interests.

Rabin joined secret talks in Oslo based on the Framework Agreement. But a lot had changed in the region since the Framework Agreement was signed in 1978. If the main objective of the Framework was a 'peace treaty between Israel and Jordan, taking into account the agreement reached in the final status of the West Bank and Gaza', in Oslo, negotiations took place directly between Israel and the PLO, an organization that Israel had deemed a terrorist outfit for years. On 9 September 1993, both parties exchanged Letters of Mutual Recognition, signed by Prime Minister Rabin and Chairman Arafat. The letters indicated that both parties recognized each other as serious partners in negotiations.[30] Four days later, on 13 September 1993, Rabin and Arafat shook hands in Washington in the presence of US President Bill Clinton and signed the Oslo Accord I. Rabin was forthright in his message to the Palestinians. 'Let me say to you, the Palestinians: We are destined to live together, on the same soil in the same land,' he said. '... we who have come from a land where parents bury their children, we who have fought against you, the Palestinians—we say to you today in a loud and clear voice: Enough of blood and tears. Enough.'[31]

The Oslo Accords were initial agreements aimed at taking some preliminary steps towards resolving the Palestine question in five years.[32] The PLO recognized Israel's right to exist and accepted the UN Security Council Resolutions 242 and 338. It also committed itself to a peaceful solution to the conflict between the Palestinians and the Israelis. In return, the government of Israel recognized the PLO as 'the representative of the Palestinian people'. The Oslo process led to the creation of the Palestinian Authority, a self-governing body, and a legislature with limited powers over the Palestinian territories.

According to the Oslo II Agreement reached between the Palestinian leadership and Israel in 1995, the West Bank was divided into three areas—A, B and C. Hebron, Nablus, Ramallah, Bethlehem and some towns and villages that do not border Israeli settlements are in Area A, which comprises some 18 per cent of the West Bank. Area B, which comprises around 22 per cent of the territory, is under Palestinian civil administration while Israel retains exclusive security control. Area C is the largest division in the West Bank, comprising some 60 per cent of the territory, and is under full Israel civil administration and security control. '[T]he jurisdiction of the [Palestine] Council will cover West Bank and Gaza Strip territory as a single territorial unit, except for: issues that will be negotiated in the permanent status negotiations: Jerusalem, settlements, specified military locations, Palestinian refugees, borders, foreign relations and Israelis; and powers and responsibilities not transferred to the Council, according to the Oslo Agreement.'[33]

The Permanence of Conflict

In the history of Israel and Palestine, there has always been a U-turn after a serious push for peace. On 4 November 1995, Prime Minister Rabin was assassinated by a Jewish extremist. His immediate successor, Shimon Peres, called for an election hoping that he could mobilize the peace dividend and take the Oslo process further. But in the 1996 election, Likud returned to power and Benjamin Netanyahu became Prime Minister for the first time.

The fate of Oslo was sealed.

Netanyahu initially refused to honour the commitments of the past governments. He made some compromises. He made some compromises.[34] For example, amid growing protests and violence by Palestinians, both sides signed the Hebron Protocol in January 1997. Under the agreement, Israel withdrew from 80 per cent of Hebron. But negotiations came to a grinding halt after the Hebron pullout. When the interim five-year period since the Oslo agreements were signed was over in May 1999, a comprehensive agreement between Israel and Palestine was still elusive. But the Oslo Accords had already reshaped the Israeli–Palestinian conflict. The Palestinian Authority was in place running parts of the West Bank. Israel, instead of directly ruling over the West Bank and Gaza, started controlling territories indirectly. The status of Jerusalem and the right of return of Palestinian refugees remained the crux of the problem with no meaningful efforts from either side to settle the issues.

US President Bill Clinton tried to revive the stalled peace process in 2000 at a Camp David summit in which he hosted both Israeli Prime Minister Ehud Barak and the Palestinian leader Arafat. All key components of the Israeli–Palestinian conflict— border of the future Palestinian state, the status of Jerusalem, the Palestinian refugees' right of return, Jewish settlements in the West Bank and Gaza and security arrangements—came up for discussions during the summit.[35] But the summit collapsed as the two sides failed to agree on the status of Jerusalem and the right of return. Israel refused to recognize Palestinian sovereignty over East Jerusalem and allow all of the Palestinian refugees who were forced to flee from home during the 1948–49 war to return to their lands, which were now already part of Israel. The collapse of the Camp David talks triggered another spell of violent protests across Palestinian territories; this came to be known as the Second Intifada. The collapse of the Oslo process, the failure of peace bids, the mushrooming of Jewish settlements in Palestinian territories and the strengthening of Islamist parties such as Hamas and Islamic Jihad among the Palestinians all contributed to the uprising.

The uprising started in September 2000, after Ariel Sharon made a visit to the Temple Mount in the Old City of East Jerusalem.[36] The Temple Mount, or Haram esh-Sharif for the Arabs, houses both the Wailing Wall and the al-Aqsa Mosque. Palestinians saw Sharon's visit as highly provocative and unleashed violent protests against Israeli security personnel. What followed was one of the most violent phases in the Israeli–Palestinian conflict. Between 2000 and 2005, over 3,000 Palestinians were killed in protests, mostly by Israeli security personnel. On the Israeli side, some 900 people were killed, mostly civilians.[37]

It was amid growing protests by the Palestinians that Prime Minister Ariel Sharon, in late 2003, announced his plan to pull out troops as well as settlements from Gaza in a unilateral move. 'The purpose of the Disengagement Plan is to reduce terror as much as possible and grant Israeli citizens the maximum level of security. The process of disengagement will lead to an improvement in the quality of life and will help strengthen the Israeli economy. The unilateral steps which Israel will take in the framework of the Disengagement Plan will be fully coordinated with the United States,' Sharon said on 18 December, in a speech at the Fourth Herzliya Conference.[38] Hamas, on the other side, claimed that Israel decided to pull out because of the Second Intifada.[39]

The government adopted the Disengagement Plan in June 2004 and in early 2015, it got the approval of the Knesset following which the Sharon government started withdrawal from Gaza. But the pullout did not bring the occupation to an end. In the West Bank, Israel continued the military occupation. In Gaza, though they had withdrawn most troops and settlers, they continued to control Gaza's air space and territorial waters and all the major entry points of the strip, except Rafah, on the Egyptian border. In practical terms, Israel continued to control Gaza indirectly.[40] Since 2007, two years after the pullout, Israel has also imposed a land, air and sea blockade on Gaza, which led many to call the enclave 'the largest open air prison in the world'.[41] Furthermore, since the pullout, Gaza has seen four major Israeli military operations, excluding the 2023–24 war—Operation Cast Lead (2008–09), Operation Pillar of Defence (2012), Operation Protective Edge (2014) and Operation Guardian of the Walls (2021)—in which thousands of Palestinians were killed. UN probes have blamed both the Israeli army and Hamas for war crimes in these conflicts.

Unsustainable Status Quo

On 18 January 2016, while speaking at a security conference in Tel Aviv, Dan Shapiro, the US ambassador to Israel at the time, said that 'at times, it seems Israel employs two standards of law in the occupied West Bank, one for Israelis and the other for Palestinians'.[42] [Though he apologized later for the timing of his critical comments, which was interpreted by many as a reference to apartheid], Shapiro was not alone in such sharp criticism. On the same day, the European Union (EU) Foreign Affairs Council unanimously adopted a resolution, stating that EU agreements with Israel applied only to the State of Israel within the pre-1967 border, not to Jewish settlements in the Palestinian territories.[43] A week later, the then United Nations Secretary-General Ban Ki-moon joined them. He said the continued settlement activity in the West Bank was 'an affront to the Palestinian people and to the international community'.[44]

These criticisms, even from unlikely quarters, demonstrated the growing levels of frustration in the international community with the freeze in the peace process and the way Israel was treating Palestinians. A new wave of violence was sweeping through Jerusalem and the West Bank. Palestinians carried out attacks against Israeli soldiers and civilians with knives, guns, vehicles and fire. Israel's response to this crisis was typical—security crackdown and provocation. It blamed the Palestinian leadership for inciting violence. The security forces shot dead the Palestinian attackers, mostly teenage boys and girls. The attackers' family members were punished, and houses demolished.

There have been several attempts to revive peace talks since the collapse of the second Camp David negotiations. In 2002, the Arab League, at its Beirut Summit, endorsed the Arab Peace Initiative, which called for normalizing relations between Arab countries and Israel, in exchange for a full withdrawal by Israel from the occupied territories, including East Jerusalem, and a 'just settlement' of the Palestinian refugee problem based on UN Resolution 194.[45] But the Israeli government rejected the offer. In the same year, the Middle East Quartet—the United States, the European Union, Russia and the United Nations—proposed a 'roadmap' for peace which called for an independent Palestinian state living side by side with Israel in peace. According to the roadmap, the peace process should start with an immediate and unconditional ceasefire that would be followed by political institutional reforms in Palestine, including elections. In phase two, the establishment of an independent Palestinian state with provisional borders was proposed. A final settlement was to be found in phase three in which issues such as the status of Jerusalem, the right of return of refugees, and Jewish settlements would be decided. The original plan suggested the settlement in two years.[46] Israel refused to freeze new settlements in the occupied territories, and the plan never took off. President Barack Obama had also tried and failed to revive talks between the Palestinians and the Israelis.[47]

After the Obama administration's efforts collapsed, the international community largely looked away from this conflict, until recently. During this period, Gaza was bombed, violence spread in the occupied West Bank, and ties between the Israelis and the Palestinians fell to a new low, closing hopes for a restart in the peace process. When the Obama administration gave up on finding or facilitating a solution to the crisis, France stepped in by announcing plans to host an international summit on Israel–Palestine peace. The conference in January 2017 was attended by diplomats from twenty-nine countries, but Israel and Palestine were absent. The summit produced few concrete steps to be taken forward. France claimed the plan was to provide a 'clear framework with defined parameters' for the resumption of negotiations. The initiative proposed the creation of two states, based on the 1967 border, with Jerusalem as the capital of both. But the ground reality of mistrust, hostility, violence and occupation was markedly different from the mood set in the conference.

During the Trump presidency, Israel stepped up the pace of the settlements. From 2017 to 2021, the number of settlers in the West Bank (excluding East Jerusalem) shot up from 3,99,000 to 4,65,000, according to data collected by Peace Now.[48] Trump's decision to move the American embassy to Jerusalem was a concession to Israel without anything in return. The Palestinians have always maintained that they won't accept any final settlement without East

Jerusalem as their capital. In a U-turn from Washington's previous position, in November 2019, the then US Secretary of State Mike Pompeo said Israeli settlements on the occupied Palestine land were not necessarily illegal. The Biden administration reversed this stand on settlements but stopped short of taking any punitive measures or pressure measures towards Israel against the settlements.

Lopsided Response

There's no level playing field between Israel and Palestine. One is the mightiest military power in West Asia, with nuclear weapons and the direct support of the US, while the other, Palestine, is not even a fully recognized nation-state. For a just solution to emerge from talks, theoretically speaking, there has to be a balance between the two sides, and that can only happen in this case through the mediation of the international community. Prime Minister Netanyahu's lack of interest in the peace process is not a secret. During the election campaign in 2015, the Prime Minister said no Palestinian state would be formed under his watch.[49] His political allies, including settler parties, are now calling for the annexation of those parts of the West Bank where settlements have been built. How can peace be possible if Israel, the superior power, continues to grab more Palestinian land while violence and occupation continue?

Israel knows that it can get away with its actions, unlike other rogue states such as North Korea or Iran. It's the only nuclear-armed nation in West Asia, though it hasn't officially declared its nuclear capability. It faced allegations, based on UN investigations, of war crimes against Palestinians in Gaza. It continues the occupation of the West Bank and Gaza in violation of UN resolutions. Despite criticisms even from its allies in the West, Israel's settlement policy remains intact. And with promises of annexation and the continuing violence, Israel was ready to deepen and tighten occupation further. Still, there was no meaningful international effort to hold Israel accountable for its actions.

Take the case of the Obama administration, which was seen as most critical of Israel's policies in the recent past. The equation between President Barack Obama and Prime Minister Netanyahu was known to be tense. Netanyahu who had travelled to Washington in 2015 while the US was pursuing a nuclear deal with Iran attacked the administration. But in the UNSC, Obama had been a consistent protector of Israel.[50] Over his eight-year tenure, the US vetoed all Security Council resolutions but one, which was specifically critical of Israel. Other Western countries were no exception.

Israel's records show that it made limited concessions only in the face of external pressure and Palestinian violence. During the Suez war, Israel was forced to pull out of Gaza amid threats and pressure tactics from both American President Dwight Eisenhower and Soviet leader Nikita Khrushchev in 1957. In the late 1970s, constant pressure from the Carter administration, and also the growing threat perception from Egypt following the Yom Kippur War prompted Israel to come to Camp David and finally sign both the Sinai pull-out and the Framework Agreements. In 1993, the Oslo process was triggered by the First Intifada. Violent Palestinian protests forced even a hard-line leader like Netanyahu, who opposed the Oslo Accords, to pull out troops from most of Hebron. Sharon's Gaza disengagement happened against the backdrop of the Second Intifada.

During the years that followed the Second Intifada, Israel thought the status quo was manageable. The Palestinians were a divided lot. The West Bank was run by Fatah and Gaza by Hamas. Palestinian Authority President Mahmoud Abbas lacked the charisma and command of the late leader Yasser Arafat. The Palestinian Authority was flush with corruption and there's widespread anger among the Palestinians towards the PA. There was no organized resistance in the West Bank. Hamas was seen as a terrorist organization by Israel, the United States and several other Western countries. There was no international pressure to make peace. And Arabs were ready to sidestep the Palestine issue to make bilateral peace with Israel. The Israelis thought they could continue the occupation without consequences.

Then came the 7 October attack.

3

A Passage to the West Bank

RAMALLAH is one of the hardest-to-access government administrative headquarters in the world, not because of geographical difficulties but rather because of the Israeli occupation of the Palestinian territories. The Palestinian National Authority (PNA), which is technically in charge of civil administration in parts of the West Bank, is based out of Ramallah, situated in the Judean Hills, roughly 10 km north of Jerusalem. The city, which has a population of roughly 40,000, has centuries-old stories of wars, conquests and occupations to tell. It was incorporated into the Ottoman Empire in the sixteenth century, and the British took over the region after the Ottomans were defeated in the First World War. Following the creation of the state of Israel in 1948, Jordan captured the West Bank, including Ramallah. But the regional map would change again after the 1967 war in which Israel seized the whole West Bank. Ever since, Ramallah, literally 'God's Height', has remained under Israeli occupation.

Today, the West Bank doesn't have an operational civilian airport, nor is the territory's airspace under the control of the Palestinian National Authority. The West Bank, the area on the western bank of the Jordan River, has an airfield in Jenin, which is today a flashpoint city, and a small airport in Kalandia, known for housing a huge, intimidating Israeli check-point, located between Jerusalem and Ramallah. The Kalandia airport has been closed to civilian traffic since 2002. Those who are going to the West Bank land either in Tel Aviv, Israel's commercial capital, or in Amman, Jordan, and then travel by road, crossing Israeli check-points, to Palestinian townships.

My first visit to the West Bank was in October 2015 to cover the visit of India's then President, Pranab Mukherjee, to Jordan, Israel and Palestine. Since we were part of the President's media delegation, our passage to Ramallah was relatively easy. I had an Israeli visa stamped on my passport, and before we left India I was told that that's what one needed to go to the Palestinian territories. We landed at Tel Aviv's Ben Gurion airport, and then boarded the media vans organized by the Israeli side.

Before leaving for Tel Aviv from Amman, we had been told that the check-in baggage would not be taken to Ramallah because of 'security reasons'. All of us were thus carrying clothing and other necessary items, including computers, in our handbags. On the Israeli side of the Beitunia check-point, we had to de-board and walk through the crossing. 'Israeli vehicles are not allowed on the other side of the wall,' the External Affairs ministry official accompanying us had briefed us earlier, referring to 'the security wall' Israel had built around the West Bank. Palestinians and human rights activists call the barrier an 'Apartheid Wall'. This wall, in places, cuts deep into the West Bank.[1]

The check-point appeared to be a massive tunnel. Heavily armed Israeli soldiers, most of whom appeared to be in their early twenties, were standing at both ends of the crossing points, their index fingers on the triggers. 'Never ever mess with the Israeli security,' the words of Venu Rajamony, the press secretary to President Mukherjee, echoed in my ears while I walked past the soldiers. On the Palestinian side, Arabs were in a queue at a terminal, waiting to cross the border to the Israeli side, where they were perhaps doing menial jobs. We boarded media vans arranged by the Palestinian Authority and strode through narrow roads connecting hilly townships. Vegetation was sparse. Palestinian soldiers in green uniforms, carrying automatic guns, were standing on either side of the road, clearing the way for the visiting Indian President. Shops were open, but with hardly any customers.

Ramallah is in 'Area A' of the West Bank. The security and civil control there are in the hands of the Palestinian National Authority. According to the Oslo Accords reached between the Palestinian leadership and Israel in 1993 and 1995, the West Bank was divided into three areas—A, B and C. Most of Israel's settlements in the West Bank are in Area C, but Israel has a huge security presence in Area B as well and it can storm into Area A towns any time. 'Life here is a little difficult. But we move on,' the bartender at the basement bar of Ramallah's Movenpick Hotel told me. A short man with a grim face who spoke in fluent English, he appeared to be older than his actual age. The bartender spoke of the wall and Israeli checkpoints that are making life 'like hell'. 'My sister is staying in Jerusalem. But I haven't seen her for the past six months. If I want to go there, I need a permit from the Israelis,' he said.

It's difficult for Palestinians to travel even from one city to another in Area A because of its numerous check-points. For example, there are ten check-points around Ramallah. At any point in time, Israel could close down these points, cutting the city off from the rest of the world. According to the United Nations Office for the Coordination of Humanitarian Affairs (OCHA), as of early 2023, there were at least 565 movement obstacles in the West Bank, including East Jerusalem. 'These include 49 check-points constantly staffed by Israeli forces or private security companies, 139 occasionally staffed check-points, 304 roadblocks, earth-mounds and road gates, and 73 earth walls, road barriers and trenches.'[2]

Palestinians holding West Bank IDs, like the bartender in Movenpick, require permits from the Israeli authorities to enter East Jerusalem through three designated check-points, except for men over fifty-five and women over fifty, according to the OCHA. And Israeli troops have the unquestionable authority to decide whom they should issue the permits to. Israel has also designated some 20 per cent of the West Bank as 'a firing zone', where Palestinians are not allowed. West Bank territories lying within the municipal boundaries of the illegal Israeli–Jewish settlements, which make up some 10 per cent of the West Bank, are also not accessible to the Palestinians.[3]

We left Ramallah for Al-Quds University in Abu Dis, situated in Area B, which is under total Israeli security control while its civil administration is managed by the Palestinian National Authority. One of the largest universities in the West Bank, Al-Quds has been a flashpoint of protests and student activism. Abu Dis is a border town in Jerusalem, but the wall Israel has built separates the town from the holy city. One can see the wall from the main entrance of the university. Anti-occupation graffiti on it, including red capital letters that read 'FREE PALESTINE', stares at those who are coming out of the university. Piles of burnt-out cars, memorials of a permanent conflict, are a common sight on the roadside.

At one check-point between Ramallah and Abu Dis, we were stopped. The white Israeli flag with its Star of David symbol was fluttering from a post. Soldiers asked for the ID of our driver. When we started taking photos from the van, they strictly said NO. As nobody was in the mood to argue with the Israeli soldiers while on Palestinian land, we set aside our cameras, phones and iPads. 'The Israeli strategy is to capsule Palestinian towns and villages. It's a deliberate policy to limit their movement within the towns they live in,' an Indian diplomat who'd come to Ramallah to make arrangements for the presidential visit told me. 'And this is frustrating the Palestinians. They can't move around. They can't go to college. They can't trade. They can't meet their relatives.' In the words of Mustafa Barghouti, a former Palestinian National Authority Minister, 'The occupation has transformed into a system of apartheid—much worse than the apartheid that existed in South Africa.' He said in an interview in late 2023, 'Today, the whole West Bank is paralysed by Israeli military check-points. The whole West Bank has been divided into 224 small ghettoes, separated from each other. And settlers are everywhere attacking Palestinians.'[4]

This complex web of check-points, roadblocks and the security wall—which is now 712 km long, and 65 per cent of which runs mostly inside the West Bank—is placing enormous limitations on the Palestine economy. 'Israel's system of policies and practices has systematically stripped the Palestinian economy of vital elements for its healthy operation, whose productive base continues to shrink, thereby exacerbating dire living conditions,' Tarik Alami, director of the Emerging and Conflict-Related Issues Division of the Economic and Social Commission for Western Asia (ESCWA), UN, said in a report in 2022.⁵ According to a 2022 UN study, the annual cost of Israel's restrictions is estimated 'at 25.3 percent of West Bank GDP and the cumulative GDP loss in 2000–20 is estimated at $50 billion, which is about three times the West Bank GDP and over 2.5 times the Palestinian GDP in 2020'.⁶

The inability of the Palestinian government led by Mahmoud Abbas, who is known by the *kunya* Abu Mazen, to resist these measures of Israel and meaningfully take forward the cause for statehood had made the Palestinian National Authority hugely unpopular among the Palestinians. 'Abu Mazen is a good man, but a very bad leader. He can't do anything but preach,' the bartender of Movenpick told me. 'His hands are also tied. He needs money from Europe to run his government. And Europe wants him to cooperate with Israel for security to keep sending money. In the West Bank, we are all collaborators in one way or the other.'

Abbas, who became the President of the Palestinian National Authority in 2005 after Yasser Arafat's death, doesn't actually have any real powers. He lost Gaza to Hamas, an Islamist militant group, in 2017. He presides over an economy that is heavily reliant on overseas aid and is tightly controlled by the Israelis.⁷ He lacks the charisma of Arafat and can neither inspire a peaceful Palestinian movement nor stop the occasional outbreak of violence. 'Abu Mazen just takes money from all around the world in the name of Palestinians, but does nothing,' an Arab salesman in an antiquities shop at West Jerusalem's famed Mamilla Mall told me two days later. It's this anger towards foreign occupation and frustration with their own leadership that gave space for Islamists such as Hamas and the Islamic Jihad to rise. In the Oslo Accords, the Palestine Liberation Organization (PLO) gave up armed struggle and supported a peaceful, negotiated solution to the conflict. But today, 63 per cent of Palestinians see 'armed struggle' as the best strategy to secure an independent state.[8]

This anger explains the occasional outbreaks of violence in the West Bank, East Jerusalem and Gaza. In recent years, the West Bank has seen a rise in attacks with knives and stones by Palestinians, mostly teenage boys and girls, who would instantly be shot dead by Israeli troops and their houses demolished. 'Our kids go and throw stones at the Israelis at the check-points, and they throw bombs and bullets back on us,' Georgy Annab, who worked in the Palestinian Authority's media department, told me. Georgy is a dynamic young man. He was running around the headquarters, known as 'Mukataa', to make arrangements for President Mukherjee's visit to the Arafat mausoleum when I met him.

As soon as the ceremonial reception was over and Presidents Mukherjee and Abbas went to the second floor of the administrative building for delegation-level talks, Georgy lit a cigarette, seemingly relaxed. He asked while shaking my hand, 'How's Palestine, my friend?' I said it's good. 'No, it's not good.' He took a step back to blow smoke out, asking if I would mind. I said I liked passive smoking, ever since I quit cigarettes. He laughed and then spread his hands as if he wanted me to look around the Presidential compound. 'Palestine is in a pretty bad shape. Do you know that you stand in the compound that was attacked several times by the Israelis earlier?'

I told him I had heard of the siege of the headquarters.

In March 2002, amidst the Second Intifada, Israel's right-wing Prime Minister Ariel Sharon launched Operation Defensive Shield, a major military operation in the West Bank that lasted for over a month. Israel sent troops to Ramallah, where Arafat was under siege at the Mukataa, Hebron, Jenin, Nablus and Bethlehem to destroy Palestinian resistance. In Ramallah, Israeli troops took control of the Mukataa and forced Arafat into one corner of his presidential compound with a few close advisers. He was not allowed to leave, while Israeli troops carried out military raids and arrests in the city.[9] In September, as suicide attacks continued in Israel, Prime Minister Sharon ordered another siege of the Mukataa. This time Israel sent bulldozers to the Palestinian presidential compound and brought down buildings, while Arafat stayed defiant in his dust-choked office in the compound. 'We are ready for peace but not for capitulation, and we will not give up Jerusalem or a grain of our soil, which we are guaranteed to us by international law,' Arafat declared from his office, surrounded by piled-up rubble.[10] He stayed in the besieged compound even after the Israeli Security Cabinet decided to 'remove' him from the Mukataa.[11] But amid his worsening health, he was transferred in October 2004 for medical reasons to a French hospital.

'We rebuilt the palace,' Georgy told me, drawing my attention to the buildings inside the Mukataa, including the Yasser Arafat Mausoleum, the 'temporary' resting place of the former chairman of the PLO. 'One day, we will rebuild Palestine,' he added.

Violence and Resistance

Back in Hotel Movenpick, I had a long chat with Husam Zomlot, Palestine's ambassador at large and one of the senior foreign policy advisers of President Abbas (Zomlot is currently the Palestine Ambassador to the UK). Asked about the effectiveness of throwing stones at the Israeli check-points, he said, 'We would have used F16s if we had them. But we don't. What we have are these stones and that's what our kids are doing.' I asked him about the violence by Palestinians. Is that helping the Palestinian cause? Zomlot said his administration didn't back any violent acts. 'Should their violence be justified? Not at all. But one has to look at the whole situation. They are hopeless people frustrated by the occupation. They can't even move freely in their own territories. Secondly, if they commit violence, the law of the land should deal with them. Not the Israeli police. What they (Israelis) are doing is just killing our children,' said the Ambassador.

Palestinian leadership had denounced violent methods several times, but they had little control over the protesters or Hamas, which won the last free elections the Palestinian territories had. Israel's military response and the check-point system they had implemented in the West Bank were actually strengthening the tide of violence. 'The kids have a sense of history. They know that whatever the Palestinians gained from the Israelis was through violent uprisings,' a psychology student at Al-Quds University told me. Nathan Thrall, an author who was a senior analyst at the International Crisis Group, agreed with her. In an op-ed article written in *The New York Times* on 18 October, he wrote: 'It is a deeply regrettable fact that, during the past quarter-century, violence has been the most consistent factor in Israeli territorial withdrawal.'[12]

Later in the day, I met President Abbas at the official dinner at the Mukataa. Wearing his trademark blue suit and gold frame glasses, he entered the dinner hall with other senior members of the PLO, including Hanan Ashrawi, a prominent woman voice of the Palestinian national movement. On one side of the wall, there was a huge image of Jerusalem, with the shiny, golden Dome of the Rock overlooking the guests, Arabs and Indians. Abbas took his seat by another wall where a large portrait of Yasser Arafat hung. Everyone was served Arabian tea. The President of the Palestinian National Authority raised a roast and others followed suit. Before everyone's attention shifted to the platter, he thanked India for its support for the Palestinian cause. After the meal, I got a chance to interact with President Abbas briefly. He held my hand and repeated, 'You are from India?' I said yes. He looked into my eyes, without saying anything. I asked if he would be willing to answer some questions. He said, 'Yes, but not today.' He asked me to coordinate with Palestine's Ambassador in Delhi.

Later in an interview, Abbas told me, 'Israel is systematically killing Palestinians.' 'The international community is dealing with Israel as a state above the international law,' he said, adding that 'Israel continues to disrespect its commitments [under the agreements both sides have reached].' Asked if he was committed to a two-state solution, Abbas said, 'I fully understand those who say the two-state solution is dead. However, I will continue with my efforts to keep it alive as all the alternatives will be more difficult and some are even impossible to implement.'[13]

Jerusalem

'What's Jerusalem worth?' Balian of Ibelin, who led the defence of Jerusalem in the twelfth century against the invading Ayyubid Army, is shown asking Sultan Salahuddin after negotiating the terms of surrender, in Ridley Scott's magnum opus, *Kingdom of Heaven*. The Sultan had told Balian, the blacksmith-turned-knight, that he would give 'every soul safe conduct to Christian lands. No one will be harmed.' 'On these terms I surrender the city,' says Balian, before asking the Sultan about its worth.

'Nothing,' says Salahudin in response and turns towards his waiting army. He then stops, turns to face the blacksmith, and then says, with both his fists tight as if he was ready for another fight, 'Everything.'

Salahudin was one of the many leaders who wanted to capture Jerusalem and win eternal glory. Christians and Arab Muslims came before him, and Ottomans came after him. The British followed the Ottomans and then the Jews. It's a city where history is frozen in every corner. Two days after meeting with President Abbas, I met a Jewish girl at Jerusalem's Inbal Hotel. A student of History of Art at the Hebrew University, Adinah (name changed) knew almost everything about Jerusalem, and she promised to take me and a few other journalists to the Old City. Later that evening, we walked along the Ottoman Walls, built in the sixteenth century by Sultan Suleiman I. I could hear *the azaan* from the al-Aqsa Mosque. An Arabic inscription on the north-eastern wall, which was originally built to prevent intruders, read, 'Suleiman the Magnificent has decreed the construction of the wall, he who has protected the home of Islam with his might and wiped out the tyranny of idols with his power and strength, he whom alone God has enabled to enslave the necks of kings in countries (far and wide) and deservedly acquire the throne of the Caliphate, the Sultan son of the Sultan son of the Sultan son of the Sultan, Suleiman.'[14]

For Muslims, the al-Aqsa mosque in Jerusalem is the third holiest place of worship in Islam after Mecca and Medina. They call the compound, which also houses the Dome of the Rock, the Dome of the Chain, four minarets and the Western Wall (the Wailing Wall for the Jews) of Haram esh-Sharif, or the Noble Sanctuary. For Jews, it's the Temple Mount, the holiest place in Judaism, where the Jewish temples once stood. Jews believe the ancient limestone wall is part of the Herod-era expansion of the Second Biblical Temple. According to Jewish tradition, the First Temple, built by King

Solomon, was destroyed by the Babylonians. The Second Temple, built in 516 BCE, was destroyed by the Romans in 70 CE. The wall is the only remaining part of the destroyed structure.

The modern story of the compound is equally complicated. The Palestinians see East Jerusalem as the capital of their future state, while Israel considers the whole city, including the western half that is, its seat of power, and the occupied eastern half as their 'eternal capital'. According to Islamic traditions, Prophet Mohammed was transported from 'the sacred place of worship' (the Great Mosque in Mecca) to the 'farthest place of worship' (Jerusalem) during his Night Journey (al-Isra) on a winged horse called al-Buraq. Later, on the same night, the Prophet is believed to have ascended to heaven (al-Mi'raj) with the archangel Gabriel from the place where the Dome of the Rock now stands.

Umar, the second Caliph of the Rashidun Caliphate, erected a prayer house at the place on the mount where the Prophet was believed to have led prayers during Isra, after the Muslim conquest of Jerusalem in the seventh century. This became al-Aqsa mosque (literally, the 'farthest mosque'). It was rebuilt and expanded by the Umayyads. The Umayyad-built structure was destroyed by earthquakes, and the mosque was rebuilt and renovated several times by the following Caliphates, including the Abbasids and the Fatmids.

After the Crusaders captured Jerusalem in the eleventh century, they turned al-Aqsa into a palace and the Dome of the Rock, which was originally built by the Umayyads, into a church. But Salahuddin, the founder of the Ayyubid dynasty, who recaptured the holy city from the Crusaders, restored the mosque. The city would remain in the hands of Muslims until the British General Edmund Allenby entered Jerusalem on foot through the Jaffa Gate on 11 December 1917 after his troops defeated the Ottomans.

In the first Arab–Israeli war that broke out after the state of Israel was declared in May 1948, the Israelis captured western Jerusalem and Jordan, the eastern half of the city, along with the West Bank. In the 1967 Six-Day War, Israel seized East Jerusalem and the West Bank from Jordan, the Sinai Peninsula and Gaza from Egypt and the Golan Heights from Syria. Later, Israel annexed East Jerusalem, taking the whole city under its control, but al-Aqsa would remain under the administration of an Islamic waqf, with the Hashemite monarchy of Jordan being its custodian.[15]

In other words, the third holiest mosque in Islam, whose custodian is the king of Jordan, exists in a compound that Jews believe once hosted their sacred temples in a city occupied by the Jewish state of Israel, which the Palestinians living under the Israeli occupation see as the legitimate capital of their future independent state. It's a place where faith, history, disputes, power and politics are all intertwined, making it extremely difficult to find peace.

'That's Jerusalem's charm and tragedy,' Adinah told me in front of the Church of Holy Sepulchre, the holiest place of Christianity, which is situated roughly 500 m from the Western Wall. The Holy Sepulchre compound contains Golgotha, where Christians believe Jesus was crucified, and his empty tomb—the tomb in which he was buried and supposedly resurrected from. Inside the compound, there is a rock where Jesus's body was believed to have been placed while taking him to the burial cave. People touch the rock and pray. On the right side, one can climb up to the site of the crucifixion. A monk with a long, silver beard, in a black robe, was sitting beside the stairs in darkness as if he was part of history like the many columns built by the Crusaders.

While walking out of the compound, Adinah talked about the complicated arrangement reached between different churches—

the Roman Catholic, Greek Orthodox, Armenian, Syriac Orthodox, Coptic Christian and the Ethiopian ones—to maintain their shared rights over the holiest place in Christianity. The agreement reached in the nineteenth century demands a 'status quo' in the literal spirit—it's called the Status Quo Agreement. In 2002, a Coptic monk moved his chair inside the compound a bit, which the other churches saw as a hostile move. There were clashes, leaving several wounded. There is a ladder up against the front wall of the church, which is today called the 'Immovable Ladder'. It's been there since the eighteenth century, and nobody can move it because doing so would be seen as a violation of the status quo.[16] 'Look at that,' Adinah told me pointing towards the ladder. 'God can't even move a ladder in his holiest city. Gods in Jerusalem are so helpless!'

~

While walking back to the hotel, passing the City of David, I asked her about Benjamin Netanyahu, the Israeli Prime Minister. 'I am not from the embassy. I can say whatever I want to.' I said that's what we would like to hear. 'I don't agree with most of his policies. I think he's taking Israel to the dark ages.'

Adinah is a secular Jew who is working for the rights of Arabs living in Israel, who make up roughly 20 per cent of the country's population. Her parents had migrated to Israel in the early 1990s from Azerbaijan and were living in Jerusalem. She and her husband had moved to Tel Aviv recently, but she said she kept coming to Jerusalem. While walking from the Jewish Quarter of the Old City to the Arab Quarter, she said, 'Look at the difference. One lives in prosperity and the other in poverty and darkness.' Lights were actually out in the Arab quarters, maybe because shops were already closed. Israeli soldiers were standing on guard at every turning. I asked Adinah what, in her view, was a solution. I told her about my conversation with Mahmoud Abbas and his undying commitment towards the two-state solution. Was the two-state solution still viable?

'The two-state solution died long ago. Only one federal state, in which Arabs, Christians and Jews coexist, is the viable solution.'

'Do you say this aloud [before others as well]?' I asked her.

'Yes, of course. They already call me and my friends traitors. They say we want Israel to be defeated. That's not true. We want Israel to live in peace.'

But in Jerusalem, peace has been just a promise for centuries.

Bethlehem

It's a hotel that bears the hallmarks of the land where it exists. Nestled against the concrete wall Israel has built, the Walled Off Hotel in Bethlehem offers its guests the 'world's worst view'. All ten rooms in the three-storey hotel, located hardly 3 km away from the Church of the Nativity, face the concrete slabs of the wall. Inside the hotel, there's a café which was decorated with original artwork by the British street artist Banksy and a small museum that explains the history of the wall, which was declared illegal by the International Court of Justice.[17]

When it was opened to guests in March 2017, the hotel made news because of its association with Banksy, who keeps his real identity secret. 'Nobody knew that Banksy was involved in the project, until the opening day. On the opening day, we invited people to this hotel, and it was a big surprise to everyone,' Wissam Salsaa, the manager of Walled Off, told me when I visited the hotel with a journalist friend in 2018.[18]

Salsaa said it had originally been a residential building, vacated in 2000, in the wake of the Second Intifada. 'This building [was] left vacant for fourteen years,' said Salsaa. 'Nobody was interested to live here because of the clashes, because of the wall. I rented the building and renovated its interiors, of course, in coordination with Banksy. It took me one year and three months to finish this project,' said Salsaa. 'The view from this hotel is the view of occupation. The view of apartheid.'

And why the name 'Walled Off'? Salsaa smiled at the question. 'Banksy gave [it] the name. It's a pun on Waldorf,' he said, referring to Waldorf Astoria, the global luxury hotel chain. Banksy, who first made headlines for his graffiti on the walls of Bristol, England, and whose works have been auctioned for millions of dollars, was frequently travelling to the Palestinian territories for over a decade, according to Salsaa.

Much before the hotel was opened, Banksy's paintings on the wall, depicting life under the Israeli occupation, became a tourist attraction. The artwork placed in the lobby in the rooms of the Walled Off signifies the Israeli–Palestinian conflict. The museum has a wax statue of Sir Arthur Balfour, the former British foreign secretary who issued the eponymous declaration in 1917 that said imperial Britain would support the creation of a Jewish homeland in Palestine. In one of the rooms, a mural on the wall shows an Israeli soldier in military fatigues and a Palestinian wearing a keffiyeh fighting with pillows. In the café, where weekly concerts happen, three cherubs hang above a piano, but all with oxygen masks because Israeli tear gas shells keep the air toxic. '(It's) a three-storey cure for fanaticism, with limited car parking,' Banksy said in a statement in 2017 when the hotel was opened.

The staff at the hotel said they were not political activists but Palestinians with a political view. 'I am a musician. We are not political. We are independent people. We send our message through music and art,' said one staffer, who did not want to be named as 'Wissam [Salsaa] is the only guy who can talk to the media'. What is the message they are sending from the Walled Off? 'Give us freedom. End the occupation. There are too many restrictions in Palestine.'

~

The next day, I took a taxi with my friend to Bethlehem again. This time we wanted to see the Church of the Nativity, which is believed to be the birthplace of Jesus. The basilica, originally commissioned in 330 CE by Constantine the Great, the first Roman emperor to convert to Christianity, is the oldest church in the holy city. The history of the basilica is as complicated as the history of the city. In 1717, when Jerusalem was controlled by the Ottomans, Catholics placed a fourteen-point silver star over what they claimed was the stone where Mary gave birth to Jesus. In 1847, Greek Orthodox monks stole the star. Five years later, Napoleon III forced the Ottoman Sultan to recognize Catholic France as the sovereign authority for all the churches of Jerusalem. This triggered massive protests from Orthodox Christians, especially those in Russia. The Sultan renounced the French treaty and restored the Greek Orthodox Church's control over a portion of the basilica.[19] Catholics were given control of another portion of the Cave. Since the mid-nineteenth century, the rights of different Christian communities over the basilica have been ruled by the Status Quo Agreement.[20]

It was a Saturday. Our work in Ramallah got done late in the afternoon, and we had two options—either go to Jerusalem, a city which I always wanted to go back to, or to Bethlehem, a city that I hadn't explored much, besides the Banksy hotel. These were not very far from each other but were separated by Israel's wall. We picked Bethlehem. Geeta Mohan, my friend, had warned me that the church would be closed by the time we reached the town. But I still wanted to give it a shot. Bethlehem lies roughly 30 km south of Ramallah. But the drive, crossing check-points and navigating the chaotic West Bank traffic, was tedious. By the time we reached the town, it was evening, and the church was of course shut.

The church, built with the famous Palestine limestone, looks like a fortress with a bell tower in the middle of a huge wall. There was a Franciscan hotel next to the church called Casanova. We asked the man at the reception if there was any chance to enter the church. He said 'Yes, tomorrow morning', with a broad smile. In front of the church is the Manger Square, where visitors come, mainly with families, to relax. Across the square, one could see the Mosque of Omar, named after the Second Caliph of Islam and built with a similar limestone. The minaret of the mosque is taller than the palm trees that border the Manger Square. The story is that Caliph Omar, after conquering Jerusalem and taking over from the Byzantines, travelled to Bethlehem, a prominent Christian settlement, and issued a law, guaranteeing respect for the church, Christians and the clergy. He prayed at a site a few metres from the church. The original mosque was built in 1860 by the Jordanians on land donated by the Greek Orthodox Church.[21] It was renovated some sixty years ago. When we were there, though the church was closed, we could hear the aazan from the mosque. Geeta told me, 'Either your God or their God, one is always up here.'

On the flanks of the square lay the Bethlehem Municipality building and the Palestinian Peace Centre. The ground floor of the Municipality building is occupied by different stores, selling 'pieces of Bethlehem', and a pub. At a store, from where I bought a wooden replica of the Nativity for my mother, I asked the burly, moustachioed man in charge how life was in Bethlehem. He said life was quiet except for the occasional flare of violence. 'The Israelis come whenever they want to come.'

'Do they come here?' I asked him, pointing towards the church.

'Yes, the church was under siege in 2002,' he said in his heavy voice while giving me the balance.

I then reluctantly asked him a question that I always try to avoid in my conversations. 'Are you a Muslim or a Christian?'

'I am a Christian, I am a Palestinian and I want freedom from occupation,' he said, clearly understanding the intention behind the question.

Outside the store, I found people sitting in front of the pub enjoying the weather and the beautiful view of the all-lit-up Manger Square, surrounded by history and faith and yet detached from their complications, sipping from their glasses. For a moment, I thought to myself: life is so simple here. On one side, you have the place where Jesus was born; just a few hundred metres across the square, you have a mosque where Islam's Second Caliph prayed! And in between is a pub where you can sit back and deliberate on what went wrong over the centuries.

4

Axis of Resistance

On 24 February 2022, the day Vladimir Putin of Russia launched the Ukraine invasion, I was in Tehran. The widespread understanding in Iran was that Russia, its most important ally, was forced to launch this war by the West. Ashraf (name changed), a young Iranian who was accompanying the visiting Indian media delegation, told me that 'the world is changing'. Ashraf, who is more than six feet tall and bulky, appears very pleasant, even when he talks about the most complicated issues of Iran. Squeezing his stubble while talking, Ashraf, a pious Shia, identified himself as a social worker associated with a think tank in Tehran, but seemed very well connected, and doors opened to him even in Iran's power corridors. He was both a facilitator and a minder.

I asked Ashraf if the Russians were making a mistake. Iran, a Shia majority theocracy, and Russia, the successor state of the communist Soviet Union with an Orthodox Christian majority, have a deep collaboration in Syria, a Sunni-majority country ruled by an Alawi family. When the regime of Syrian President Bashar al-Assad, the only state ally of Iran in West Asia (Middle East), was on the brink of collapse, the Russians came to their rescue in 2015. Iran-trained troops as well as Hezbollah, a pro-Iran Shia militia group based in Lebanon, fought alongside the Syrian army under Russian air cover against Assad's rivals during the civil war.[1] By the time the Ukraine war broke out, Assad had almost won the civil war, recapturing most of the territories he had lost to rebels and jihadists. But Syria remained dependent on the Russians and the Iranians for security.

The civil war produced a new security challenge for Syria. As Iran deepened its footprint inside Syria, Israel got alarmed as it continued to occupy the Golan Heights, which it captured from Syria in the 1967 war. Israel was also worried about Iran's continued arms supplies to Hezbollah through Syria. In recent years, Israel has carried out dozens of air strikes inside Syria, mainly targeting shipments for Hezbollah. Russia, which practically controls Syria's airspace, never challenged Israel's air strikes in Syria. In November 2022, a senior Israeli official told me at the Ministry of Foreign Affairs in Jerusalem that 'there is an unwritten understanding between us and the Russians. We won't hurt the Russian troops in Syria and the Russian interests in general, and they won't screw our operations in Syria. It's mutual tolerance.'

Ashraf was aware of Russia's limitations in Syria. My question was, if Russia got stuck in Ukraine, how was it going to affect Iran's interests in West Asia? 'My friend,' he put his big arm on my shoulder while we were standing at the top floor of Tehran's Milad Tower, 'the Russians came into the picture only after the civil war broke out in Syria. We've been playing this game in this region for centuries.'

The Milad Tower and the Azadi Square are two of the most favoured tourist destinations of Tehran. The Azadi Square, which has a 45-metre marble tower known as Azadi Tower (formerly Shahyad, Shah's Memorial Tower), was commissioned by Shah Mohammed Reza Pahlavi, Iran's last monarch. The square was the centre of the revolutionary activities in 1978–79 that led to the fall of the Shah's regime, following which the Mullahs captured power. 'Mehrabad Airport, where Imam Khomeini landed after the revolution in 1979 is just 2 km from here,' Ashraf said to me. When the Shah fled the country amid widespread protests, Ayatollah Ruhollah Khomeini, then Iran's senior-most Shia cleric, was in exile in Paris. He returned on 11 February 1979 in a chartered Air France Boeing 747-100. When the Air France captain accompanied him out of the aircraft at the Mehrabad Airport, hundreds of thousands of Iranians, who had thronged to the airport and Azadi Square, welcomed the Ayatollah. 'I will appoint the government... With the support of the people, I will appoint the government. I will do this because the people approved me,' Khomeini said to the cheering crowd.[2]

For Ashraf, the only significance of Azadi Square was its role in the revolution. But he was quite proud of Milad Tower, the tallest tower in Iran, which was built by the revolutionary regime. If Azadi Tower was the symbol of Iran's monarchy, the Milad Tower, 435-m high, including a 120-m antenna, was a symbol of the revolution for the Islamists. Its octagonal concrete shaft joins a pod with twelve floors that come with their observation decks, a cafe and a museum. The antenna, on top of the pod, pierces into Tehran's smoggy sky. In the museum, there is a huge eighteenth-century map of the Persian Gulf by a French cartographer on display. Our guide told us, pointing at the map, 'You may have heard some calling the Persian Gulf the Arabian Gulf today,' referring to the body of water that separates the Arabian coast from the Iranian coast. 'Look at this map, reach your own conclusions,' said the guide, a young woman who was a huge fan of Amitabh Bachchan and Aishwarya Rai. From the deck of the twelfth floor, the highest point of the tower where visitors are allowed, one can see the whole city, which was made the capital of the Persian empire in the eighteenth century by Agha Muhammad Khan, the first king of the Qajar dynasty. In the north lies the Alborz mountains, the natural barrier that separates the Iranian plateau from the Caspian Sea. Looking at its white peaks from some 350 m above the ground, exposed to the icy February Tehran winds, I could sense how geopolitics shaped Iran's past and present. 'The Americans and the Israelis think they can destroy Iran,' Ashraf told me from the deck. 'You look at those mountains that ring this beautiful city. Who can destroy us?'

I didn't answer his question. The next day, I was at Tehran's National Garden. The area had been a military shooting range in the nineteenth century during the Qajar period. Reza Shah Pahlavi, the founder of the Pahlavi dynasty who became the Shah of Iran in 1925, turned the range into a public park. Subsequently, key government buildings came up in the area. Today, building number nine is the Ministry of Foreign Affairs. I was there on a Friday. The building looked deserted. There was a huge cannon in front of the main part, flanked by cropped palm trees. The evening sun reflected on the Persian inscription on the main entrance. Inside the ministry, we passed the briefing hall and entered a conference room. Portraits of Ayatollah Khomeini and Ali Khamenei, the former and current Supreme Leaders, were hanging from the wall.

There was a full-size cut-out of Gen. Qassem Soleimani, the slain charismatic Iranian commander, at the entrance to the hall. I had a free-wheeling conversation with a senior Iranian diplomat on the condition that I should not name him. We talked about the nuclear deal, which Iran signed with world powers in 2015 but collapsed in 2018 after the then US President Donald Trump unilaterally pulled his country out of the deal, Tehran's foreign policy challenges, ties with India and its rivalry with Israel.

A shadow war was already going on between Israel and Iran. Israel's opposition to the Joint Comprehensive Plan of Action, or the Iran nuclear deal, was not a secret. Israeli leader Benjamin Netanyahu publicly campaigned to scuttle the deal when the Barack Obama administration was in talks with Tehran and other world powers. Israel carried out covert operations inside Iran, targeting the latter's nuclear and missile programmes, in what former Israeli Prime Minister Naftali Bennett called the 'Octopus doctrine', hitting the octopus at its head, not just at its tentacles.[3] A number of Iranian nuclear scientists, including Mohsen Fakhrizadeh, who oversaw Iran's nuclear programme, were assassinated, which was then blamed on Israel.[4] Israel has never denied the accusations. Iran responded with drone attacks, targeting what it claimed was a compound used by Israeli operatives in northern Iraq. A naval conflict between the countries, where ships linked to them came under attack in the Persian Gulf and in Arabian and the Mediterranean waters, was escalating. Former Iranian President Mahmoud Ahmadinejad had described Israel as 'a disgraceful blot' and threatened to 'wipe it off the map'.[5] And Israel sees Iran's growing military capabilities and its close ties with Islamist militia groups in the region as an existential threat. 'I will never allow Iran to obtain nuclear weapons,' the current Israeli Prime Minister Benjamin Netanyahu once said.[6]

I asked the Iranian diplomat whether the regime stood by the comments made by former President Ahmadinejad on Israel. He ignored the question and said it's Israel that is orchestrating destabilizing activities inside Iran. I reframed my question and asked him, 'Is there a chance for peace between Israel and Iran?' The answer came at once. 'No. Not as long as Jerusalem is under Zionist occupation.'

'Why Jerusalem? Why does Iran continue to support the Palestinians when most Arab countries have opted to live in peace with Israel?' I asked him, feigning ignorance.

'You should understand one thing.' His demeanour changed abruptly, making him serious. 'We are an Islamic Republic. Jerusalem is our holy city. Palestinians are our sisters and brothers. Our foreign policy has a commitment towards the Palestinians. It's our moral and spiritual responsibility. We will never abandon that.'

The Persian Octopus

Ties between Iran and Israel have not always been *this* hostile. On the contrary, before the 1979 revolution, Israel was one of the closest partners of the Shah's Iran, which saw Arab countries across the Persian Gulf as its main rivals. The partnership had led to nuclear cooperation, and Israel, which today is hell-bent on preventing Tehran from going nuclear, had then promised to supply nuclear missiles to Iran.

In July 1977, Shah Mohammad Reza sent Lieutenant General Hassan Toufanian, his deputy minister of war and armaments, to Israel to hold secret talks with the newly formed right-wing Likud government of Menachem Begin. In April that year, the Shah had signed six 'oil for arms' contracts with Shimon Peres, the defence minister in the previous government. One of the contracts, code named 'Flower', sought Israel's help to modify its advanced surface-to-surface missiles and sell them to Iran. Gen. Toufanian's mission was to ensure that the change of government in Israel would not affect the deal. He met Major General Ezer Weizman, defence minister in the Begin government, and both of them agreed to build a military co-production line—Israel was to provide the technical know-how and Iran the finances and test sites. As part of it, Israel promised to supply Iran ballistic surface-to-surface missiles with a range of 700 km that could carry a nuclear warhead.[7]

Counterfactually speaking, had the Islamic Revolution not taken place, Iran would have, in the 1980s, had Israel-supplied nuclear missiles that could strike deep inside the Sunni kingdoms across the Persian Gulf. But the 1979 revolution that brought down the Shah's monarchy and turned the country into a theocratic republic radically altered not just Iran but the whole region as well. West Asia would never be the same again. The revolution moved Iran, one of the natural powers in the region in terms of resources, geography and population, to change from an American ally to its top enemy. For the Sunni Gulf monarchies, a Shia theocratic republic across the Gulf waters not only posed geopolitical challenges but also existential and ideological threats. For Israel, the region's only nuclear power, its most prominent rival was just born. Ever since, the power struggle between these three pillars has been one of the defining factors of West Asia's geopolitics.

A year after the revolution, Saddam Hussein's Iraq, backed by Gulf monarchies and the West, attacked Iran, launching a disastrous war that lasted for eight years. They expected the war to overthrow the revolutionary regime; instead, it helped the Ayatollahs consolidate their position within the country. Isolated in West Asia, Iran knew that it was not a conventional military power compared to its rivals. Saudi Arabia spends almost five times more on its military than Iran's defence budget.[8] Israel, its key rival, is a de facto nuclear power and the mightiest military force in West Asia, and has the unconditional support of the United States. As Iran cannot beat its opponents in a conventional power projection, it has turned to the doctrine of forward defence—build and aid a network of militia groups in faraway regions that could pose security threats to Tehran's conventional rivals.[9] This approach is what makes Iran the 'strategic octopus' of West Asia. The regime is the head, the militias are the tentacles. Of these tentacles, the most prominent ones are Hezbollah and Hamas, both training their guns at Israel.

Even if Iranian leaders and diplomats, like the one I met in Tehran, say that Iran's commitment towards Palestinians is ideological, there is a fair amount of realpolitik in its support for pro-Palestinian groups. Over the years, the Islamic Republic, grappling with US sanctions and practically isolated in the region that is politically dominated by Sunni Arab countries, saw that its support for the Palestine cause would help it garner some legitimacy in West Asia, especially among the masses. Besides, supporting militia groups on the Israel border, such as Hamas and Hezbollah, also provided Iran some strategic leverage in the immediate conflicts Israel was fighting. When Arab countries, mostly allies of the United States, gave up their old hostility with Israel and moved towards either formally recognizing the Jewish nation or doing backroom business, Iran emerged as the most prominent pro-Palestine and anti-Israel nation-state voice in West Asia. It maintained its anti-Israel rhetoric while continuing to support Hezbollah and Hamas.

The Party of God

The roots of Hezbollah go back to Israel's 1982 war on Lebanon, which the then Likud Prime Minister, Menachem Begin, launched to oust the Palestine Liberation Organization (PLO) from the neighbouring country. Once the PLO was ousted from Lebanon, 'there would be a historic period of peace, of 40 years, or 50 years', Begin reportedly said on 4 August 1982, while addressing some 200 American members of the United Jewish Appeal in Jerusalem.[10] Lebanon was in the grip of a devastating civil war that began in 1975. According to Lebanon's post-French Constitution, power was divided among the different communities in the country—the Presidency was reserved for Christians, the Premiership for Sunnis and the Speakership for the Shias.[11] Roughly 40 per cent of Lebanon's population are Arab Shias. The influx of the Palestinian refugees into Lebanon and the relocation of the PLO to Lebanon from Jordan in 1971 created fissures in the country's delicate confessional system, which would lead to the civil war. While the Sunnis and Maronite Christians were the powerful sects there, Shias were the invisible majority, sidelined by the major players and post-colonial institutions.

Israel attacked Lebanon in 1978 and 1982, first to push the PLO out of the border region and then out of the country. 'If they do not go, well, we shall have to solve the problem. They will not stay in Beirut. That is out of the question,' Prime Minister Begin said in August 1982, referring to the PLO.[12] Yasser Arafat, the PLO chairman, finally agreed to leave Lebanon, but if Begin expected the PLO's departure to bring him peace, he was thoroughly mistaken.

One community that bore the brunt of Israel's disproportionate bombing was the already marginalized Shias. The Iran revolution had taken place just three years ago. Iran's Supreme Leader Imam Khomeini had already called on the world's 'oppressed Muslims' to rise against their oppressors. Iran sensed an opportunity in the chaos that engulfed Lebanon immediately after Israel's invasion. The Islamic Revolutionary Guard Corps (IRGC), an elite branch of the Islamic Republic, formed immediately after the revolution, despatched a group of soldiers to Lebanon to mobilize Shias. They formed a loose network, what was then unofficially called the 'Islamic Resistance', and provided them arms and training. Iran sensed two strategic opportunities in Lebanon. One, organize the Shia community and turn them into a powerful entity in Lebanon's complex political system and two, build a strong Shia militia that could fight the Israeli occupation of southern Lebanon, bogging down the Israelis in Lebanon's morass through asymmetric warfare.

One of the first targets of the Islamic Resistance was the Multi-National Force (MNF) deployed in Lebanon. In April 1983, the US Embassy in Beirut was bombed, killing sixty-three people. In October, 305 people, mostly American and French soldiers, were killed in suicide attacks on their military barracks. Following these attacks, the MNF would leave the country, providing the first victory to the newly organized Shia militants. Israeli troops retreated to a 'security zone' in southern Lebanon. In 1985, the Islamic Resistance came up with a manifesto, calling for 'the destruction of the state of Israel', vowing to oust occupied forces from Lebanon and declaring allegiance to Iran's Supreme Leader. 'This enemy is the greatest danger to our future generations and to the destiny of our lands, particularly as it glorifies the ideas of settlement and expansion, initiated in Palestine, and yearning outward to the extension of the Great Israel, from the Euphrates to the Nile,' reads the manifesto. 'Our struggle will end only when this entity is obliterated. We recognise no treaty with it, no cease fire, and no peace agreements, whether separate or consolidated,' it adds.[13]

Over the years, Hezbollah has built sprawling social, political and military networks with deep roots in Lebanon's Shia community. In southern Lebanon, a Shia stronghold, it carried out a disciplined, effective, popular guerilla war against the occupying Israeli forces, turning the Israeli 'security zone' into what Adam Shatz calls an 'insecurity zone'.[14] The party organization has been built in a Leninist order, centralizing authority in the hands of the secretary general. The chief would oversee a seven-member Shura council, like the Polit Bureau of a communist party, and then there are sub-councils. Their social network caters to the Shia working class, offering support, including healthcare and education assistance, in a country where the state is systemically weak, while the political and parliamentary councils have played the role of a kingmaker in Lebanon's fractured polity ever since 1992, when Hezbollah participated in the elections for the first time.[15] Yet, the most important arm is the Jihad Council, which controls its military infrastructure.

Israel assassinated Hezbollah's co-founder Abbas al-Musawi in 1992 as part of a policy of targeted killings to weaken rival outfits. But the man who succeeded Musawi, Hassan Nasralla, turned Hezbollah into a socio-politico militant behemoth, 'a state within the state', though it had been designated as a terrorist outfit by Israel and several of its allies.[16] In 2000, after eighteen years of occupation, Israeli Prime Minister Ehud Barak decided to unilaterally withdraw troops from southern Lebanon, which Hezbollah celebrated as 'the first Arab victory in the history of Arab–Israeli conflict'.[17] But Israel's withdrawal did not quieten the Lebanese border. Hezbollah had no plans to disarm itself and become a normal political movement in

Lebanon. For Nasrallah, who, like Khomeini, was driven by pan-Shiism, the bigger battles were yet to come. He continued to build up Hezbollah's arsenals, in collaboration with Iran. He said Hezbollah would continue to fight the Israelis as long as its occupation of Shebaa Farms, a contested region between the Lebanese–Israeli border, and Palestinian territories continued. 'As an Arab nation, it's our duty and responsibility to free Jerusalem from the Israeli occupation,' Nasrallah said.[18]

In 2006, after Hezbollah carried out a raid and abducted two Israeli soldiers, Prime Minister Ehud Olmert declared war against the militant group. The war lasted for over thirty days and even on the last day of fighting, Hezbollah launched hundreds of rockets into Israel. Israeli air strikes and ground attacks destroyed much of Hezbollah's military infrastructure, but the group survived, and emerged politically stronger in Lebanon. 'Nasrallah wins the war,' screamed *The Economist*'s cover on 17 August 2006.[19] In the subsequent years, Hezbollah rebuilt its military power, mainly with help from Iran and Syria. From the 1980s, Syria's Baathist regime has been a conduit between Iran and Hezbollah. After the 2003 American invasion of Iraq, which led to the fall of Saddam Hussein and the rise of Shia parties, with close historical links to Iran, in Iraq, Tehran strengthened its influence across the Shia crescent, from Tehran to Baghdad, Damascus to Beirut all the way up to Israel's northern borders.

When Bashar al-Assad's regime in Syria was losing control in the midst of the civil war that broke out in 2011, Nasrallah did not have to think twice before despatching thousands of Hezbollah soldiers across the border to fight alongside the Syrian Army. He knew it was a do or die battle. If Assad fell, Iran's critical geographical link with Hezbollah would be broken, exposing the organization to the wrath of Israel. Hezbollah emerged stronger out of the Syrian conflict, with its newly gained battlefield experience. It has also strengthened the Iran-Syria-Hezbollah axis.

Israel today sees Hezbollah as a serious rival. In its 2009 updated manifesto, Hezbollah had reiterated its commitment for the destruction of Israel. 'Our problem with them (the Israelis) is not that they are Jews,' Hassan Nasrallah said when he announced the manifesto on 30 November 2009, 'but that they are occupiers who are raping our land and holy places.'[20] According to the International Institute for Strategic Studies, London, the militia has up to 20,000 active, well-trained fighters and as many reservists, with an arsenal of small arms, tanks, drones and long-range rockets.[21] In November 2022, I was on Israel's northern border, travelling with a group of journalists and an Israeli brigadier. The brigadier, a short, pleasant man wearing a sweatshirt and jeans, spoke to us matter-of-factly about the security challenges Israel was facing. We went to the Golan Heights, which Israel had captured from the Syrians in 1967. Today, Israel sells Golan as a key tourist destination. From Golan we moved to the border where Israel, Syria and Lebanon meet. There were barbed wires beyond which an isolated UN outpost was lying vacant. The brigadier pointed towards the buildings in the valley and told us that it was a Shia settlement. 'In 2006, we fought pitched battles with Hezbollah fighters along the border,' he said. I asked him how he assessed Hezbollah as an enemy. 'Hezbollah is a tough enemy. They have very good military equipment. They are very well-trained. They are like a proper army that has now amassed more than 1,00,000 rockets,' he said. 'See, we are soldiers. Our assessment is not political. Hezbollah is not Hamas. We have respect for the way Hezbollah fights. But we are ready to fight them any time.'

'Will there be another war between Israel and Hezbollah?'

'They take orders from Tehran. We take orders from our government and generals. You can't rule out another war. If one breaks out, it would be bloodier than 2006,' said the brigadier. His words came true on October 1 2024, when Israel launched its fourth invasion of Lebanon, after killing the Hezbollah chief, Hassan Nasrallah, days earlier.

The 'Zeal' of Resistance

If Hezbollah was the most successful story of Iran's forward defence, the second leg of this strategy is Hamas, the Palestinian Islamist group that carried out the 7 October 2023 attack inside Israel. Unlike Hezbollah, Iran was not involved in Hamas's creation. Hamas is Sunni and doesn't subscribe to Iran's Shia theocratic ideology either. Yet, Iranians saw Hamas as an important partner in its fight against Israel and have cultivated deep ties with the organization, designated as a terrorist outfit by Israel and its Western allies, over the years. For Hamas, which saw Arab nations warming up to Israel, bypassing the Palestine question, Iran emerged as a critical supporter and supplier. If Hezbollah was born as a tentacle of the Persian octopus, Hamas was recruited as one.

The roots of Hamas go back to the Muslim Brotherhood, one of the oldest political Islamist organizations present today. The Brotherhood, established by Egyptian Islamist Hasan al-Banna in 1928, made a presence in British-ruled Palestine in the 1930s. In 1935, Banna sent his brother Abd al-Rahman al-Banna to Palestine to build contacts. His focus had been on reorienting Muslim society, while the Palestine Liberation Organization (PLO), founded in 1964, championed the Palestinian nationalist sentiments.[22] After Israel captured the West Bank and East Jerusalem from Jordan, and Gaza Strip from Egypt in 1967, the PLO, vowing to liberate the whole of Palestine, started a guerilla group. The Muslim Brotherhood still stayed away from politics, but their leadership was increasingly critical of the PLO's secular nationalism.

The Brotherhood's approach was that the time for 'jihad' had not come yet and they should first rebuild a stronger, pious Islamic society—they called it 'the upbringing of an Islamic generation'.[23] During this time, Israel established contacts with the Brotherhood leadership in the occupied territories. Sheikh Ahmed Yassin, the physically challenged, half-blind cleric of the Brotherhood, established al-Mujamma' al-Islam (The Islamic Centre) in 1973. Israel recognized the Centre first as a charity and then as an association. This allowed Sheikh Yassin to raise funds, build mosques and set up educational institutions, including the Islamic University of Gaza.[24] After the 1979 Islamic Revolution in Iran, Islamist organizations, having witnessed the political success of the Mullahs, started becoming more ambitious and active. The 1980s saw repeated clashes between the left-wing supporters of the PLO and the Islamists in the occupied territories.

Hamas was established after the First Intifada broke out in 1987. On 8 December 1987, several Palestinians were killed in a traffic incident in Gaza, involving an Israeli driver, leading to a wave of protests. This incident led to an explosion of pent-up anger of the Palestinians, who, despite the PLO's fighting and activism, were not seeing an end to the occupation. The occupied territories were swept by a mass uprising. The PLO called on its supporters to join the Intifada. The Brotherhood also found it an opportunity to enter the struggle against the occupation. On 14 December, the Brotherhood, under the leadership of Yassin, issued a leaflet, asking Palestinians to stand up against the Israeli occupation. In January, they issued another leaflet under the name Harakat al-Muqawamah al-Islamiyyah (the Islamic Resistance Movement)—in short, Hamas, which means 'zeal' in Arabic. In 1989, Hamas launched its first attack, abducting and killing two Israeli soldiers. Israel cracked down on the group, arresting Yassin and jailing him for life.

Unlike the PLO, which was modelled around the leftist guerilla national movements in the Third World, Hamas had a completely different vision. The charter it issued on 19 August 1988 was studded with anti-Semitic remarks. Palestine is 'an Islamic Waqf land consecrated for Moslem generations until Judgement Day', reads the Charter. 'There is no solution to the Palestine problem except jihad' and all peace initiatives are a 'waste of time and acts of absurdity'. It cites a Hadith, quoting the Prophet Mohammed, 'The Day of Judgement will not come about until Moslems fight the Jews, when the Jew will hide behind stones and trees. The stones and trees will say, O Moslems, O Abdulla, there is a Jew behind me, come and kill him. Only the Gharqad tree would not do that because it is one of the trees of the Jews [related by al-Bukhari and Moslem].'[25]

In the 1990s, Hamas leadership toned down its blatant anti-Semitic rhetoric. 'We don't hate Jews and fight Jews because they are Jewish. They are a people of faith, and we are a people of faith, and we love all people of faith,' Sheikh Yassin said in an interview. 'The Jews lived with us all of our lives and we never assaulted them. But if they take my home and make me a refugee? Who has more right to this land? We don't hate the Jews, we only ask for them to give us our rights.'[26] In a 1997 speech, Sheikh Yassin repeated his position. 'I want to proclaim loudly to the world that we are not fighting Jews because they are Jews! We are fighting them because they assaulted us, they killed us, they took our land, our homes, our children, our women, they scattered us, we became scattered everywhere, a people without a homeland.'²⁷ But this did not mean that there was any meaningful improvement in Hamas–Israel ties.

When the PLO moved to join peace efforts seeking a solution to the Palestinian issue, Hamas hardened its position. It opposed the Oslo Accords, which allowed the formation of the Palestinian National Authority with limited powers within the occupied territories. When the PLO recognized Israel, Hamas rejected the two-state solution and vowed to liberate the whole of Palestine 'from the [Jordan] River to the [Mediterranean] Sea'. It has built an organization with several branches, following the Hezbollah model—the social wing is involved in Islamic education and charity works, while the Izz ad-Din al-Qassam Brigades, the military wing, is in charge of military planning and weapons acquisitions. It also has a political bureau. In October 1994, a year after the first Oslo Accord was signed, Hamas carried out its first suicide attack in Israel, killing twenty-two people in Tel Aviv.

In the 1990s and early 2000s, Hamas conducted several suicide attacks, targeting Israelis. In 2000, when the Second Intifada broke out, Hamas was in the driving seat. Hamas's supporters fought pitched street battles with Israeli troops, who used brute force to crush the protests. Hamas, by that time, had taken a mixed approach towards the Palestine question. It refused to stop violence; it refused to recognize the state of Israel, like the PLO did, but at the same time, it offered a ceasefire based on the 1967 border. In 2004, in the midst of the Second Intifada, Sheikh Yassen urged his movement and the Israelis to be 'realistic'. 'We are talking about a homeland that was stolen a long time ago in 1948 and again in 1967. My generation today is telling the Israelis, "Let's solve this problem now, on the basis of the 1967 borders. Let's end this conflict by declaring a temporary ceasefire. Let's leave the bigger issue for future generations to decide.'"[28]

On 22 March 2004, weeks after this truce offer was made, Sheikh Yassin, then sixty-seven, who was always seen in a white robe and skull cap, was returning from a mosque near his residence in the Sabra neighbourhood of Gaza City after offering the first prayer (Fajr) of the day. When the quadriplegic Sheikh was being escorted home by his bodyguards and supporters, Israeli missiles hit them, killing at least ten Palestinians, including the Sheikh. 'Blood spattered the walls of surrounding buildings. I could not recognize the Sheikh, only his wheelchair,' a witness said.[29] Israel's policy was to weaken Hamas by taking out its leadership. Abdel Aziz al-Rantisi, Sheikh Yassin's successor, was also killed a month later. Khaled Meshal, another top leader, had survived an attempt on his life by Mossad in Jordan, in 1997. But the killings did not weaken Hamas. The movement continued to remain defiant, targeting Israeli troops and settlers. In 2005, faced with Hamas's violent attacks, Israel, under right-wing Prime Minister Ariel Sharon, unilaterally decided to pull out of Gaza. It would return to the enclave eighteen years later, following Hamas's 7 October 2023 attacks.

Hamas's violent tactics and Israel's collective punishment of Palestinians in return seemed to have helped the Islamists gain popularity. In the January 2006 legislative elections in Palestinian territory, Hamas won 74 out of the 132 seats, while the Fatah party, the PLO's backbone led by President Mahmoud Abbas, got only 45 seats.[30] In its election manifesto, Hamas showed, for the first time, signs of moderation. It dropped the call for the destruction of Israel, which was mentioned in the 1988 charter, and said its first priority was to change the situation for Palestinians. Hamas formed the government in the Palestinian territories, but faced opposition from both Israel and Western powers. As tensions rose between Fatah and Hamas in the West Bank, Palestinian National Authority President Abbas dissolved the Hamas government and declared a state of emergency. This led to violent clashes between Fatah and Hamas. Fatah ousted Hamas from the West Bank, and Hamas ousted the former from Gaza in 2007. Since then, Hamas has been Gaza and Gaza has been Hamas, a new reality that would shake the whole of West Asia on 7 October 2023.

While Hamas never gave up its right to armed resistance, the organization signalled changes in its outlook over the years. It still refuses to recognize Israel but has offered hudna (a lasting ceasefire) if Israel returned to the 1967 border. In 2017, it adopted a new charter from which the anti-Semitic remarks of the original manifesto were expunged. The new document states that Hamas is not seeking war with the Jewish people—only with Zionism, which drives the occupation of Palestine. 'Hamas advocates the liberation of all of Palestine but is ready to support the state on 1967 borders without recognizing Israel or ceding any rights,' it reads.[31] The new charter also doesn't have any mention of the group's parent organization, the Muslim Brotherhood.

'The change in the charter means nothing. It was just to make them more presentable before the world. That's it,' an Israeli diplomat based in India told me in December 2024, two months after the 7 October attack by Hamas. 'If they were a changed organization, why did they attack us? Why did they kill our kids? Why did they rape our women?' asked the diplomat. I said the Hamas offer was to cease fire based on the 1967 border. 'Will Israel withdraw to the 1967 border in return for peace?' I asked the diplomat. 'You know, those issues should be decided through talks later. Hamas is a terrorist organization. They get support from Iran, and they take orders from Iran. We have evidence. They go to Iran for training. They smuggle weapons in through the Rafah crossing (on the Egyptian border),' the diplomat said.

'What should we do? Should we go to the terrorists and beg for peace? We are not going to talk to the terrorists who want to destroy us. Our priority is to destroy them.'

The General's Daughter

In Tehran, in February 2022, Ashraf took us to an apartment in an upscale neighbourhood. He told us we were going to meet an important host, without telling us who the host was. At the ground floor, we were told to deposit our mobile phones and back bags at the counter. I told Ashraf that we were allowed to carry a phone even into the Foreign Ministry building. He just smiled me away, stroking his stubble. I took the stairs to the second floor. On the wall, there were multiple framed pictures of Qassem Soleimani, the former commander of al-Quds, the elite foreign wing of the Islamic Revolutionary Guard Corp. In one picture, Soleimani, wearing a grey suit, was offering prayers at Imam Khomeini's mausoleum on the outskirts of Tehran. In another, he was in a battlefield, wearing military fatigues, giving instructions to soldiers. A third picture showed him wearing his green military uniform, being decorated with the award of the Zolfaghar Order, the highest military honour of Iran, by Ayatollah Ali Khamenei, the Supreme Leader, who had described him as 'a living martyr of revolution'.[32]

Qassem Soleimani joined the Iranian Army immediately after the revolution. He was on the frontlines during the 1980–88 Iran–Iraq war. His commanders were so impressed by his bravery during the war that they promoted the young soldier, in his twenties, to head the 41st Tharallah Division of the IRGC. When the war ended through a ceasefire in 1988, the Mullahs in Tehran, who Saddam Hussein and his Gulf allies wanted to overthrow, were totally in control of Iran. Gen. Soleimani was rewarded for his war performance. In 1990, he was named the IRGC commander of Kerman Province.

Iran had laid the foundations of its 'forward defence' doctrine during the Iraq war. The Quds Force was in charge of building Iran's network of operatives, organizations, militias and parties—its tentacles. By the time Gen. Soleimani was appointed the head of the Quds Force in 1998, Iran had already established a network of resistance, including Hezbollah and Hamas. His job was to take it to new levels. And he did just that.

A pious Shia Muslim, Gen. Soleimani was the hardliner of hardliners. He never hid where he stood in Iran's complex power dynamics in which the hardliners, moderates and reformists compete for influence through elections and other means. In 1999, when students revolted against the regime demanding more freedoms, Gen. Soleimani and other senior military figures wrote a letter to the reformist Mohammad Khatami, who was the President then, demanding action against protesters. 'Our patience has run out,' they wrote, warning that if the government didn't crush the protests, the military would. It was a blunt warning from the establishment, which is loyal to the Supreme Leader, to a more popular wing of the regime, the elected government. The police finally cracked down on the protesters.

In the subsequent years, when Iran rapidly expanded its presence in both Iraq and Syria, and ties between Tehran and Washington were fast deteriorating, Gen. Soleimani, as the commander of Iran's foreign missions, was very much in focus. In 2018, he responded directly to a warning from President Donald Trump against the Iranian President not to threaten the United States. Gen. Soleimani said, 'It is beneath the dignity of our President to respond to you. I, as a soldier, respond to you.'³³ Understandably, he was extremely popular among the Revolutionary Guards. When Mike Pompeo, the US Secretary of State, called for global efforts to deter Gen. Soleimani in July 2018, the IRGC retorted, 'Gen. Soleimani is not a single person. The great people of Iran support him.'³⁴

When the Syrian civil war broke out in 2011, Iran got alarmed. If the regime of Bashar al-Assad fell, Tehran would be weakened. Gen. Soleimani's mission was to stop it happening. 'The Syrian army is useless,' he once told an Iraqi politician.³⁵ What he did was to build and train Shia militias and send them to Syria to fight the rebels and the Sunni jihadists along with the regime. He coordinated with Hassan Nasrallah, the Hezbollah leader, whose life he'd once saved from an Israeli attack, strategizing the war.³⁶ In 2013, the regime troops, Shia militias and Hezbollah fighters captured Qusayr, a town on the Syria-Lebanon border, from the rebels in a joint operation, which was one of the early victories of the Assad regime in the civil war. Though the Russian intervention in 2015 actually turned around the conflict, the real ground support for the Assad regime came from the Iranians and their militias. And it's Gen. Soleimani who oversaw that ground support. Syria was his war.

As the main driver of Iran's forward defence, which helped the Islamic Republic deepen its influence across the region through militias, Tehran's rivals, mainly the United States and Israel, saw Gen. Soleimani as a key threat. On 2 January 2020, amid escalating tensions between Iran and the United States in the region, an American drone struck the convoy of Gen. Soleimani outside the Baghdad airport. The General was on his way to meet the Iraqi

Prime Minister, Adi Abdul Mahdi. He was killed instantly. Millions of supporters across West Asia took to the streets to mourn his death, including Palestinians in Gaza. 'We are loyal to those who stood with the resistance and with Palestine and we hold the US administration and the Zionist occupation fully responsible for the consequences of this deplorable crime,' Hamas said then, referring to the General's killing.[37]

Back in Tehran's apartment, we were asked to take a seat at one side of a long table. Iranians are known for their hospitality. The table was crowded with Iranian tea, fresh fruits, nuts, cupcakes and packaged juice. Ashraf asked us to 'refresh ourselves' while we wait for our host. Nearly ten minutes later, Zeinab Soleimani, accompanied by two bodyguards, walked into the hall. In a black abaya that didn't fully cover the baggy jeans she was wearing and a black hijab, Zeinab, who was then thirty-one, greeted all of us with a warm smile and took a seat on the opposite side of the table. She spoke, in fluent English, of the achievements of the Iranian revolution, the brutalities of the 'Zionist regime' and the significance of the martyrdom of her 'beloved father'.

Zeinab, the youngest of Gen. Soleimani's four children, was virtually unknown till January 2020. Because of security reasons, the general's personal life was hidden from the public eye. But after his death, Zeinab emerged as the most visible face of the General's family. In March 2020, on Nowruz, the Iranian New Year, Zeinab shared a photo of her father and a dog tag on Instagram, and wrote: 'You gave me this when we went to Syria and asked me to keep it so they would know that I'm your daughter ... You told me you'd be happy if we were martyred together. You flew away and left me behind. Maybe my wings were too small.' In 2016, at the peak of the Syrian civil war, while visiting the family of an Iranian soldier killed in Syria's Aleppo, Gen. Soleimani said, 'I have a daughter, who is a guerilla in her own right.'[38] I asked Zeinab whether she had accompanied her father to battlefields as some accounts had claimed. She did not give a direct answer. 'My father was a very busy man. He had dedicated his life for the revolution; for the oppressed. We hardly got to meet him or spend time with him. Whenever we could, we cherished every moment of it.'

Zeinab is now running an NGO that is working among Iranian women—at least that's what her associates told me. They, however, remained tight-lipped on her other whereabouts. After Soleimani's death, Iranian state media gave her prime slot coverage. The then President Hassan Rouhani met her and promised to retaliate for the General's killing.[39] In an interview with *Al Manar*, the Hezbollah-run Lebanese TV, she asked 'uncle Hassan Nasrallah' to avenge her father's death. Iran carried out a missile attack at a US air base in Iraq in retaliation for Soleimani's death, injuring dozens of American soldiers. Tensions between the two countries have stayed high ever since. 'This is not over. Crazy Americans and Zionists should not think that my father's martyrdom is the end of the resistance. It will only strengthen the resistance,' Zeinab said.

'How long will the resistance continue?' I asked the General's daughter.

'Till we defeat our enemies,' Zeinab Soleimani said, standing up, putting her right arm on her left chest and bowing a little in a gesture to indicate that she would now take my leave. 'Till we liberate Jerusalem.'

5

The Partisan Superpower

IN February 2024, four months after Hamas's 7 October attack in Israel, I was at the British Foreign Office. I was part of a group of foreign policy enthusiasts from India who were travelling in the UK as part of the Foreign, Commonwealth & Development Office's (FCDO) Indo-Pacific Thinkers' Programme. Weather forecasters had predicted a pleasant day in London. 'The only prediction about London's weather that can't go wrong is that it's unpredictable,' Shruti, who had studied in London and was part of the delegation, told me. We were walking from the hotel, close to the Thames River, to King Charles Street, where the Foreign Office is located, while braving the cold February winds. The FCDO building, commissioned in the nineteenth century, is just another old London white building from the outside. We would have walked past it if the young British diplomat who was leading the pack hadn't stopped us and announced that we'd reached our destination. There were no barricades or security personnel outside the office.

Inside the building, we were seated in the Durbar Hall where the glass windows opened on to the famous Durbar Court. The court, designed by Sir Matthew Digby Wyatt, a nineteenth-century architect and a surveyor of the East India Company, was originally built as an open-air hall surrounded by the columns, piers and arches of the three-story structure on all four sides (now, it's roofed). In 1867, the British government had thrown a reception for the visiting Ottoman Sultan Abdülaziz at the Court. In 1902, some of the coronation festivities of King Edward VIII had been held there. While we were sitting inside the hall waiting for British diplomats to join us, I got busy reading about the historical vanity of the Court.

In our conversations, British diplomats mainly talked about the Ukraine war, which was about to enter its third year, the war in Gaza, which had seen high civilian casualties, China's rise, India's foreign policy and the possibility of a Trump presidency. A few weeks earlier, then British Foreign Secretary David Cameron had said in London that Britain would consider recognizing a Palestinian state, including at the United Nations, as part of efforts to bring about an 'irreversible' peace settlement. 'Palestinians must have a political horizon so that they can see that there is irreversible progress to a two-state solution,' said Lord Cameron.[1] The then Prime Minister Rishi Sunak immediately said there was no change in the British government's policy towards Israel and Palestine. In an interview with Piers Morgan, Sunak said, 'Our position is the same. David was saying that we are committed to a two-state solution. We absolutely are committed and that's been a long-standing position of the UK government.' He said the United Kingdom would recognize the state of Palestine only 'at a point where it is most conducive to the [peace] process'.[2]

Cameron's comments, amid reports that more countries were considering offering recognition to the Palestinians, had angered the Israeli government, which introduced a resolution in the Knesset, Israel's Parliament, opposing any unilateral recognition of a Palestine state. Ninety-nine of the Knesset's 120 members supported the resolution. 'The Knesset came together in an overwhelming majority against the attempt to impose on us the establishment of a Palestinian state, which would not only fail to bring peace but would endanger the State of Israel,' Israeli Prime Minister Benjamin Netanyahu said after the vote.[3]

Even when violence was raging in Gaza, the British government was treading a cautious line. It did not support the global call for a ceasefire; instead, Prime Minister Sunak called for a humanitarian pause. It joined the United States' Operation Prosperity Guardian, a naval coalition the Biden administration set up to carry out attacks against Yemen's Houthi militants who started attacking vessels in the Red Sea after the Gaza war broke out.

At the FCDO, I asked a senior British diplomat about Cameron's comment and Prime Minister Sunak's response. 'In a sense, both were correct,' said the diplomat. 'What the foreign secretary said was that Britain would consider recognizing the Palestinian state. That shows our commitment to the two-state solution, and we are committed to the two-state solution. And secondly, the Middle East can't go back to the pre-7 October status quo after this war. There is now an urgency to push for a political solution to the crisis. That's what the foreign secretary meant.'

Britain has historically played an important role in the Israel–Palestine conflict. Britain was the first major global power that recognized the Zionist demand for the creation of a Jewish homeland in Palestine, through the 1917 Balfour Declaration. When Britain issued the Balfour Declaration, it had no powers over Palestine, which was part of the Ottoman Empire. After the First World War, Palestine came under Britain's Mandatory rule. It was during this period that the Zionists started building a parallel state in Palestine, which became the state of Israel on 14 May 1948, the last day of the British Mandate over Palestine. In post-war West Asia, Britain's influence progressively eroded, while the United States emerged as the most powerful force in the region. During this period, Britain's foreign policy also largely aligned with that of the United States.

Two days later, I was in Cambridge talking to a former diplomat who had served as Britain's ambassador in Israel. I asked the ambassador how he assessed the war in Gaza. 'Israel doesn't seem to be meeting its objectives in Gaza—mainly dismantling Hamas. A lot of civilians are getting killed. On 7 October, the whole world's focus was on what Hamas did. But now, what the international community is talking about is what Israel is doing. This is what Hamas wanted. They must be happy with what's happening in Gaza today.'

I brought up the contrasting positions the West has taken towards Ukraine and Gaza for discussion. The United States and the United Kingdom had mobilized the Western world, imposed sanctions on Russia and supplied weapons worth billions of dollars to Ukraine to fight the Russian aggression. But when it comes to Israel, there is not even a strong call for a ceasefire. The former diplomat ignored the comparison with Ukraine, and then said: 'There still are fears of a wider war [in West Asia]. The United States' focus is on preventing such an outcome. Secretary [of State Antony] Blinken travelled to the Middle East several times and met both Israeli and Arab leaders. They are trying really hard to douse the flames. They are doing a lot of talking. But they are not *doing* enough. They keep resupplying Israel as quickly as they can during the war.'

'Is Britain doing what it can to bring the war to an end?' I asked him.

'Listen. We are no longer living in the nineteenth century. We are a relatively smaller power today with a lot of challenges, including in Ukraine and in the Indo-Pacific. In the Middle East, America is the power. They should lead. We will follow,' said the former diplomat.

Back in Delhi in the first week of March, a former Indian diplomat, who was in India's National Security Board, used similar words. 'The United States' focus is not on bringing the Gaza war to an end, but to prevent the Gaza war from escalating into a regional war. But the problem is that the source of the regional conflict is the Gaza war. If you don't address that and work on its regional spread, it's like treating the symptoms, not the disease,' he told me.

Exactly after a month, Iran launched a barrage of missiles and drones at Israel in retaliation against the latter's bombing of its embassy compound in Damascus, bringing the region to the brink of a direct war between the two powers. On July 31, Israel killed Fuad Shukr, a top commander of Hezbollah, in an air strike on Beirut, and Ismail Haniyeh, the political chief of Hamas, in a mysterious attack in Tehran. Haniyeh was in the Iranian capital to attend the swearing in ceremony of the new President of the Islamic Republic, Masoud Pezeshkian. Britain and America do not want a wider war. But they seem either helpless or disinterested in reining in their ally which is relentlessly expanding its operations across West Asia.

Recognition in Eleven Minutes

The United States' ties with Zionists go back to the days of the Balfour Declaration, which was strongly supported by President Woodrow Wilson. He was informed of the proposed resolution in September 1917, two months before it was announced. The British first told Col Edward M. House, an American diplomat, who was then in London, about the resolution and asked if the President would favour 'a declaration of sympathy' with the Zionist cause. House, who was a close adviser of Wilson, warned the President of the 'dangers lurking in' the declaration. 'If I were British, I would be chary about going too definitely into that question,' he said.[4] Wilson initially refused to respond to the British overtures. In October, the British government sent another message via the American Embassy in London:

> His Majesty's Government views with favour the establishment in Palestine of a national home for Jewish race and will use their best endeavours to facilitate achievement of this object; it being directly understood that nothing shall be done which may prejudice civil and religious rights of existing non-Jewish communities in Palestine or rights and political status enjoyed in any other country by Jews, who are fully contented with their existing nationality and citizenship.[5]

Subsequently, Wilson sent a message to the British government, through Col House, stating that he was in favour of the declaration. On 3 March 1919, two years after the declaration was issued, Wilson publicly announced his support for it. 'The Allied nations with the fullest concurrence of our government and people are agreed that in Palestine shall be laid the foundations of a Jewish Commonwealth,' he said.⁶ By 1920, a consensus emerged in the American establishment in favour of the Zionist cause. The First World War was over. The San Remo Conference of April 1920 awarded the Palestine Mandate to Britain. In July that year, Sir Herbert Samuel, author of *The Future of Palestine*, took over his new position as high commissioner and civil administrator of Palestine, replacing the British military. The new administration recognized the World Zionist Organization as the official representative of the Jewish people. If the United States had faced Arab pressure from taking a public stand on the Zionist cause, that pressure waned in the years that followed the First World War. On 1 September 1922, the same day the British Mandate for Palestine was approved by the League of Nations, the US Congress passed the Lodge-Fish Resolution, stating that:

> ... the United States of America favors the establishment in Palestine of a national home for the Jewish people, it being clearly understood that nothing shall be done which should prejudice the civil and religious rights of Christian and all other non-Jewish communities in Palestine, and that the holy places and religious buildings and sites in Palestine shall be adequately protected.⁷

During the interwar period, the US largely saw Palestine as a British problem even though it remained sympathetic towards the Zionist cause. President Franklin D. Roosevelt had promised the Arabs that the United States would not intervene in Palestine without consulting both parties. When Harry S. Truman became

President, he endorsed the Balfour Declaration, saying it was in line with Woodrow Wilson's 'self-determination' principle. Truman also believed the Jews, having survived the Holocaust, were in need of a homeland. However, the Departments of War and State advised caution and warned the White House against interfering in the Palestine issue, fearing that Arabs would turn against America, especially after the Second World War broke out. But after the War, Washington, the new superpower, started showing an inclination to take an active leadership role in pressing global issues, including the Jewish question. Jews also enjoyed the sympathy of the post-war world after the horrors they went through in Europe.

Ralph Bunche, an American diplomat who won the 1950 Nobel Peace Prize for his role in mediating the armistice between Israel and Arab nations after the war of 1948, was an assistant to the UN Special Committee on Palestine (UNSCOP). Bunche, whose sympathies for the Jews were hardly a secret, strongly argued for the partition of Palestine and the creation of a Jewish state.[8] UNSCOP recommended the British Mandate of Palestine be ended and the territory be partitioned into a Jewish state, an Arab state and an international city (Jerusalem). Arabs strongly opposed the partition plan. In October, the Arab League asked its governments to move troops to the borders of Palestine. But President Truman, overcoming opposition from within his administration, asked the State Department to support the plan. The administration lobbied in favour of the partition resolution (181), which was adopted in the UN General Assembly on 29 November 1947. The resolution never made it to the UN Security Council. But at midnight on 14 May 1948, the last day of the British Mandate, Zionists declared the state of Israel.

Immediately after the state was declared, Eliahu Eilat (Epstein), a Zionist leader who would become the first Israeli ambassador to the United States, sent a message to US President Harry S. Truman. 'With full knowledge of the deep bond of sympathy which has existed and has been strengthened over the past thirty years between the Government of the United States and the Jewish people of Palestine, I have been authorised by the provisional government of the new state to tender this message and to express the hope that your government will recognise and will welcome Israel into the community of nations,' Epstein wrote in the communication.[9]

The Truman administration's response came in eleven minutes.

This Government has been informed that a Jewish state has been proclaimed in Palestine, and recognition has been requested by the provisional Government thereof.

The United States recognizes the provisional government as the de facto authority of the new State of Israel.

(sgn.) Harry Truman

Approved,

14 May 1948[10]

The Three Wars

Though the United States offered the state of Israel its support right from the latter's birth, the initial two decades of their relationship had not been very smooth. The United States remained supportive of Israel but was also cautious of the Cold War realities. Its priority was to maintain its good relationship with the Arab world, mainly for two reasons. One, it did not want energy supplies from West Asia, which were critical for America's booming post-war economy, to take a hit; two, it did not want to take overtly pro-Israel policies that could push Arab countries, especially those in the Persian Gulf, into the Soviet embrace. So, Washington offered diplomatic protection to Israel at the UN Security Council and provided limited aid, mainly food supplies, but stopped short of sending weapons to the newly created state.

But three wars in the three decades that followed the creation of the state of Israel would reshape America's Israel policy and lay the foundations of the 'special relationship'. On 29 October 1956, Israeli forces invaded Egypt with the declared objective of reopening the Straits of Tiran, the narrow sea passage between the Sinai and the Arabian Peninsula, and the Gulf of Aqaba, the deep, narrow gulf on the eastern side of the Sinai that opens into the Red Sea. An Egyptian blockade of these waters had prevented the passage of Israeli ships. But the real objective of the war was something else.

On 24 October, in a private villa in Sèvres on the outskirts of Paris, British, French and Israeli officials held a secret meeting. They had one thing in common—they all hated Gamal Abdel Nasser, Egypt's charismatic socialist President. A few months earlier, Nasser had nationalized the Suez Canal Company, a joint British-French enterprise that had owned and operated the Suez Canal.[11] The 193-kilometre-long canal across Egypt's Isthmus of Suez connects the Mediterranean Sea in the north and the Red Sea in the south—thereby bringing the Atlantic Ocean and the Indian Ocean closer. It had been a critical artery for global trade since the mid-nineteenth century. Nasser was also a key source of support for the National Liberation Front (FLN) in Algeria, which was fighting a guerilla war against the French. For David Ben-Gurion, the Israeli Prime Minister, Nasser, the tallest Arab leader and a champion of pan-Arabism at the time, was the obvious enemy number one.

In the Sèvres meeting, they agreed on a secret plan, which came to be known as the Protocol of Sèvres. Israel would attack Egypt first, and Britain and France would join the war later. Ben-Gurion presented a comprehensive plan. The war would be over only after Nasser was toppled from power. France and Britain could retake their control of the Suez Canal. Britain would restore its hegemony over Jordan and Iraq and continue to control the major waterways and energy supplies in West Asia, and France would consolidate its influence in West Asia and North Africa, through Lebanon, Israel and Algeria.[12] 'So that lets us off the hook. We have no obligation, it seems, to stop the Israelis attacking the Egyptians,' Sir Anthony Eden, the British Prime Minister, said during the talks about the tripartite plan.[13] On 5 November, just six days after Israel attacked Egypt in Sinai, France and Britain sent troops to fight the Egyptians. The invading forces made quick gains in the early stage of the war. Ben-Gurion claimed that the island of Tiran, located at the opening of the Straits of Tiran, 'would now be part of the third kingdom of Israel'.[14]

But where France, Britain and Israel erred was in judging the mood in Washington. The United States was not happy with the fact that two of its allies, France and Britain, had launched this war without proper consultation. The world was changing, and the United States was the new leader of the Western world—not Great Britain. President Eisenhower was also concerned that the Soviet Union, whose intervention in Hungary in the same week was slammed by America, would come to the defence of Egypt, pushing the most populous Arab nation deeper into the Red embrace. Washington voted in favour of a resolution at the UN that publicly condemned the invasion, and put pressure on London and Paris to accept a UN ceasefire. Soviet leader Nikita Khrushchev warned Israel to withdraw from the captured territories or face Soviet rockets.[15] US President Eisenhower also issued an ultimatum to Israel, asking it to unconditionally withdraw in return for continued aid and support from the United States. Israel obliged within a day.

The Suez Crisis was a moment of reckoning for both Israel and the United States. Israel realized that the era of the British Middle East was over and that the United States was the new sheriff in town. Washington, on the other side, saw the military potential of Israel. The United States wanted a loyal ally who would not turn to the Soviet Union and could act as a balancer against the Arabs. Israel, a multiparty Jewish democracy, ticked all the boxes. President Kennedy ended the arms embargo that his predecessors had placed on Israel. In 1960, when he was a senator, Kennedy, while speaking at a convention of the Zionist Organization of America, had said, 'The ideals of Zionism have, in the last half century, been endorsed by both parties, and by Americans of all ranks in all sections. Friendship for Israel is now a partisan matter.' He added, 'It is a national commitment.' As the thirty-fifth President of the United States, he began a security partnership between America and Israel. On 27 December 1962, in a meeting with then Israeli Foreign Minister Golda Meir, President Kennedy said, 'The United States has a special relationship with Israel in the Middle East, really comparable only to that which it has with Britain over a wide range of world affairs.'[16]

If the Suez Crisis set the stage for the security cooperation between the United States and Israel, the 1967 Six-Day War further strengthened the special relationship. Until that year, the United States was wary of angering the Arab world by openly embracing Israel. But in June 1967, Israel defeated Jordan, Syria and Egypt, all in six days, and captured swathes of territories from all of them. The whole historical Palestine, including East Jerusalem, came under Israel's control. Two of the Arab countries Israel defeated—Egypt and Syria—were close Soviet partners. For the United States, which at that time was bogged down in Vietnam, Israel's quick military victories, without any major assistance from Washington, were loud messages from West Asia. From then on, the United States started seeing Israel as a stable ally that could check the expansion of Soviet influence in West Asia.

If it was Israel that launched the 1956 and 1967 wars, on 6 October 1973, the Yom Kippur holiday, Israel was caught by surprise when Egypt and Syria launched a joint attack in the Sinai Peninsula and the Golan Heights. Within a day, Israel's defence positions along the Golan Heights in the north and the Suez Canal in the south collapsed. Hundreds of Israeli soldiers were killed. Israel immediately dispatched its reservists, who helped the troops maintain the line in the Golan, but in Suez, Israeli troops continued to face setbacks. On 8 October, after an Israeli counterattack in Suez failed miserably, the then defence minister Moshe Dayan visited the frontline and warned his generals that the 'Third Temple is in danger'. The First Temple in Jerusalem was destroyed by the Babylonians, the second by the Romans. By using the metaphor of The Third Temple, Gen. Dayan, a hero of the 1967 war, was referring to the state of Israel.[17] It was one of the darkest phases in the history of the Israeli Defence Forces.

In the initial days of the war, Israel lost some 50 fighter jets and 500 tanks. '500 tanks!' Henry Kissinger, the then national security advisor, expressed his shock when Israeli ambassador Simcha Dinitz told him about the losses the IDF suffered in just three days. According to Dayan, Israel was fast approaching the point of 'last resort', indirectly raising a nuclear threat. Prime Minister Golda Meir ordered thirteen nuclear bombs to be readied for use by missiles and aircrafts. Jericho missiles, which could carry nuclear warheads, were put on high alert. By that time, it was an open secret that Israel had up to twenty nuclear weapons.[18] Ambassador Dinitz pleaded with the United States for an immediate airlift of weapons to help Israel win the war. If the United States did not airlift supplies, 'very serious conclusions may occur', said the ambassador, in a reference to the nuclear option.[19]

There were concerns within the Nixon administration about the airlift. In a Washington Special Action Group meeting, held on 6 October 1973, then Secretary of Defence James R. Schlesinger warned against American supplies to Israel. 'Our shipping any stuff into Israel blows any image we may have as an honest broker,' he said.[20] But Kissinger argued that if the United States did not go to Israel's defence, the Soviets would take a victory in the region against a crucial American ally.

On 10 October, in a White House meeting, President Nixon told Kissinger and his other close aides that 'the situation in the Middle East ... has developed into something tougher than the Israelis anticipated.'

'The Israelis were caught with their pants down—unmobilized,' said Kissinger about the Egyptian attack.

'The Israeli tank losses have been extremely heavy. We won't violate the confidence by giving you figures, but they are far heavier than anticipated,' said Nixon.

During the conversation, Nixon expressed his concern about the Soviet Union getting itself involved in the conflict or the war getting wider with other Arab countries joining in it. 'Now, as to what we say Henry?' he asked Kissinger.

'You can say you are confident we are working toward an end of conflict and a just peace in the Middle East. We are in contact with all the parties. The less said about details, the better,' said Kissinger.

'We will not let Israel go down the tube,' proclaimed President Nixon. [21]

Two days later, Nixon ordered the largest airlift in American history. Codenamed Operation Nickel Grass, its aim was to resupply Israel's losses. Within a month, the US airlifted about 22,325 tonnes of supplies, including tanks, artillery, shells and ammunition, in multiple flights of C-141 Starlifters and C-5 Galaxys.[22] With help from the United States, Israel would push Egyptians back to the pre-war frontline. But the war was a wakeup call for Israel's leadership, indicating to them that close ties with the United States was an imperative for the Jewish nation's survival. In the United States, Nixon's axiom would continue to guide each and every President, from Gerald Ford to Donald Trump and Joe Biden—'No American President can afford to let Israel go down the tube'.

Exceptional Ally

Today, Israel is an exceptional ally of Washington. The United States offers practically unconditional financial, military and political support for the Jewish state. Israel's undeclared nuclear status has never faced any global scrutiny or pushback, thanks to the protection offered by the United States. Israel is also the largest recipient of America's aid—it has received $158 billion in aid from the United States since the end of the Second World War. Currently, Israel gets $3.8 billion in military aid every year from the United States—which accounts for about 16 per cent of Israel's total military budget.[23] In April, in the midst of the Gaza war, in which 34,000 Palestinians had already been killed by then, the US Congress approved a special package of $17 billion in defence aid for Israel.[24]

The United States is also Israel's largest trading partner, with annual two-way trade in goods and services hovering around $50 billion. 'Several treaties and agreements, including the 1985 US–Israel Free Trade Agreement (FTA), solidify bilateral economic relations,' according to the State Department.[25] Both Israel and the United States also have a deep defence partnership, which involves joint research and development and weapons production. For example, the Iron Dome, Israel's famed missile defence shield, uses parts built in the United States and the system is financed in part by the United States. With US help, Israel has built a highly advanced defence manufacturing base, which has made the country the world's tenth largest military exporter.[26] Since 1972, the United States has used its veto power over fifty times to strike down resolutions critical of Israel in the United Nations Security Council.

From the 1973 Yom Kippur War onwards, the United States has also offered solid military support to Israel in its conflicts. In 1982, when Israel invaded Lebanon in an attempt to push the Palestine Liberation Organization (PLO) out of the neighbouring country, the United States sent the Multinational Force to Lebanon.[27] After the First Intifada, the first uprising in the Palestinian territories against the Israeli occupation, the United States supported the Oslo process and the two-state solution, but without compromising its relationship with Israel. In October 1995, the US Congress passed the Jerusalem Embassy Act, which recognized Jerusalem as the capital of the state of Israel and asked the administration to establish the US Embassy in the disputed city.[28]

American Presidents continued to get themselves involved in the peace process without any results. President Bill Clinton played a key role in the 2000 Camp David negotiations between Yasser Arafat and Israeli Prime Minister Ehud Barak, which eventually failed to reach a deal. But since the collapse of the Second Camp David talks, American Presidents have largely looked away from the issue. President George Bush's 2007 Annapolis Conference was no more than a photo-op in the last days of his presidency. President Barack Obama's focus was on the Iran deal, while his administration offered full support to Israel at the United Nations. Donald Trump offered support to Israel without any qualms. His administration recognized, in December 2017, Jerusalem as Israel's capital and moved America's embassy to the city the next year. 'It was 70 years ago that the United States, under President Truman, recognized the State of Israel. Ever since then, Israel has made its capital in the city of Jerusalem—the capital the Jewish people established in ancient times,' said President Trump. 'Israel is a sovereign nation with the right like every other sovereign nation to determine its own capital,' he declared.[29] The Trump administration also recognized Israel's annexation of the Golan Heights, the Syrian territory Israel captured in 1967 and held under its occupation ever since, in violation of UN Security Council resolutions.[30]

While there were personality clashes between American Presidents and Israeli Prime Ministers, such clashes never led to a breakdown in what President John F. Kennedy called 'the special relationship'. In the 1970s, President Jimmy Carter heaped pressure on Israel to make peace with Egypt and give concessions to the

Palestinians. Israel, shocked by the Yom Kippur War, finally agreed to withdraw from Sinai and sign the Framework for Peace Agreement in return for Egypt's recognition of the state of Israel. This was the last time Israel fully withdrew from an occupied territory as part of a peace agreement.

During the Second Intifada in 2002, President George W. Bush pressed Israel to show restraint in the occupied West Bank, and in return Israeli Prime Minister Ariel Sharon accused him of appeasing the Arabs. 'Don't repeat the terrible mistake of 1938 when the enlightened democracies of Europe decided to sacrifice Czechoslovakia for a temporary solution. Do not try to placate the Arabs at our expense ... Israel will not be Czechoslovakia,' Sharon said, drawing parallels between British Prime Minister Neville Chamberlain's surrender before Hitler as part of the 1938 Munich Agreement and Bush's policies towards the Arabs.[31] Sharon later apologized for the comparison. President Bush asked Israel to pull back from the West Bank and end its military operations 'without delay', but the Israelis never obliged. Sharon had Bush 'wrapped around his little finger', Brent Scowcroft, the national security advisor of President George H.W. Bush, said in October 2004 about Bush Jr's policy towards Israel. 'I think the President is mesmerized. When there is a suicide attack [followed by a reprisal] Sharon calls the President and says, "I'm on the front line of terrorism," and the President says, "Yes, you are ..." He [Sharon] has been nothing but trouble,' Scowcroft said in an interview.[32]

But these tensions never affected their special relationship. The United States, which is otherwise very vocal about human rights violations in Asia, Africa and Latin America, always overlooks allegations of war crimes levelled against Israel, even when they are backed by UN investigations. The United States, which imposed crippling sanctions on Iran against its nuclear programme, doesn't even publicly talk about Israel's nuclear arsenals. The United States, which threw Russia out of the Group of Eight countries and imposed sanctions on Moscow after its 2014 annexation of Crimea through a referendum, has recognized Israel's annexation of Syria's Golan Heights, and moved its embassy to the disputed city of Jerusalem. Israel's illegal occupation of Palestinian territories never cast a shadow over the special relationship, which, according to political scientist John Mearsheimer, 'is the closest two nations can ever get'.[33]

President Barack Obama and Israeli Prime Minister Benjamin Netanyahu had also clashed over the Iran nuclear deal. Netanyahu had visited the Republican-controlled US Congress and attacked Obama over his Iran policy. But the same Obama vetoed all resolutions at the UN Security Council critical of Israel, except one during his eight-year presidency. Obama, during his last months in office, also cleared a $38 billion aid package for Israel. The Biden administration had earlier criticized the Netanyahu government's plan to overhaul the country's judiciary. But after the 7 October attack by Hamas, the United States threw its full weight behind the Netanyahu government's war on Gaza. Even when international public opinion turned against the way Israel was conducting the war in Gaza and a vast majority of UN members called for a ceasefire, the Biden administration continued to support Israel, militarily, politically and diplomatically.

There are different theories explaining the depth of this special relationship. One argument, made by the likes of American conservative geostrategist Walter Russel Mead, is that Israel's strategic value in a volatile yet critical region makes it appealing for Washington. During the Cold War, the United States saw Israel as a powerful bulwark against possible Soviet expansion in the Arab world.³⁴ After the Cold War, when the United States started becoming more and more involved in West Asia, it continued to see Israel as a force of stability, along with Saudi Arabia and Egypt. Mead argues American policy towards the Jewish state follows a 'logic of realpolitik', which reflects the sentiment of a majority of Americans who feel 'sympathetic' towards Israel. This support has its origins in 'the Anglo-American Christian spirit', which is highly influential in America's domestic politics and is 'less anti-Semitic and more pro-Zionist than other forms of Christianity'.³⁵

Historically, Israel has enjoyed near unanimous support in the US Congress, and a vast majority of Americans have favourable views about Israel. American Jews and evangelical Christians are two powerful, politically active groups in the United States. They are important constituencies for both parties, and they are both pro-Israel. Then there's a powerful Israel lobby in the United States, which according to Mearsheimer and Stephen Walt, heavily influences US policy towards Israel. The lobby helps amplify pro-Israel voices, backs pro-Israel politicians and works toward playing down or neutralizing voices critical of Israel. 'The lobby pursues two broad strategies. First, it wields its significant influence in Washington, pressuring both Congress and the executive branch. Whatever an individual lawmaker or policymaker's own views may be, the lobby tries to make supporting Israel the 'smart' choice. Second, it strives to ensure that public discourse portrays Israel in a positive light, by repeating myths about its founding and by promoting its point of view in policy debates,' write Mearsheimer and Walt.³⁶

The American Israel Public Affairs Committee (AIPAC), a powerful pro-Israel lobbying group, hosts top leaders from both countries, including Presidents, Senators and Prime Ministers, for its annual gatherings. Pro-Israel groups also support both parties in the United States financially. For example, during the 2020 campaign, pro-Israel groups contributed over $30 billion (63 per cent of which went to the Democrats and the rest Republicans), according to OpenSecrets.org.[37] Besides, there are strong ties between the military industrial complexes of both countries. All these factors together—Israel's strategic value, America's domestic politics, the presence of the pro-Israel lobby and the military-industrial interplay—make sure that there's an institutional consensus in the United States about its relationship with Israel, irrespective of which party or President is in power in Washington DC.

'Go back to the 1956 war, the United States took a very tough position against Israel, and demanded that Israel, the United Kingdom and France vacate their aggression on Egypt,' Talmiz Ahmed, India's former ambassador to Saudi Arabia, said in February, four months after the Hamas attack, in a show in which I was also a participant. 'After the 1967 war, the Israelis very carefully worked with various sections of the US establishment, utilizing the full force of the Jewish community. Despite their size being very small, they are very influential people—in politics, media, Wall Street, etc. They are now influential on behalf of Israel. It's a consolidated force. A new element that has come in favour of Israel are the Christian evangelists in America,' he said.

'Israel is not a foreign policy issue as far as the United States is concerned. It is an integral part of their domestic politics. This is something Israel has achieved since the 1967 war,' added the former ambassador.[38]

6

A Troubled Brotherhood

I met Khaled (name changed) in October 2015. He was a faculty member at the University of Jordan, located in the plush Jubaiha neighbourhood of Amman, the Jordanian capital. I was at the university, with a reporting assignment. The University of Jordan is the oldest and largest public university in the Hashemite Kingdom. Inaugurated by King Hussein bin Talal in 1962, the university has emerged over the years as a pioneer of social studies and medical sciences in the Arab world. It's also known for its pro-Palestine activism. Festooned with cypress and pine trees, the campus, with its wide roads and yellow brick buildings, looked like a luxury oasis in the middle of a city that's home to 4 million people, roughly half of Jordan's population.

Khaled, a PhD in international studies, was an alumnus of Jawaharlal Nehru University (JNU), New Delhi. He got excited when I told him I'd finished my PhD at the same university two years earlier. He knew my supervisor. 'Prof. Dietl is quite an authority on the Middle East,' he said, with a wide smile and a glint in his eyes. I said, 'Yes, quite an authority, but she prefers West Asia over the Middle East.' Then both of us laughed. My professor used to tell us that if one wants to be geographically precise, they have to call the region 'West Asia'—the region between Central Asia on the east and the Mediterranean Sea in the West and the Black Sea in the north and the Arabian Sea in the south, which falls 'in the western part of the Asian continent'.

A big man, Khaled, wearing beige trousers and the same-coloured blazer, spoke fast and moved even faster. Each sentence ended with a laugh, irrespective of the merit of what he was talking about. While walking around the campus, which reminded both of us of JNU, we spoke about Delhi, a city he said he instantly fell in love with, and the student activism and academic discourses in JNU. 'Were you there when Hugo Chavez visited the campus?' he asked me, referring to the late Venezuelan socialist President. Yes, I was there. I told him how eventful the day was. When two JNUites meet, there is no dearth of topics of mutual interests.

Eventually we moved to the topic of Jordan. I told him I saw King Abdullah II, Jordan's reigning monarch, the previous day at the Al Husseiniya Palace in Amman during a guard of honour. 'God save the King,' said Khaled, bursting out into laughter again. I asked him about life in Jordan and its support for Palestine while coexisting with Israel. The Hashemite Kingdom made peace with Israel in 1994, a treaty which has stood the test of time. For the first time, Khaled paused before talking. His pleasant, clean-shaven face instantly turned serious. 'Brother, you know the history. I know the history. What's there to discuss?' I said that I look at the region from afar, but for Khaled, that is where he lives. It's part of his life. 'We have a complicated past with the Palestinians—that's hardly a secret. At the same time, we are also enraged by the injustice meted out to the Palestinians. But, Israel is a reality. And we have to live with reality. You can always find this balancing in Jordan's foreign policy,' he said, unapologetically.

To say Jordan had a complicated history with the Palestinians would be an understatement. From the very beginning, the history of Jordan and Palestine has been intertwined. Jordan is the only Arab country that fully integrated the Palestinian refugees of 1948. The sizeable population of Palestinians in exile are settled in Jordan. Roughly 2.3 million people living in Jordan have registered as Palestinian refugees—this is as much as the total population of Palestinians in Gaza.[1] This included Queen Rania, King Abdullah II's wife, who was born to Palestinian parents in Kuwait. Jordan has fought two wars with Israel over Palestinian territories—1948 and 1967. But Jordan had also occupied the Palestinian West Bank between 1948 and 1967 and conducted a brutal crackdown on the Palestinian Liberation Organisation (PLO) in 1970. It also became the second Arab country, after Egypt, to sign a peace treaty with Israel in 1994.

'You can't understand Jordan's policy towards Palestinians without understanding the history of Jordan and Palestine. We were all one people. And then came the Zionists and then the colonialists. The Arab lands were divided and stolen. When we started nation building in Jordan, we had to do what every nascent nation state had to do,' said Khaled, referring to the emergence of Jordan as an independent kingdom on the eastern banks of the Jordan River (locally known by its Arabic name, Nahr al-Urdunn).

During the Ottoman period, the land that today is recognized as Jordan, Syria, Israel and Palestinian territories were all part of the Syria Vilayat. The Ottomans had a governor in Damascus who ruled over the vast Arab lands. (Jerusalem, though territorially was part of the Syria Vilayat, was an independent sanjak, or administrative district, that reported directly to Istanbul, not Damascus.)[2] During the First World War, in a correspondence with Sharif Hussein of Mecca, the British promised that they would support Arab independence if Arabs revolted against the Ottomans. Hussein, whose Hashemite family had autonomy over the holy cities of Arabia, called for a revolt, and the Syria Vilayat became a crucible of Arab rebellion. After the Ottomans were defeated in the Levant, the British and the French, along with local Arab chieftains, established the Occupied Enemy Territory Administration (OETA) over the Levant provinces (Syria, Jordan, Lebanon, Israel and Palestine). They agreed to divide the Syria Vilayat into three subunits—OETA South (Palestine), under British rule; OETA West (Lebanon), under French rule; and OETA East (Syria and Jordan), under Arab leadership.

In 1918, Prince Faisal, son of Sharif Hussein, entered Damascus and announced the establishment of a fully independent Arab constitutional government in OETA East, with support from the British military. But the French, who had already established their authority in Lebanon, were not ready to completely give up their influence in Damascus. Britain withdrew its troops from OETA East in 1919. This provided two different opportunities to Faisal and the French. On 8 March 1920, Faisal proclaimed the Arab Kingdom of Syria in a region encompassing modern-day Syria and Jordan.[3] Faisal thought the British, who had promised Arab independence to his father, would support his kingdom. But he failed to get recognition for any major power. Four months later, the French troops attacked Syria, dethroned Faisal and established a civil administration in the northern part of the kingdom, leaving the southern part, which lay on the eastern bank of the Jordan River across Palestine, and was then called 'Transjordan', a no-man's land. In the words of Sir Herbert Samuel, the first British representative to Palestine, 'Trans-jordan was left politically derelict after the Franco–Syrian war.'[4]

By this time, Britain had already established its control over Palestine, on the western bank of the river. According to some accounts, Samuel, a known Zionist and author of the 1915 memorandum 'The Future of Palestine', which called for British support for the Zionist claim over Palestine, had supported the idea of extending the frontier of British Palestine's territory beyond the river to include Transjordan. But this proposal was rejected. The British Foreign Secretary Lord Curzon believed that Britain's interests would be best served if London retained some influence in Transjordan without establishing direct colonial rule. Britain also wanted to accommodate the Hashemite family, its Arab ally against the Ottomans during the war, who lost their kingdom to the French. In August 1920, a month after the Franco-Syrian war, Samuel travelled to Transjordan from Jerusalem and held meetings with local Arab chieftains. 'No centralised government was at that time possible. I took steps to establish [three] local councils. These councils assumed the administration of affairs, with the assistance of a small number of British officers who were sent from Palestine for the purpose,' Samuel wrote later about the visit.[5]

Prince Abdullah bin Hussein, the second son of Sharif Hussein, arrived in Ma'an, in southern Transjordan, from Hejaz in Arabia, by train in November 1920. His aim was to fight for the restoration of the Arab Kingdom. But Britain did not want anti-French violence to break out from a region that's next to British-controlled Palestine. The colonial powers were also faced with a complex geopolitical post-war scenario at that time. Britain had promised to support the Zionist claim for a homeland 'in Palestine'.[6] Britain and France had reached a secret agreement to divide up Ottoman West Asia between their spheres of influence, despite Britain's promise to the Hashemites.[7] In March 1921, Winston Churchill, the newly appointed colonial secretary, called a conference of British military leaders and administrators in the region in Cairo to discuss the post-war situation and find solutions.

In the Cairo Conference, Britain decided to give the throne of the British Mandate of Iraq to Faisal, the Arab king dethroned by the French from Damascus, and Transjordan to Abdullah, Faisal's elder brother. Before Faisal could sit on the throne, he was required to sign a new friendship treaty with the Great Britain. Britain also clarified that Transjordan would be technically incorporated into the British Mandate for Palestine, which would allow London to retain its influence in the territory even when Abdullah built new administrative structures.[8] After the Cairo Conference, Abdullah met Churchill in Jerusalem where they finalized the Transjordan deal. 'A conference with the Emir was held at Jerusalem, and an agreement made, under which the mandatory power recognized him, for a period, as administrator of Transjordan, with the condition that any action hostile to Syria must be abandoned,' wrote Samuel about the Churchill–Abdullah meeting.[9]

But Abdullah still had apprehensions regarding the deal. Britain had committed itself to supporting the creation of a Jewish homeland in Mandatory Palestine. Tens of thousands of Jewish immigrants from Europe were settling in the area every year. Sir Samuel was appointed the British representative and administrator of Mandatory Palestine. And Britain was planning incorporate Transjordan into the mandate, as, according to the Colonial Office, 'the two areas [Palestine and Transjordan] are economically interdependent, and their development must be considered as a single problem'.[10] Abdullah was ready to take over the administration of Transjordan as a British protectorate, but he wanted guarantees from the Crown that Jewish settlements would not be permitted in his territory.

Britain, looking for a solution that would keep all four sides— the Empire, the French, the Zionists and the Arabs—mollified, agreed to Abdullah's demand. On 11 April, 1921, the Emirate of Transjordan was established.[11] In 1992, Britain passed the Transjordan Memorandum at the Council of the League of Nations as an addendum to the Mandate for Palestine, which included Transjordan in the mandate without applying the provisions about Jewish settlement.[12] A year later, Britain officially recognized the Emirate of Transjordan. 'Subject to the approval of the League of Nations, His Majesty's Government will recognize the existence of an independent Government in Transjordan under the rule of His Highness the Emir Abdulla, provided that such Government is constitutional and places His Britannic Majesty's Government in a position to fulfil its international obligations in respect of the territory by means of an agreement to be concluded between the two Governments,' Herbert Samuel said in April 1923.[13]

Britain considered the Cairo Conference and its outcome as a success. T.E Lawrence, the British diplomat who was better known as 'Lawrence of Arabia' for the role he played in the Arab revolt against the Ottomans, was Churchill's special advisor during the Cairo Conference. In Lawrence's words, Churchill made 'straight all the tangle' and that Britain had fulfilled 'our promises in letter and spirit ... without sacrificing any interest of our Empire or any interest of the people concerned'.[14]

The Arab Occupier

If Churchill and Lawrence thought creating a separate kingdom of Transjordan and keeping it apart from Palestine would help them establish peace in the region and protect the Empire's interests, they were mistaken. There were bigger historical forces at play. When new Arab countries were created on the former Ottoman lands, they became increasingly apprehensive about the continuing Jewish migration to British-controlled Palestine. Abdullah, the ruler of Transjordan, had his own ambitions. In his talks with Churchill, Abdullah had suggested the unification of Palestine and Transjordan under an Arab ruler, or the unification of Transjordan and Iraq (which was given to his brother Feisal). The British rejected both suggestions.[15] Abdullah finally settled for Transjordan, but never gave up his ambitions for a 'greater Jordan'.

Across the river, in British-held Palestine, tensions were on the rise between the indigenous Arab population and the Jewish settlers since the early 1930s. After the UN General Assembly passed Resolution 181, which recommended the partition of Palestine into three territories—an Arab state, a Jewish state and Jerusalem as an international city—violence between Jewish paramilitary groups and Palestinian irregulars and Arab volunteers escalated. This was a particularly tense period. Britain, whose mandate would expire on 15 May 1948, had already expressed its intent to leave Palestine. The Jewish Agency, the representative of the Jewish settlers in

Palestine, with its paramilitary groups, was preparing to declare a state of Israel. And Arabs, who rejected the UN Partition plan, were mobilizing troops for a potential conflict.

Zionists declared the state of Israel on 14 May 1948. The next morning, a coalition of seven Arab countries (Transjordan, Egypt, Syria, Lebanon and expeditionary troops from Iraq, Saudi Arabia and Yemen) crossed into Mandatory Palestine, triggering the first Arab–Israel war. When the war came to an end in 1949, Israel captured more territories than what the UN plan had promised, including Upper Galilee, Western Jerusalem, Jaffa and parts of Negev; while Egypt took what came to be known as the 'Gaza Strip', on its Sinai border; and Transjordan seized territories on the western bank of the Jordan River, including East Jerusalem (which came to be known as the 'West Bank').[16] King Abdullah immediately laid claim to the West Bank.

'I will save the Arabs by expelling and annihilating all Zionists and Jews,' Abdullah said in Jerusalem, in November 1948, when Israel and Transjordan were still technically at war. He was speaking at the Coptic Convent in the Old City, before a crowd of believers and clergy. A Coptic Bishop rose from the crowd and stated: 'As the Christian Church welcomed Omar Ikn Khatib (the second Rashidun Caliph), handing over to him the boys of the Holy Sepulchre, so we proclaim you today [the] King of Palestine.'[17]

After the coronation of Abdullah as the king of Palestine, Transjordan moved fast to consolidate its control over the West Bank and East Jerusalem. A month later, the royal court called a conference of Palestinian notables and Jordanian military officials in Jericho to discuss the future of the Palestinian territories. The outcome of the Jericho Conference was hardly a surprise. Who, from the select crowd, was going to challenge the authority of the king who had already declared himself the ruler of Palestine, at a conference that was called by his court? Four resolutions were passed that expressed 'gratitude to Arab states for their efforts on behalf of the liberation of Palestine' and supported the call for unity between Transjordan and Arab Palestine.[18] On 24 April 1950, the West Bank and East Jerusalem were formally annexed into Transjordan and the name of the new united country was changed to the Hashemite Kingdom of Jordan.

Jordan gave citizenship rights to the Arabs living in the West Bank, which more than tripled the population of the country to 1.3 million. The Palestinians were given half of the seats in Jordan's sixty-member Parliament. But Jordan's annexation of the vast Arab territories did not go down well with its Arab allies, who fought alongside Amman in the war against Israel. For many, the annexation was part of Abdullah's Greater Jordan ambitions. Saudi Arabia and Egypt demanded Jordan's expulsion from the Arab League. The expulsion motion did not get enough support, but the Arab League's initial response was that the 'annexation of Arab Palestine by any Arab state would be considered a violation of the League Charter, and subject to sanctions'.[19] Later, in June 1950, the Arab League adopted a resolution 'to treat the Arab part of Palestine annexed by Jordan as a trust in its hands until the Palestine case is fully solved in the interests of its inhabitants'.[20]

But for Jordan, the annexation was not temporary. In the Gaza Strip, which was under the military occupation of Egypt, Cairo had established an all-Palestine government under the leadership of Ahmed Hilmi Pasham, which claimed authority over the whole of Mandatory Palestine. The all-Palestine government had the backing of most members of the Arab League, but Jordan refused to recognize a Palestinian authority over Palestinian territories.[21]

In the subsequent years, Amman took measures to tighten its control over the West Bank, and its rulers repeatedly said the West Bank was a legitimate Jordanian territory. In April 1948, at the Arab League meeting in Cairo, King Abdullah stated, 'Palestine and Jordan are one, for Palestine is the coastline and Transjordan the hinterland of the same country.'[22] King Hussein bin Talal, Abdullah's grandson who ascended the throne in 1952 at age seventeen, said a year later that East Jerusalem 'was the alternative capital of the Hashemite Kingdom and would make up an integrate and inseparable part of Jordan'. Six years later, Hazza Majali, the then Jordanian Prime Minister, declared: 'We are the government of Palestine, the Army of Palestine and the refugees of Palestine.'[23]

During the same period, the Palestinian national movement emerged stronger. The Palestine Liberation Organization (PLO), as a conglomerate of Palestine national liberation movements, was formed in May 1964. The PLO, which vowed to liberate 'the land between the river and the sea', launched guerilla attacks against Israel. Yasser Arafat, the PLO chairman, also launched a diplomatic outreach, trying to mobilize Arab and global support for the Palestinian cause. Several Arab countries, mainly Egypt under President Gamal Abdel Nasser, strongly backed the PLO. But Amman, under King Hussein, continued to maintain its post-1948 position that 'Jordan is Palestine and Palestine is Jordan'.

The 1967 Six-Day War would change the borders of the region once again. In 1948, even though Arab forces failed to defeat Israel, they had taken over and defended most of the Arab-populated parts of Palestine. But in 1967, Israel inflicted a crushing defeat on its neighbours, Jordan, Egypt and Syria, in just six days. Israel captured the West Bank and Jerusalem from Jordan, the Gaza Strip and Sinai Peninsula from Egypt and the Golan Heights from Syria. For the first time in history, Israel came to control the whole of historical Palestine. It would never retreat since then.

Black September

Hundreds of thousands of Palestinian refugees, along with them nationalist guerillas, fled the West Bank to the other side of the Jordan River. In the subsequent months, Jordan, the new base of the PLO, emerged as a hotbed of Palestinian resistance. The PLO, headquartered in the border town Karameh, and with support from other Arab countries, grew in strength and popularity. They stepped up cross-border attacks against Israel from Jordan, often inviting reprisals from the Israelis. This posed a security challenge to Amman. Inside Jordan, the PLO factions, including the radical left-wing groups such as the Popular Front for the Liberation of Palestine (PFLP) and the Democratic Front for the Liberation of Palestine (DFLP), emerged as a parallel state.

King Hussein was also wary of the PLO's republican nationalism at a time when Baathist, socialist pan-Arabist movements were taking deep roots in Arab societies. When Hussein took measures to curtail the activities of the PLO, it led to clashes between Jordanian forces and the guerillas, deepening the internal security crisis and making the king look weaker at home. Many foreign diplomats thought the monarchy's days were numbered. Henry Kissinger, US President Richard Nixon's national security adviser, said, 'The authority and prestige of the Hashemite regime will continue to decline. The international credibility of Jordan will be further compromised ... Hussein faces an uncertain political future.'[24]

The monarch himself was concerned about the developments of the late 1960s. 'We had thousands of incidents of breaking the law, of attacking people. It was a very unruly state of affairs in the country and I continued to try,' Hussein later recalled. 'I went to Egypt, I called in the Arabs to help in any way they could—particularly as some of them were sponsoring some of these movements in one form or another—but without much success, and towards the end I felt I was losing control ... I feared that the army would fracture along Palestinian–Jordanian lines,' he said.[25]

The relationship between the guerillas and the Jordanian monarchy reached a breaking point in 1970 when the leftist PLO factions called for overthrowing the Hashemite monarchy. They called King Hussein 'a Zionist tool' and 'a reactionary puppet of Western imperialism'. Initially such rhetoric came from the PFLP and the DFLP. But on 15 August 1970, Yasser Arafat, the chairman of the PLO, declared, 'We have decided to convert Jordan into a cemetery for all conspirators—Amman shall be the Hanoi of the revolution.'[26] This was a wake-up call for the monarchy. In September that year, after a string of plane hijackings by Palestinian guerillas based in Jordan, King Hussein dissolved his civilian administration, established a military government and ordered his troops to attack the PLO bases and camps inside the kingdom.

On 17 September, Jordanian troops attacked PLO positions, including the Palestinian refugee camps in the capital city, with tanks, mortars and artillery. Hussein's generals expected a victory in three days, but Palestinian guerillas put up a strong resistance. A force from Syria, under the banner of the Palestine Liberation Army, marched towards Jordan to fight alongside the guerillas. What began as a three-day military raid turned into a full-blown civil war, with the Jordanian air force launching strikes at enemy bases on Jordanian soil. Heavy fighting lasted for weeks, in which, according to Arafat, the Jordanian Armed Forces killed at least

25,000 Palestinians.[27] The events would be remembered by the Palestinians as 'Black September'.[28] The military operation dealt a body blow to the PLO, leaving Arafat with no choice but to leave Jordan. On 27 September, Hussein and Arafat signed a ceasefire agreement brokered by Gamal Abdel Nasser. Nasser died the next day of a heart attack.

The PLO relocated to Lebanon. Having resolved the security crisis at home, Hussein emerged politically stronger. But he knew that the wounds were deep and that history would not be kind to him. Later, when Adnan Abu Oudeh, an army major in the General Intelligence Department (also known as the Mukhabarat), who was made the Minister of Information, asked Hussein, 'What was the most difficult decision you had to make?' The monarch replied, 'The decision to recapture my own capital.'[29]

The Winds of Change

Even after Black September, Jordan continued to maintain its claims over the West Bank. On 2 February 1970, a few months after the crackdown on Palestinian guerillas, Prince Hassan, King Hussein's brother and the Crown Prince, said, 'There is only one land with one history and one and the same fate. Palestine is Jordan and Jordan is Palestine.' In 1972, Hussein repeated this claim. 'We consider it necessary to clarify to one and all, in the Arab world and outside, that the Palestinian people with its nobility and conscience is to be found here on the East Bank [of the Jordan River], the West Bank, and the Gaza Strip. Its overwhelming majority is here [on the East Bank] and nowhere else,' he said.[30]

But after its defeat in the 1967 war, Jordan never challenged Israel militarily. It continued to lay claims to the Palestinian West

Bank and East Jerusalem, but the kingdom had no practical plans to retake the territories back. This was not the case with Egypt and Syria, though. Jordan lost a territory in 1967 which it had annexed in 1948. But for Egypt and Syria, the losses were their sovereign territories—Sinai Peninsula and Golan Heights, respectively. Cairo and Damascus made military plans to take them back, when Jordan preferred peaceful co-existence with Israel. On the Yom Kippur Day of 1973, Egypt and Syria launched a surprise joint attack on the Israeli troops stationed in the occupied territories.

The Yom Kippur War made Israel realize that Egypt, despite its defeat in 1967, remained a potential strategic threat, which led to talks between the two sides. And for Egyptian President Anwar Sadat, who launched the war, the primary objective was to get Egyptian territory back from the Israelis. His nationalist objectives triumphed over his pan-Arabist Palestinian sympathies. This marked a decisive shift in the Arab approach towards the Palestine question. Unlike Jordan, which had occupied and annexed Palestinian territories and still laid claims to the West Bank, Egypt had always remained a supporter of the PLO and the Palestinian cause. And Egypt's decision to become the first Arab nation that recognized the state of Israel as part of the 1978 Camp David Agreement in return for the Israeli withdrawal from the Sinai Peninsula showed that if there's a clash between their national interests and their support for the Palestinian cause, the Arabs would pick the former.

But given the mood in the Arab world in the 1970s, Sadat couldn't have ignored the Palestine question completely. He insisted Palestinians get something out of his normalization with Israel. After much deliberation, the Framework for Peace in the Middle East was included in the Camp David agreements in which Israel promised to establish a self-governing authority in the Palestinian territories.

This was the first time Israel recognized the idea of Palestinian nationalism. The PLO by that time became synonymous with the Palestinian national movement and Arafat, who was then based in Lebanon, was given a hero's welcome in several foreign capitals. The Arab public opinion was largely in favour of creating a Palestinian state.

At the Arab Summit 1974 held in Rabat, Morocco, a unanimously approved resolution recognized the PLO as the 'sole legitimate representative of the Palestinian people'.[31] Jordan knew the winds were changing. It supported the Rabat resolution, but was still not ready to give up its claims over the Palestinian territories. The Jordanian parliament continued to have representatives from the West Bank. But after Camp David and Israel's de facto recognition of Palestinian nationalism, it became practically impossible for Amman to continue to treat the West Bank as a Jordanian territory. It was clear that Jordan would have to abandon its claims and support the Palestinian nationalist movement like other Arab countries, and the question was when, not if. The Twelfth Arab Summit, held in Fes, Morocco, adopted another resolution, with support from Jordan and other members, that called for the withdrawal of the Israeli troops from all the Arab territories it had captured in 1967, and the 'establishment of an independent Palestinian State with Jerusalem as its capital'.[32]

On 30 July 1988, nearly ten years after the Camp David Agreement was signed and eight months after the First Intifada (the Palestinian uprising) broke out, King Hussein dissolved the Jordanian Parliament, ending the West Bank representation in the legislature. The next day, he cut off the administrative and legal ties to the West Bank, except the custodianship to the Muslim shrines in Jerusalem. In an address to the nation, Hussein abandoned Jordan's claims over the West Bank, and offered support to the creation of a Palestine state. 'We respect the wish of the PLO, the sole and legitimate representative of the Palestinian people, to secede from us as an independent Palestinian state. We say that while we fully understand the situation, nevertheless, Jordan will remain the proud bearer of the message of the Great Arab Revolt, adhering to its principles, believing in one Arab destiny, and committed to joint Arab action,' said the monarch. 'Jordan is not Palestine and the independent Palestinian state will be established on the occupied Palestinian territory after its liberation, God willing. There the Palestinian identity will be embodied, and there the Palestinian struggle shall come to fruition, as confirmed by the glorious uprising of the Palestinian people under occupation,' he added.[33]

Cold Peace

Jordan had selfish interests. It knew that the West Bank would never return to its control. The region had been under the direct military occupation of Israel, and Amman had no plan to go to war with Israel for the West Bank. The Palestinian nationalism had grown to become a powerful political force in the Arab world. The Arab League had already supported the establishment of an independent Palestinian state and recognized the PLO as the legitimate representative of the Palestinian people. The Israelis themselves had, in theory, agreed to having a Palestinian self-governing authority in the occupied territories. Hussein knew the tides of history had turned. He decided to do the inevitable, but before that he wanted to try one last time to resolve the Palestine question through a bilateral deal with Israel.

In 1987, a year before Hussein formally declared Jordan's decision to abandon claims over the West Bank, Amman reached out to Israel. In April that year, King Hussein held a secret meeting with Shimon Peres, the Labour leader who was serving as foreign minister in the Likud-led national unity government in Israel, at the London residence of Lord Victor Mishcon, a prominent British Labour politician. Hussein's proposal, which came to be called 'the Jordan Option' was to resolve the Palestine question 'peacefully' through Jordan's sovereignty and based on the UN Security Council Resolutions 242 and 338.[34] Both Hussein and Peres secretly agreed to the Jordan Option as part of which an international conference was to be called to discuss the Palestine question. The Jordanians would represent the Palestinian side as the PLO would be excluded from the peace process—a suggestion welcomed by the Israelis. Both sides agreed to send their proposals to Washington to take it further.[35] The Ronald Reagan administration was open to the proposals. But Peres never got approval for the Jordan Option from the right-wing Prime Minister Yitzhak Shamir, who thought an international conference on Palestine would impose an unfair deal on Israel. It was after the collapse of the Jordan option and the outbreak of the First Intifada that Hussein decided to abandon Jordan's claims of sovereignty over the West Bank and East Jerusalem.

But the king still wanted peace with Israel, which had a huge military presence just across the Jordan River in the occupied West Bank. Egypt had already broken ranks with other Arab countries and signed a peace treaty with Israel in 1979—an agreement which survived the many upheavals that followed in the Israel–Palestine conflict. Egypt proved that Arabs could successfully engage Israel bilaterally, bypassing or giving lip service to the Palestine question, if their interests were at stake. King Hussein wanted to do what Egypt's President Anwar Sadat did, but the time was not ripe in the late 1980s when the Palestinian territories were in an uprising against Israel's occupation.

The tides turned in the 1990s. An international conference in 1991 between Israel and Arab countries focused on the Palestine question was eventually held in Madrid, Spain, largely based on the framework agreed between Hussein and Peres in their London meet. The PLO sent an advisory delegation to the Madrid Conference, which saw, for the first time, the Israelis and the PLO coming close to each other at an international peace conference.[36] Three years later, the first Oslo Accord would be signed, where a two-state solution to the Israel–Palestine conflict got international approval and legitimacy. Jordan and Israel lost no time in reviving direct talks.

The first breakthrough came on 25 July 1994 when King Hussein and Prime Minister Yitzhak Rabin of Israel signed the Washington Declaration in the US capital, bringing an end to the state of war between the two countries, in the presence of President Bill Clinton. 'Out of all the days of my life, I do not believe there is one such as this,' Hussein said before signing the declaration at the Rose Garden in the White House. 'It is dusk at our homes in the Middle East. Soon darkness will prevail. But the citizens of Israel and Jordan will see a great light,' said Prime Minister Rabin, with a pen in his hand, seconds before he signed the eleven-page accord.[37] The Washington Declaration cleared the decks for a peace treaty between the Hashemite kingdom and the Jewish state.

There was genuine appetite on both sides for a peace treaty. The regional situation, after the Oslo Agreement, was favourable to Jordan and Israel. The Labour government in Israel, led by Prime Minister Rabin, was seen as a serious party for peace. The US was actively pushing both Amman and Jerusalem to take the Declaration to the next level. It did not take much time.

On 26 October, in Arava (a Negev desert outpost on the Israel–Jordan border south of the Dead Sea basin), Israel and Jordan, in the presence of more than 4,500 guests, including US President Clinton, signed the Wadi Araba Peace Treaty, leaving behind forty-six years of troubled relations and launching new beginning. In the treaty, the countries agreed to settle their land and water disputes, broaden economic cooperation and trade and, more importantly, not to let each other's territory be used as a staging ground for attack by third parties. They also agreed to establish full diplomatic relations and exchange ambassadors within a month. Israel also pledged to recognize the Kingdom's claims to Islamic shrines in Jerusalem.[38]

Fifteen years after Egypt signed a peace treaty with Israel, the Hashemite Kingdom of Jordan, which had occupied the Palestinian West Bank and East Jerusalem for nineteen years and laid claims over the territories for forty-six years, became the second Arab country to normalize relations with the Jewish state.

'Peace between Jordan and Israel is no longer a mirage,' President Clinton stated from the venue of signing. 'It is real. It will take root in this soil ...' he said, referring to the Arava Valley, ' ... the bleak desert that hides great signs of life.' He added, 'It will grow to great heights and shelter generations to come.' King Hussein said the countries turned Arava into a 'valley of peace.'[39] But history is more layered than the triumphal rhetoric of the royals and politicians. In a sign of what's to come, when Yizhak Rabin and his Jordanian counterpart Abdul-Salam al-Majali signed the treaty, Hezbollah guerillas fired mortar bombs from Lebanon into northern Israel. Hamas and PLO factions had called for a strike. Thousands of Palestinians marched in the West Bank cities of Hebron and Nablus in protest against the treaty. Yasser Arafat denounced it. And in Jordan, many saw it as the kingdom's surrender to the Zionist regime.

But King Hussein was undeterred. He called the Wadi Araba treaty 'peace with dignity' and that Jordan supported 'every word and every letter' of the treaty. He added, 'This is our gift to our peoples and to generations to come.'[40] The next day, the monarch's Royal Jordanian plane, a Lockheed L-1011 TriStar, escorted by Israeli F-15s, circled over Israel-controlled Jerusalem. The Hashemite monarch and his wife had a bird's eye view over the Old City, where his grandfather's coronation as the king of Palestine had taken place forty-six years ago.[41]

The Arab Apathy

In the University of Amman, while walking with Khaled in 2015, I asked him about the Wadi Araba treaty. He said, 'It's cold peace', recalling what King Abdullah II, Hussein's son who ascended the throne in 1999, once said. While speaking to *La Repubblica* in October 2009, Abdullah II said Israel's relationship with Jordan 'is getting colder'.[42] The bonhomie of the Hussein was already lost. Abdullah II had taken a pragmatic view of the crisis. He opposed Israel's efforts to change the status quo in the Palestinian territories and strongly backed the two-state solution, but did not rock the Wadi Araba agreement. 'There is an attempt to change the political aspect, as we start to see Israelis encroaching on East Jerusalem, which is part of Palestinian territories occupied in 1967. You can't change realities on the ground while negotiations are ongoing ... Jerusalem is of tremendous importance for Jordan, this is a red line that can not be crossed. Even more so regarding the issue of the Mosque,' said the king in the interview.

When the Wadi Arab was signed, there was a promise of a Palestinian state based on the Oslo process. Israel had also pledged to respect Jordan's ties to Jerusalem's Muslim holy places. But the Oslo process has collapsed ever since. Israel has expanded its settlements in the West Bank. And Haram al-Sharif (Temple Mount) in the Old City, which hosts the Western Wall, the Dome of the Rock and al-Aqsa Mosque, has emerged as a flashpoint, particularly after Ariel Sharon's controversial visit to the place in 2000.[43] Did Israel keep the promises it made in the Wadi Araba treaty? Khaled said 'No', without thinking twice. So does it make for Jordan to continue to stay in the treaty, especially when the king himself slams Israel's violations? 'See, peace with Israel is not only about their commitments towards Palestine. It's also about Jordan's relations with a nuclear-armed neighbour, which has the full-throated backing of the United States. We fought two major wars in the past with Israel. We don't want to go back to those days,' he said.

'There was a time when Arabs thought, especially Jordanians, that the Palestine problem was theirs. That has changed. It changed when Egypt broke with the Khartoum consensus and made peace with Israel,' he said referring to the 1967 Khartoum resolution of the Arab summit, which vowed 'no talks with Israel, no peace with Israel and no recognition of Israel'.[44]

'Jordan did the same in 1994. Trust me, more countries will follow. The regional dynamics of the Middle East is changing,' said Khaled, keeping his hands on his hips. He continued as if he was giving a lecture to his students. 'The Palestinians are divided. You tell me why there are two governments in Ramallah and Gaza. Arabs are increasingly worried about Iran. Then you have the Muslim Brotherhood and the Islamic State—both threaten our regimes. And then there are Americans. Arabs have a lot of challenges to deal with on their own, and the Palestine question doesn't come on top of the list any more.' Khaled paused. The smile returned to his face. 'We are not petrodollar sheikhs. We need American aid. We have an Islamist opposition at home, and a population that's largely Palestinian. We have to keep the border peaceful, and keep our people happy. It's a balancing act,' he said, adding after another pause, 'The King is the protector of Jordan, not of the West Bank. Not any longer.'[45]

Khaled asked me if I was going to the West Bank. I said, 'Yes, in two days.'

'Trust me, life is terrible under occupation. You go and see what life looks like in the West Bank. It's an injustice. But Palestinians should also realize that the Palestine problem is no longer an Arab–Israel problem. It's an Israel–Palestine problem.'

Years later, when I was writing about the Abraham Accords—in which four Arab countries, the UAE, Bahrain, Morocco and Sudan, reached normalization agreements with Israel under the aegis of the Donald Trump administration—I was reminded of Khaled's words. When Egypt signed a peace treaty with Israel, Anwar Sadat insisted that a Framework Agreement for the Palestinians be signed. Jordan signed a treaty in the immediate aftermath of the Oslo process where hopes for a Palestinian state were high. But when the Abraham Accords were signed, the Palestinians got no concession from Israel.

US President Joe Biden, the democratic President who succeeded Republican Donald Trump, was keen on expanding the Abraham Accords. The Biden administration promoted talks between Israel and Saudi Arabia. If Saudi Arabia, custodian of Islam's two holiest mosques and arguably the most powerful Arab country today, normalizes ties with Israel, it would be a coup of sorts. In November

2020, Israeli Prime Minister Benjamin Netanyahu secretly met Mohammed bin Salman, the Saudi Crown Prince, in the kingdom.[46] In September 2023, MBS, as Prince Salman is widely known, said in an interview that Saudi Arabia was 'moving closer each day' towards reaching an agreement with Israel. 'It seems it's for the first time a real one, serious. We're gonna see how it goes,' said the Prince. Asked about his demands from Israel for a normalization deal, MBS said the agreement would 'reach a place that will ease the life of the Palestinians', stopping short of calling for the establishment of a Palestinian state, which has been the Saudi position for decades.[47] The Palestinian question looked certain to be pushed to the margins of West Asia's present.

In the following month, hundreds of Palestinian militants from Gaza crossed the border to Israel and carried out the worst attack in Israel's history, killing at least 1,200 people and taking some 240 hostages. Israel was shocked and agonized. Fire and fury followed.

7

7 October 2023

'YOU might be witnessing a massacre.'

Vivian Silver, the seventy-four-year-old Canadian-born Israeli peace activist, texted her son in the early morning of 7 October 2023. She was living in Be'eri Kibbutz, a Jewish commune in southern Israel near the Gaza border. Residents of the kibbutz, home to over 1,200 people, woke up to alarm sirens followed by sounds of gunshots on that fateful morning. Images of militants holding guns roaming around the kibbutz were soon circulated in a community WhatsApp group. Be'eri, which was established as a commune in 1946 and named after Berl Katznelson, one of the intellectual founders of Labour Zionism, lies just 3 km from the Gaza border. It had a ten-member security team. But the kibbutz was attacked by some seventy militants of the Nuseirat Battalion of al-Qassam Brigades, Hamas's military wing. They overpowered the security personnel and entered the kibbutz.

When violence and panic spread, amid rocket sirens and gunshots, Vivian took shelter in the safe room of her home. From there, she took a call from a public radio broadcaster. Nobody still knew what exactly was happening and what was coming for the Israelis. 'They are insane. Look how they are interrupting us on a holiday,' said the show host. It was a Shabbat day. It was also Simchat Torah, a Jewish holiday that celebrates the conclusion of the annual cycle of public Torah readings. In 2023, Simchat Torah fell between sunset on 6 October and nightfall on 7 October.

Vivian was unhappy with the host. 'We can talk more about this if I survive,' she said. After the interview, she texted Yonatan, her son. 'Where is our Army?' she asked. At 10.41 a.m., she sent another text. 'They are in the house now.'

'Mom,' Yonatan wrote.

'I am afraid to breathe,' she said.

'I have no words. I'm with you,' texted Yonatan.

'I feel you,' she wrote.

'Are you safe now?' he asked.

...

'Mom???'

She didn't respond.[1]

Vivian's first visit to Israel was in 1968, a year after the Six-Day War in which Israel captured the whole of Palestine. She studied psychology and English literature at the Hebrew University of Jerusalem. She immigrated to Israel in 1974, a year after the Yom Kippur War, and started living in kibbutz Gezer in central Israel. She moved to Be'eri in 1990, in the midst of the Palestinian First Intifada (uprising), along with her husband and two sons. Gaza then had Israeli troops and settlers. Before Israel imposed a blockade on Gaza in 2007, Vivian, who had co-founded the Arab-Jewish

Center for Equality, Empowerment and Cooperation, a non-profit, had organized several cross-cultural projects with Palestinians in Gaza. In the post-blockade years, she emerged as one of the most vocal critics of Israel's treatment of Palestinians. She was a former board member of B'Tselem, a Jerusalem-based non-profit which documents the human rights violations in the occupied Palestinian territories. In 2014, shortly after that year's Israel–Hamas war in Gaza, she co-founded Women Wage Peace, a grassroots peace movement, whose main objective was to prevent more conflicts and promote a peaceful solution to the Israel–Palestine conflict. In 2011, *Haaretz* named her as one of the '10 Most Influential Anglo Immigrants' to Israel.[2]

I visited Vivian's home in Be'eri in April 2024, roughly six months after the kibbutz was attacked. The yellow-painted two-storey house was totally destroyed. Tiles were strewn in front of the building amid overgrown lantana plants with unattended yellow and orange flowers. The building, with its main door blown away and scarred walls, stood, under the clear April skies, like a memorial of the greatest tragedy of Israel. The smell of death was hanging in the air.

'They entered the community and randomly attacked everyone,' Ela, a spokesperson of the Israeli Defence Forces (IDF), told me and a group of journalists, standing in front of Vivian's house. By the time Israeli troops arrived in Be'eri on 7 October, it was too late. The militants had already killed around a hundred people and kidnapped thirty. 'They came with RPGs and brought petrol in Toyota trucks. They attacked houses after houses, threw grenades and burnt down buildings,' Ela, who must be in her twenties, wearing a dark green military jacket and trousers, said unsentimentally in fluent English. The soldiers went from building to building to clear militants.

At Vivian's charred house, they couldn't find her body. Everyone thought she was taken to Gaza. Her sons launched a campaign, highlighting her peace activism, to get her released. Later, human remains were found among the ashes in her house. Five weeks after the attack, the remains were identified as Vivian's via her DNA.

'In this house lived Vivian Silver who was brutally murdered in the Hamas terror attack on 7 October,' read a banner that's hanging from the blackened wall of her house. Inside the building, there was a huge pile of ash. The roof was broken in parts, walls black and cracked and furniture charred. 'Alarms go off every time there is a rocket attack from Gaza. Those living in Southern Israel were familiar with it. My commander calls it the symphony of war,' said Ela, standing inside the burned-out safe room of Vivian's house. 'But on 7 October, it was different. There were ongoing alarms for over fifteen minutes. Then people living here realized that this time, it's unusual. It was not only about sirens. People also heard shooting outside their homes and shouting in Arabic. Then they knew that the safe rooms were not going to protect them.'

Ela walked around the room, letting journalists shoot the scars of the attack. 'The terrorists came very well-prepared. They knew people would hide inside their safe rooms. In Vivian's case, they burned the house, and they burned her body,' she said. After a pause, she continued, 'This room looks now clean, but after the attack, it was filled with ashes about 40-cm high.' Ela said so while pointing to the wall whose paint had partly been peeled off. 'This is why it took so long to identify her body. When we brought experts who scanned through the ashes, they found one tooth—that helped us realize that she was actually murdered here.'

Vivian's house was not an exception. On her lane in Be'eri, all houses were attacked and most of them burned. Walls had both the numbers left by Israeli troops after securing them and the Arabic inscriptions left by the attackers. Of the thirty hostages taken from Be'eri, nineteen were released as part of a ceasefire agreement with Hamas in November. The remaining eleven were still in Hamas's captivity in Gaza when I was in the kibbutz, and their family members did not know how many of them were alive. Only seven families were then living in Be'eri, which also had a strong IDF presence. 'This is comparable to Holocaust. One thousand and two hundred people were killed in a single day,' an Israeli diplomat, who had been posted in India earlier, told me in Be'eri, outside one of the destroyed homes on Vivian's lane. 'Can you imagine this? Terrorists swooping in on your homes in the wee hours and start shooting at your parents and children in front of you and burning down your houses and communities? This is what Israel endured on 7 October,' he added.

Massacre at the Festival

It's a rural farmland area. The tree-lined Re'im park is located some 500 metres from Route 232, a busy southern road that connects Highway 25 with the kibbutzim in the south. The van I was travelling in took a diversion from Route 232 to a smaller, unpaved road. After a few minutes, the driver, a big, clean-shaven man, who'd immigrated to Israel from Russia, announced in his heavy voice that we had arrived at the 'festival ground'.

I saw dozens of people wandering through the trees, stopping at the memorials and small gardens set up for those killed and kidnapped on 7 October at this park. At one location, where there was a thicket of poles, visitors stood by in silence, while some others walked through the poles. Each pole had portraits of those who were killed at the park. Israel's blue and white flag, with the Star of David in the middle, was fluttering from one of them. Some 3,500 people were at Re'im for a full-night party on 6 October. Billed as a celebration of 'Friends, Love and Infinite Freedom', the music festival had a camping zone in the forest and a food court. When the day broke, the site of the Nova festival turned out to be a graveyard.

At first, at 6.30 a.m., sirens went off, after which rockets appeared in the sky. Then there was another siren, warning of impending rocket attacks. The festival-goers, scattered in fear and scrambling for their belongings, started fleeing the field. Then came armed militants, mostly on motorcycles and paragliders, wearing army attire. They opened fire at the crowd indiscriminately, according to the account given by survivors.[3] There was no place to hide. The trees were not thick enough to guard them from the bullets. There was nobody to protect the crowd, either. Some of them took their cars in a last-ditch move to escape the fire. But the cars were attacked by Rocket-Propelled Grenades (RPGs). A pileup of burned vehicles created a traffic jam on the main road. Then the militants raided the cars stuck on the road and shot at those inside or burned them.

I walked around the park, lost in thought. Despite it being an open field, an eerie silence filled the space. Young soldiers, mostly in their early twenties, were roaming around in plain clothes, wearing automated guns. Visitors offered prayers at the memorials or paid tributes to the dead. 'We were frightened to death,' a survivor, a woman in her thirties, told me. I took a seat under the shade of a tree on a public bench. She used to live in a kibbutz nearby. Now, her family is living in government-arranged accommodation. The trauma of 7 October refuses to leave her. 'As a Jew, as a Zionist, and as an Israeli, for the first time, I felt that history is repeating again,' she said, clasping her own palms, referring to the Holocaust. According to Israeli authorities, more than 360 revellers were killed at the Re'im park and on the nearby roads. The massacre was recorded by the car dash cameras and the Hamas militants themselves, which were telecast on Telegram channels. At least forty hostages were also taken from the site.

Hundreds of cars were destroyed or burned. The cars as well as the motorcycles that the Hamas attackers used were taken to an open ground near Netivot. Locals now call it the 'car cemetery', another memorial for the 7 October victims. The IDF guards the car cemetery, with a tent which offers reprieve from the scorching summer sun for the visitors, and a shelter closer to the main gate, which is to be used if the siren goes off. 'This is a fifteen-second alert zone from Gaza. If you can't make it to the shelter in fifteen seconds, lie down on the ground with your hands on the back of your head,' Adam, a spokesperson of the southern district of the Northern Command of the IDF, told me. On the vast ground, there were cars and trucks that were fully burned and vehicles that were bullet-ridden and partly destroyed. The burned-out cars were stacked up in four levels on one side of the ground. It looked like a huge wall with rusted iron skeletons of vehicles. Cars with bullet holes were kept in lines, as if they were parked in an open-air parking lot. At another corner lay motorcycles and Toyota trucks with RPG launches mounted on them. Adam, wearing military fatigues, jumped on to a truck, took the RPG's handle, turned it towards us, faking to aim at the targets, and then said, 'This is how they fired at our people.'

A drone was circling the ground from above. There was a burned-out upturned vehicle near the front fence. Adam asked me whether I could say what the vehicle was. I said it could be a van. 'This was an ambulance. Hamas attackers didn't spare even ambulances. There were sixteen different human remains in this ambulance by the time we reached here.' He added, 'Three hundred cars were completely burnt by the terrorists. They came to the roads to deliberately hunt for civilians. And they came with petrol bombs, RPGs and other explosives.'

The war had already entered the seventh month, and there were no signs of an end. I told him the world sympathized with Israel on 7 October. And asked him about the way Israel is conducting the war in Gaza, in which most of the victims were women and children. 'Look,' he said, stretching his bulked-up hands towards the huge wall of burned vehicles. 'How cruel our enemy is! Israel is fighting in Gaza with Western values, to minimize civilian casualties.' I said the facts on the ground did not support his claims. He continued as if that didn't matter. 'We are fighting a vicious enemy, who is using civilians as human shields. Hamas started this war. This war is still going on because of Hamas. Hamas can end the war today if they agree to release the hostages.' But Adam was aware of the international debate about Israel's occupation of Palestinian territories. 'This is not a dispute about land. This is a (?) Jew-hatred agenda that Israel is battling. It's not the war we wanted. It's not the war we started. But we must win the war. There is no other choice.'

Hamas launched at least 3,000 rockets from Gaza on 7 October. At least 5,000 militants breached the Gaza-Israel barrier, and drove into southern Israeli villages, towns and military facilities.[4] Some of them used powered paragliders to land in Israel. Several communities such as Be'eri, Kfar Aza, Nir Oz, Netiv Haasara and Alumim came under attack. Hamas's military chief Mohammed Deif, who announced the attack to the world, called it Operation al-Aqsa Flood. 'Today, the people claim their revolution,' Deif said in the speech that was released by Hamas on 7 October.

'The Israelis have attacked [our] worshippers and desecrated al-Aqsa [Mosque], and we have previously warned them. The enemy desecrated al-Aqsa and dared to harm the Prophet's path. Hundreds have been martyred and injured this year due to the occupation's crimes... We have decided to put an end to all of the occupation's crimes. The time is over for them [Israel] to continue to act without accountability. Thus, we announce the "al-Aqsa Flood" operation,' said Deif.[5]

Deif, commander of the Qassam Brigades, has been on Israel's kill list at least since the early 2000s. In 2002, he lost an eye in an Israeli strike. In 2006, Israel struck a building in which Hamas leaders had assembled. The attack seriously injured Deif, but he survived. In August 2014, after an initial ceasefire was announced following weeks of fighting, Israel carried out an airstrike targeting him. The attack killed Deif's wife and two children, but he escaped again. The escapes earned him the nickname among the Palestinians: 'the cat with nine lives'. Over the years, Deif emerged as one of the most powerful figures of Hamas in Gaza. According to Gen. Giora Eiland, a former Israeli National Security Advisor, 'Deif is the decision-maker in Hamas ... He believes every day they continue to fight is another achievement for them.'[6]

After Deif took over the Brigades, Hamas carried out a host of suicide attacks inside Israel. Israel holds him personally responsible for the deaths of many of its citizens. In the 7 October message, he called on Islamic resistance forces in the Palestinian-occupied territories as well as the larger Arab street to march towards Palestine. 'We call for mobilization towards Palestine ... Today, whoever has a gun, let him bring it out; it's time. Everyone should come out with their trucks, cars, or tools. Today, history opens its most pure and honourable pages,' he said.[7]

By the time, the Hamas attack was brought to an end, 1,139 people had been killed—695 Israeli civilians, including 38 children, 71 foreign nationals, and 373 members of the security forces. This was the biggest terror attack in Israel's history. And this was the first time Israel's borders had been breached by a ground force since 1948, the year the state of Israel was created. Hamas leaders, including Mohammed Deif, 'are dead men walking,' declared Israel's Defence Minister Yoav Gallant.[8]

'A big fuck-up'

In November 2022, eleven months prior to the Hamas attack, I was in southern Israel. With a group of journalists and an IDF spokesperson, we went to Kerem Shalom, a key border crossing between Israel and Hamas, and the walled border beyond the crossing point. Lt Col Jonathan, the IDF spokesperson, took us to a tunnel from Gaza, a few kilometres from Kerem Shalom, which the IDF unearthed inside Israeli territory. 'This is one of the longest cross-border tunnels Hamas has built,' said a uniformed IDF officer, opening the iron door of a concrete structure in the middle of barren lands on the Israeli–Gaza border. The door opens to concrete steps that disappear underground. It was dark, muddy and suffocating inside. The officer asked journalists to turn on the flashlights.

The IDF built the steps for easy access to the mouth of the tunnel, which is roughly 50 m underground. The steps were muddy and slippery. The northwestern Negev region gets rains only a few days a year. It was one of them. 'Rains lash the mud in the tunnel onto the steps, which makes the going tough,' said the officer, stepping into darkness.

The 2.5-km-long tunnel, of which 900 m is inside Israeli territory, is roughly a ten-minute drive from Tel Gama, the mound in southern Israel that saw Australian and New Zealand troops, under British command, mount a successful cavalry charge against the Ottomans in the First World War. The IDF detected and destroyed the tunnel in 2016. 'This is largely a military area. This is a historically important area. But Hamas can build tunnels to any points in the border region,' Jonathan, who was wearing jeans and a T-shirt with a thick black jacket, told me while we were inside the tunnel. I could barely stand upright. If I stretched my hands, I would have hit the muddy walls. The strong smell of mud was attacking my nostrils. 'Hamas built these tunnels to smuggle their militants into Israel from Gaza,' Jonathan said.

'Hamas has an elaborate network of tunnels, for various purposes. Narrow tunnels like these are mostly built for infiltration and to launch attacks inside Israel. On Gaza's Egyptian border, Hamas and the Islamic Jihad have built wider, more sophisticated tunnels and they get everything they want smuggled through these tunnels. This includes weapons, contraband, cigarettes, fuel and clothes,' said Jonathan. The uniformed IDF officer said his forces had destroyed dozens of tunnels from Gaza in recent years. 'We have developed a technology to detect tunnels at the early stages of digging. And we wait for the right time to attack and destroy them,' said the officer.

'The people in Gaza might have a different story to tell,' one of my journalist colleagues whispered in my ears while the officer was speaking of infiltration from the enclave. They indeed did. In recent years, Gaza, the tiny Mediterranean strip of 2.3 million people, has emerged as a hotbed of Palestinian resistance against Israel's occupation. Unlike the West Bank, whose Palestinian Authority is controlled by Fatah, Gaza has been run by Hamas since 2006. Even before Hamas took control of the enclave, Gaza was the centre of operations for Islamist groups, whose violent resistance differed from the Fatah's secular nationalism and dialogue-driven approach. Gaza's political character in part was shaped by its tumultuous history.

When Palestine was incorporated into the Ottoman Empire in the sixteenth century, it was divided into six administrative districts. Gaza Sanjak (District of Gaza) was one of them, stretching from Jaffa in the north (now part of Israel) to Rafah (now, the border crossing with Egypt) in the south. For over four centuries, it remained an Ottoman district. In 1917, during the last leg of the First World War, the British captured Palestine, including Gaza, from a crumbling Ottoman Empire.[9] After the state of Israel was created in May 1948 in Palestine, which resulted in the displacement of over 7,00,000 Arabs, mostly from areas that became part of the new Jewish state, refugees took shelter in neighbouring regions. Most of them moved to what was then called the Gaza Strip. Within months, the 356 sq. km territory saw its population swelling to over 2,00,000. The people of Gaza, who lived under Ottoman rule for centuries and British occupation for decades subsequently, would continue to see their fate being determined by external rulers. Israel captured the enclave in 1967 and kept it under its control, either through direct military occupation or blockades.

If two different streams of Palestinian national movements—the secular nationalism championed by Fatah and the Palestinian Liberation Organisation (PLO), and the Islamist awakening promoted by the Muslim Brotherhood—emerged under the Israeli occupation, Gaza became a hotbed of the latter. The Brothers established deep roots in the enclave. From the 1970s, Israel had promoted Jewish settlements in the West Bank and Gaza. In 2005, faced with Hamas's violent resistance, Israel unilaterally decided to pull back its troops and settlers from Gaza. For the first time in centuries, Palestinians got a chance to establish their own rule in the enclave, even though Israel's direct occupation of the West Bank and East Jerusalem continued. In the first elections held in the Palestinian territories, in 2006, Hamas came to power, defeating Fatah. The Islamists and the secularists initially formed a unity government. But it fell apart quickly, particularly after Western countries refused to sanction funds to the Palestinian Authority led by Hamas, which they see as a terrorist outfit. A brief Fatah–Hamas civil war broke out. Fatah ousted Hamas from the West Bank and the latter captured Gaza in 2007. Ever since, Hamas has been the government in Gaza.

'We withdrew from Gaza. We pulled back every soldier and every Jew from Gaza. But did that bring peace? Hamas took over Gaza, and started firing rockets into Israel. So, who is to blame for the wars?' Jonathan asked me emphatically. Israel saw the takeover of Gaza by Hamas, as a security challenge. It imposed an illegal land, air and naval blockade on Gaza from 2007 onwards, to control what and who went in and out of the enclave. At the Kerem Shalom check-point, Ami Shaked, its director, told me in November 2022 that for Israel there's no difference between Hamas and ISIS. 'They don't want any solution but the Islamic solution. They think we don't have the right to live here,' Mr Shaked said. Kerem Shalom has been hit several times by mortars and rockets from Gaza. 'There are Israeli communities living in this region. They live under constant fear and trauma of rocket attacks from Gaza.'

Hamas, on the other side, did not see Israel's withdrawal from Gaza, which is only a part of Palestine, as an end to the conflict as Jonathan claimed. The Islamist group said it retained 'the right to resist' as long as Israel continued the occupation of Palestinian territories, including East Jerusalem. Constant tensions led to occasional wars. Between the Hamas takeover of Gaza in 2007 and the Hamas attack on Israel in 2023, there were four major conflicts between Israel and Hamas in which thousands of Palestinians and hundreds of Israelis were killed.

Gaza is often described as the world's largest open prison.[10] It's one of the most densely populated regions in the world. Israel has built barriers along the border—both overland and underground—with limited check-points. It issues a limited number of permits to the Gazans to get out of the enclave. The unemployment rate in Gaza was roughly 47 per cent, which shot up to almost 80 per cent after the war started.[11] Electricity is scarce—eight-hour power cuts were common before 7 October. Israel destroyed Gaza's only airport years ago and restrained access for the Gazans to the Mediterranean Sea. The enclave's economy is mostly run on contributions from abroad, which dried up after the war.

When I was at the Gaza border in 2022, the region was largely calm, even though violence continued in the occupied West Bank. '[But] Gaza has been like this since 2005. A spell of tense calm can be broken any time with a spark. And then a full-scale war will come,' I wrote in *The Hindu*, after I returned to India.[12] From Tel Gama and Kerem Shalom, one could see the border fence that separates Israel from Gaza. There were not many soldiers in the vicinity, but Israel's observation posts, overlooking Gaza, were visible from a long distance. 'The IDF has some very sophisticated surveillance tech so that we can keep monitoring Hamas through those posts,' Jonathan told me, pointing to the towers.

The IDF has built barbed wires over land and a deep concrete fence underground. 'The purpose is to stop infiltration. Underground fences with tunnel detectors sound us out if Hamas is building a tunnel towards the border.' How deep is the fence?

'That's confidential information,' he said, with a smile. 'But I can tell you that it is deeper than the deepest tunnel Hamas has built.' With tunnel-detection technology, underground fences and the Iron Dome anti-missile defence system, the IDF hoped to put an end to Hamas's tunnel and rocket threats as well as infiltration. 'Hamas and the Islamic Jihad are getting support from other countries. They have amassed thousands of rockets. But we have equipped ourselves better to deal with those threats,' Jonathan said.

But, as it turned out, none of this helped Israel prevent the 7 October attack. Hamas had planned its attack in detail. They had specific maps of southern Israel's towns, military facilities and infiltration routes, including tactical guides identifying weak spots in Israel's armoured vehicles.[13] They underwent months-long training before flooding Israeli towns. Mossad, Israel's external intelligence agency which has a mythical status among the world's spy circles, knew that Hamas had plans to carry out a large-scale attack. Agents had prepared a document code-named 'Jericho Wall', outlining Hamas's plans and sent them to their superiors. But Israel's military and intelligence leadership ruled out the report, saying such a plan was largely aspirational and beyond Hamas's capabilities. Rather, Israel had, like Jonathan and the military officer I met on the Gaza border, super confidence in the measures they had taken along the border. Perhaps that's what Hamas also wanted.

On 7 October 2023, Hamas fired thousands of rockets, and sent drones to knock out security cameras and automated machine guns at the unmanned surveillance posts on the border. They used bulldozers to pull down the security barrier Israel had built, and dispatched militants en masse on motorcycles, paragliders and on foot. Hamas followed what Jericho Wall had detailed with 'shocking precision'.[14] Yet, Israel was caught unawares.

In January 2024, three months after the Hamas attack, I met an Israeli diplomat in India. I asked them how Hamas amassed its weapons. 'Gaza is practically under your blockade. You control the land borders, you control the coast. Then how do they get sophisticated weapons and foreign training?' The diplomat said, 'We don't control all the crossings. The Rafah crossing is a huge one. It's manned by Hamas and the Egyptians. Hamas has also built deep tunnels into the Egyptian side which they use to smuggle in weapons. Their commanders also travel abroad. They get training from Iran or Hezbollah. And they come back and train other terrorists.'

'Are you saying that Egypt, which has signed a treaty with you, is permitting this? I thought Egypt itself doesn't like Hamas much,' I said. 'I am not suggesting anything like that,' replied the diplomat. 'My point is that it's a myth that Israel is controlling all the checkpoints. We are controlling only our border points. And Rafah is being used to smuggle in weapons and fighters.'

Then I asked the diplomat the obvious question that had plagued many of us since 7 October. 'See, you have one of the best intelligence services in the world. You have the support of highly advanced tech. I was on the Gaza border in 2022 where I was told about the surveillance measures you had put in place. Then, how did 7 October happen?'

'It's a big fuck-up, a big fuck-up' said the diplomat, twice. 'They had the intelligence. But nobody took it seriously. And now we all are paying the price.'

Two-State Illusion

After the Hamas attack, Israel launched a devastating bombing campaign on Gaza. 'Israel is at war,' declared Prime Minister

Benjamin Netanyahu, vowing to take 'mighty vengeance' against Hamas.[15] Israel stated that it had the right to respond to Hamas's terror attack. The world stood by Israel. The United States offered full support. President Joe Biden, who travelled to Israel and met with Netanyahu and his Cabinet members, said, 'I don't believe you have to be a Jew to be a Zionist, and I am a Zionist.'[16]

Netanyahu set two goals for the IDF. 'Crush Hamas' and release the hostages. The IDF carried out air strikes across Gaza for weeks, before launching a full-scale invasion, first in the north, and then expanding to the whole of the enclave. In the initial stage, more than 1 million people in northern Gaza were ordered by the IDF to leave their homes within 24 hours.[17] Gaza City in northern Gaza, the largest city in the enclave, was turned into a pile of rubble within weeks.

The use of disproportionate force against the enemy is a well-known Israeli method (the Dahiya doctrine). Dahiya in Lebanon was a stronghold of Hezbollah, the Shia militia. In the 2006 war with Hezbollah, Israel carried out widespread bombing of Dahiya, flattening the town. In October 2008, while warning Hezbollah amid tensions in northern Israel, General Gadi Eisenkot, then head of the Army's Northern Division, said Israel would use 'disproportionate force' to destroy Lebanese villages from where Hezbollah was firing rockets. 'What happened in the Dahiya quarter of Beirut in 2006 will happen in every village from which Israel is fired on... From our standpoint, these are not civilian villages, they are military bases,' said Gen. Eisenkot, who later became Israel's Chief of General Staff and then a minister in Netanyahu's Cabinet.[18] Post-7 October, the IDF followed the same tactics in Gaza.

In April 2024, I met an Israeli journalist, who calls himself a right-winger, in Jerusalem. We had an open discussion about the war and Israel's objectives at a restaurant in the Old City.

The effects of the war were visible everywhere. When I was in Jerusalem the last time, the flea market near Jaffa Street was so crowded that I found it difficult to walk in between traders and shoppers. This time, it looked like a ghost street, with only a few shops being open. Restaurants were mostly empty. A tour guide I had met on my previous trip told me the war took a huge hit on the economy. At the Church of Holy Sepulchre, the fourth-century church that is considered the holiest place of worship in Christianity, there was hardly anyone besides our group when we visited the place in the evening. The journalist told me that like every war, 'this one also has a cost. And Israelis are bearing it'.

He said 7 October changed everything. Things can't just go back to the 7 October status quo, he said. I raised the issue of collective punishment of Gazans. The journalist, a kippah-wearing, bearded man in his early forties, said there was a debate on whether the people of Gaza were culpable in the whole disaster or not.

'In what sense?' I asked him.

'They voted for Hamas,' he said.

'So are you saying that they should be punished as a whole?'

'No, that's not what I am saying. Hamas is part of Gaza's society. You look at their charter. They are committed to the destruction of Israel. And they were still voted to power.'

'But in that case Likud's founding charter also lays claims to the land between the River and the Sea,' I said. 'And Likud has been in power in Israel for how many years!' [19]

'You can't compare a legitimate ruling political party with a terrorist entity,' he said.

He then told me he didn't agree with the military tactics the IDF is using in Gaza. By that time, almost all of Gaza's population had been displaced. People in the north and central Gaza have been pushed to the Rafah border in the south. There was a growing international demand to let Gazans return to their homes in the north. 'Everybody says people in Gaza should be allowed to return to Gaza City and Khan Younis. But where will they go? There is not a single building standing in northern Gaza. The whole city has been brought to the ground,' he said.

'Isn't this mindless vengeance? Does this help Israel meet its long-term strategic objectives?' I asked him.

'I don't know. I don't even know if there's a strategy,' he replied.

Two days later, at a Committee Room in the Knesset, the Israeli Parliament, I met Boaz Bismuth, a Member of the Knesset (MK) from Netanyahu's Likud Party. I asked him if he saw an end to the war. Six months into the war, Israel had not met any of its declared objectives. 'The war will be long. At least one year. We are making progress. We will meet our objectives,' said the MK.

Bismuth, a bespectacled, clean-shaven, tall man with dark hair, wore a dark blue suit and tie. He seemed to be in a hurry, but was careful with the words he used. 'I was also a journalist,' he said, probably recalling his stint as the editor of *Israel Hayom*, a Hebrew language daily. In 2022, he joined Likud and became an MK. Ever since the 7 October attack happened, Bismuth has taken a hardline position on the war, calling for erasing Hamas. 'The cruel and monstrous people from Gaza took an active part in the pogrom in the Israeli settlements, in the systematic murder of Jews and the shedding of their blood, in the kidnapping of children, old people, and mothers, and in tying up babies and burning them alive!' he wrote on X (formerly Twitter), on October 16. 'One mustn't pity the cruel, there is no place for any humanitarian gesture—the memory of Amalek must be erased!' he added, referring to the biblical enemy nation of the Israelites.

'We have two objectives,' Bismuth told me in the Knesset committee room. 'One is to bring back the hostages. And the other is to eliminate Hamas.' While asked about the mounting civilian casualties in Gaza, he said, 'I am not at war against civilians. I am at war against Hamas. People in Gaza elected Hamas. Still, I am not at war against them.'

For Bismuth, sustainable peace is possible in the region only if Hamas is defeated. 'If we lose the war, we lose the idea of peace. If I lose, I lose everything. So, I am not going to lose it,' he said, adding that other countries, including India, should support Israel in this war instead of attacking the way Israel is conducting the war. 'Every country that respects itself should call Hamas what it is—a terrorist entity.'

This was the politician's view of the war. Later in the day, I went to the Israeli Foreign Ministry in Jerusalem, where, inside a meeting room, I met Michel Ronen, a senior diplomat who headed the Bureau of Southeast Asia at the ministry. I asked him about the diplomatic fall-out of the war. By that time, much of the global opinion had turned against Israel. There were cracks in Israel's relationship with the US, its biggest backer, which was becoming increasingly impatient with the mounting civilian casualties in Gaza. 'We are working to make sure that the political and international legitimacy stays for our military operations. We are aware of the dangers. We lost international support for our military operation in 1973. The UN demanded a ceasefire in three weeks. But this time, we see more flexibility,' the ambassador told me.

When I met him, Qatar and Egypt, with the blessings of the United States, were already mediating ceasefire talks between Israel and Egypt. Cairo hosted the talks. I asked the ambassador about the military goals Israel had set and the role of diplomacy in the midst of the ongoing war. 'We are not looking at a victory formula. We want hostages back. That's what our urgent priority is,' he said. But will a hostage deal lead to a permanent ceasefire in Gaza? Hamas, which struck a limited deal with Israel in November and released some 100 hostages in return for a week-long ceasefire, later demanded a permanent ceasefire for another hostage deal. 'I cannot guarantee what would happen after a deal. There could be a ceasefire or there could be more attacks,' said Ambassador Ronen.

I asked him about the larger Palestine question. He gave the standard reply: Israel will continue working with its partners for peace.

'Ambassador, as a diplomat, do you still believe a two-state solution is possible?' I asked him, before wrapping up our conversation.

'Some here call the two-state solution a two-state illusion,' came his quick reply.

The War in the North

'War is bad for everyone. And we live in constant fear,' Asiya, who lives in a village near the Israeli–Lebanon border, told us in April, 2024. Hailing from Israel's minority Druze community, Asiya hosts tourists and visiting delegations at her home in Yanuh-Jat for lunch. She offers traditional Druze food in a large house on a hill. From her balcony, the heights on the Lebanese–Israel border that have been on fire for six months are visible. 'After the war began, business was down. We get practically no tourists these days,' said Asiya, a mother of three who lost her husband a few years ago.

Ever since the Gaza war, Israel's northern border has seen a slow-burning war between the Israeli forces and Shia and Palestinian militias on the other side. Southern Lebanon is the stronghold of Hezbollah. Hamas's Qassem Brigades and the Islamic Jihad's al-Quds Brigades also have some limited presence in southern Lebanon. These groups have launched multiple rocket attacks into northern Israel since 7 October 'in solidarity' with Palestinians and Israel has carried out hundreds of retaliatory strikes in Lebanon.

Yanuh-Jat, which was hit by rockets from Lebanon in April 2023, has relatively been quiet in the latest round of conflict. But Asiya was worried that if the tensions escalated on the border, her village and its over 6,000 residents, mostly Druze, would get caught in the war. Like most houses on Israel's border, Asiya's house also has a bunker. 'I have 15 seconds to take shelter in the bunker once the alarm goes off in the event of a rocket attack,' she said.

Israel had fought a month-long war with Hezbollah in 2006, which did not end well for the Jewish nation. Hezbollah, a well-trained guerilla army, has hundreds of thousands of rockets and drones among its weapons. Hezbollah has repeatedly launched rockets into northern Israel and the occupied Golan Heights, targeting both Israeli military personnel and civilians. In retaliation, Israel has carried out air strikes. Between 7 October and 15 March, Hezbollah and other militias in Lebanon and Israel exchanged at least 4,733 attacks across the border, according to the Armed Conflict Location and Event Data Project (ACLED), a non-profit. Of these, Israel accounted for 83 per cent of the attacks, totalling 3,952 incidents, while Hezbollah, Amal Movement and Palestinian militias launched 781 attacks.

Hezbollah has stated that it would continue attacking Israeli positions as long as the Gaza war continues. According to Hassan Nasrallah, Hezbollah's charismatic leader, his fighters were 'pressuring' Israel from Lebanon. 'This battle concerns Palestine, but also concerns the future of Lebanon and its water and oil resources. This front is a support front that is part of the battle that will determine the fate of Palestine, Lebanon and the region strategically,' said Nasrallah.[20] 'We have been at war since 7 October,' said Sarit Zehavi, the founder and president of Alma Research and Education Centre, a think tank focused on Israel's security. Ms Zehavi, a former Lieutenant Colonel in the Israeli Defence Forces, said Hezbollah was carrying out a well-calculated campaign from Southern Lebanon. 'It's not a full-scale war. But Hezbollah has managed to terrorize the whole Upper Galilee region,' she said.

According to Alma's research, Hezbollah carried out over 2,000 attacks on Israel between 7 October 2023 and 31 March 2024. Over 57 per cent of these attacks have targeted military facilities, while 43 per cent were aimed at civilians. Hezbollah and other militants have used anti-aircraft and anti-tank guns, drones and mortars in these attacks. And Israel's repeated air strikes inside Lebanon targeting Hezbollah positions and commanders did little to deter or blunt Hezbollah's fire power, according to Alma. After the northern border turned into a war zone, Israel evacuated forty-three communities (61,000 people) in the Upper Galilee region, located up to 5 km from the border. Most of them have taken temporary shelter in hotels in the Northern District. The displacement has added pressure on the government of Prime Minister Netanyahu to calm the border region and allow the displaced to go back to their homes.

'Hezbollah has always set their eyes on Upper Galilee. Now they have managed to push Israelis out of the region. Hezbollah's plan is to occupy Galilee,' Zehavi told me at her office in Upper Galilee, from where the border heights were visible. She said there has never been real peace on the northern border even after the 2006 war. 'The war did not deter Hezbollah. They have been amassing strength all these years. And now they are testing it,' she said.

'I can't say how the situation is going to play out,' said Zehavi. 'Israel wants to take the displaced back to their homes. But that's not possible as long as cross-border firing continues. And Hezbollah says there won't be a ceasefire unless there's a ceasefire in Gaza. Even if there's a ceasefire, it would only embolden Hezbollah,' she said.

Five months after I met Zehavi in the Israel-Lebanon border region, Prime Minister Benjamin Netanyahu decided to escalate Israel's war with Hezbollah. While Nasrallah wanted to fight a limited war keeping some military pressure on the IDF which was fighting in Gaza, Netanyahu went for full-force punches. On 17 and 18 September 2024, thousands of handheld pagers and hundreds of walkie-talkies exploded across Lebanon, mainly targeting Hezbollah's ground-level functionaries. Before Hezbollah recovered from the shock, Israel launched waves of massive bombings in southern Lebanon and the suburbs of Beirut, killing several of Hezbollah's top commanders. And then, on 27 September, an IDF strike on a Beirut suburb killed Hassan Nasrallah, who was Hezbollah's secretary-general for over three decades and one of the most influential men in the Axis of Resistance. While Hezbollah was still mourning the death of their leader, Israel launched a ground invasion of Lebanon on 1 October.

What started as a war against Hamas a year earlier is now a two-front war for Israel. The war in Gaza remains unfinished. And the war in Lebanon has just begun. For Hezbollah, with or without Nasrallah, this was the moment it had been preparing for from 2006.

8

The View from India

'MODI is a supporter of Israel. He knows that Israel can contribute to India's growth,' a senior Israeli diplomat told me in April 2024 at the Ministry of Foreign Affairs in Jerusalem, referring to India's Prime Minister. We were sitting in a relatively small conference room at the ministry. At the oval-shaped table, the Israelis had kept cut fruits and snacks. A painting of Theodor Herzl, the father of modern political Zionism, was hanging on the wall. 'Modi coming to power in 2014 was a significant moment in India—Israel ties,' said the diplomat. 'We have been a reliable partner in times of need. And now, there is a government in Delhi that values our contributions,' he said.

The diplomat, who was talking about Israel's diplomatic challenges in the aftermath of the Gaza war, suddenly looked relaxed when the topic shifted to India. After the 7 October 2023 attack by Hamas in Israel, Narendra Modi was one of the first global leaders who condemned the attack and offered solidarity. 'Deeply shocked by the news of terrorist attacks in Israel. Our thoughts and prayers are with the innocent victims and their families. We stand in solidarity with Israel at this difficult hour,' he posted on X (formerly Twitter). Modi's post triggered speculations in India and abroad on whether New Delhi's position towards Israel–Palestine was witnessing a dramatic change post-7 October.

A retired Indian diplomat, who was part of the National Security Board, told me in March 2024 in New Delhi that he was 'surprised' by the Prime Minister's 'sweeping solidarity'. 'Such declarations go against the basic premise of the work people like me do in our lifetime. But then the MEA stepped in,' said the diplomat, referring to India's Ministry of External Affairs. On 19 October, Arindam Bagchi, the official spokesperson of the MEA said in Delhi that India supported a two-state solution to the Israel–Palestine conflict. 'We have strongly condemned the horrific terrorist attack on Israel. The international community must stand together in combating terrorism in all its forms and manifestations, and there can be no equivocation on this. There was also the issue of Palestine, and on that, we have reiterated our position in favour of direct negotiations for establishing a two-state solution,' he said at a press conference. 'We have also expressed our concern at the civilian casualties and the humanitarian situation. We would urge the strict observance of international humanitarian law.'[1]

Back in Jerusalem, I asked the Israeli diplomat about India's support for the two-state solution (meaning, creation of an independent Palestinian state, as the state of Israel has already been existent). 'India has condemned the 7 October attack. We see it. India's support for UN resolutions doesn't signal a policy change.

India supports a two-state solution. In theory, we also support a two-state solution,' he said.

'Are you saying that Israel supports the creation of an independent, sovereign Palestine state?' I asked.

'We are not against the two-state solution,' he continued. 'Details should be reached in negotiations. But who do we talk to? Hamas, which wants to eliminate us? Or Abu Mazen [Palestine Authority President Mahmoud Abbas]? Does he have any powers? We live with the threat of terrorism. So a future Palestine state, whenever it's formed, should be unarmed.'

If Israel says a future Palestine state should be unarmed, it would not be a sovereign state. But the diplomat's views are relatively moderate compared to the mainstream opinion in Israel's political circles about the two-state solution. Prime Minister Benjamin Netanyahu has repeatedly said there wouldn't be a Palestinian state on his watch. 'I think that anyone who moves to establish a Palestinian state today, and evacuate areas, is giving radical Islam an area from which to attack the State of Israel,' he said in 2015.[2] Naftali Bennett, the former Prime Minister, said in a 2013 interview, before he formed his government, 'There is not going to be a Palestinian state within the tiny land of Israel.'[3] By 'the tiny land of Israel, he was referring to the land between the Jordan River and the Mediterranean Sea, which was historical Palestine. The Knesset, Israel's Parliament, has passed resolutions rejecting the Palestinian statehood. 'A Palestinian state would pose an existential danger to the State of Israel and its citizens, perpetuate the Israeli–Palestinian conflict and destabilise the region,' according to a resolution passed in the 120-member Knesset in July 2024, with 69 votes in favour and nine against.[4]

So the two-state solution, which India and a vast majority of the countries support, remains practically dead in Israel. But the diplomat seemed unperturbed about this contradiction. 'You may have a position on the two-state solution. I may have my own position,' he said. 'But that need not affect India–Israel relationship. From our side, we are clear. We want to further improve our ties with India. India has also de-hyphenated Israel and Palestine so that we can deepen our bilateral partnership irrespective of the Palestine factor.' With his crisp comment, the diplomat was actually laying bare India's position towards Israel–Palestine, which has seen both changes and continuity over the years.

A Historical Overview

In November 1947, when the United Nations General Assembly voted on a resolution to partition Palestine into a Jewish state, an Arab state, and an international city (Jerusalem), India, which had got independence just three months earlier, came under intense pressure to vote in favour of the resolution. The partition plan was put forward by the UN Special Committee on Palestine (UNSCOP), and had the backing of powerful Western countries, including the United States. Thirty-three countries, roughly 72 per cent of the total votes, cutting across the East–West divide, supported the resolution, including the United States, France, the Soviet Union and Czechoslovakia. The United Kingdom, which at that time still had a Mandatary administration in Palestine, and China, which was then ruled by the nationalist Kuomintang, abstained. Thirteen countries, roughly 28 per cent of the total votes, voted against the resolution. One of them was India.[5]

India's decision at the UNGA voting was hardly surprising. Even before Independence, leaders of India's freedom movement had expressed their support for the Palestinians. In 1936, while speaking on Palestine Day (27 September) in Allahabad, Indian National Congress Working Committee member Jawaharlal Nehru said India's fight for independence was 'part of a world struggle against imperialism and fascism, including the struggle that's going on against British imperialism in Palestine'.[6] Two years later, Mahatma Gandhi wrote in *Harijan,* the weekly magazine he founded in 1933, that '[I]t is wrong to impose the Jews on the Arabs. What is going on in Palestine today cannot be justified by any moral code of conduct'.[7] The 1939 Session of the Indian National Congress adopted a resolution on Palestine and looked forward 'to the emergence of an independent democratic state in Palestine in which the rights of all communities would be protected'.[8]

At the UN in 1947, India, along with Iran and Yugoslavia, proposed an independent Palestine as a federated State where Jews, Muslims and Christians could co-exist, with Jerusalem as its capital. Under this plan, Arabs, who made 68 per cent of Mandatory Palestine's population, would get some 56 per cent of the territory and Jews would get 44 per cent. The federal government would control immigration, defence and foreign policies, while the national governments of Jews and Arabs would run day-to-day affairs of their territories. 'The federal State is also in every respect the most democratic solution, both as regards the measures required for its implementation and in its operation, since it requires no undemocratic economic controls, avoids the creation of national minority groups, and affords an opportunity for full and effective participation in representative government to every citizen of the State. This solution would be most in harmony with the basic principles of the Charter of the United Nations,' it stated.[9] But this proposal did not get the support of majority members at UNSCOP, which put forward the Partition Plan.[10] At the UNGA voting, India voted alongside Pakistan and the Arab bloc against the Partition Plan.

India's position was rooted in the overall foreign policy framework the new republic had set for itself. Born into a bipolar world, India, which won independence through a decades-long freedom movement, took a strong position against colonialism and for self-determination, particularly in the context of Asia and Africa. Having gone through the horrors of Partition in which hundreds of thousands of people were killed, India said it would not support the partition of Palestine. For Nehru, Palestinians were 'a people struggling for independence against imperialist control and exploitation. It's not a racial or religious one.'[11] India was also concerned about Pakistan's efforts to inflame the Kashmir issue at global stages, and it did not want to go against the Arab consensus on Palestine. The government was also mindful of the sensitivities of the country's large minority population. So anti-imperialism, lessons from its own history, political calculations and a pragmatic assessment of its relationship with the Muslim world all influenced India's decision to oppose the creation of the state of Israel by dividing historical Palestine.[12]

But when the state of Israel was declared on 14 May 1948, which won quick recognition from both the United States and the Soviet Union, India accepted the reality and offered recognition to the Jewish state in 1950. 'We would have recognized Israel long ago, because Israel is a fact. We refrained because of our desire not to offend the sentiments of our friends in the Arab countries,' Nehru said about his government's decision in 1950.[13] But New Delhi did not establish full diplomatic relations with Israel. In 1953, Israel was allowed to open a consulate in Bombay, but India was yet to open a diplomatic mission in Israel. Israel's repeated attempts to establish full diplomatic relations were futile. A frustrated David Ben-Gurion, Israel's first Prime Minister, said in 1960, 'I cannot understand how Mr Nehru fits his behaviour to Israel with Gandhi's philosophy of universal friendship.'[14]

India's foreign policy those days were shaped by its commitment to non-alignment. India wanted to stay out of the two powerful blocs—the US-led capitalist bloc and the Soviet-led communist bloc—and be a voice of the newly decolonized countries. Being a champion of anti-colonial struggle, India continued to support national self-determination of countries that were still living under colonial rule or foreign occupation. This gave a moral footing to India's foreign policy. But the non-alignment and support for the newly emerging countries also helped India chart a realistic path to expanding its influence in an international order that was marred by great power rivalry.

Almost all countries in the Non-Aligned Movement (NAM), especially Gamal Abdel Nasser's Egypt and Josip Broz Tito's Yugoslavia, co-founders of the movement, along with Nehru's India, were strong advocates of the Palestinian cause. Israel, on the other side, had increasingly identified itself with imperial powers. If India–Israel relations had a bad start in 1950, the 1957 Suez war made it worse. Nehru was aggravated and shocked by Israel's attack on Egypt, a fellow non-aligned country, with support from France and Britain, both former colonial powers. On 31 October 1956, India issued a statement, saying Israel's attack was a 'flagrant violation of the UN Charter and in opposition to all principles laid down in the Bandung Conference [of 1955]'. The war, which Nehru called a 'dastardly action', hardened India's position towards Israel, and deepened its friendship with Egypt.[15]

During the Six-Day War of 1967, when Israel captured the West Bank and East Jerusalem from Jordan, the Gaza Strip from Egypt and the Golan Heights from Syria, all in six days, India took a strong position against Israel, which launched the war. In Parliament, Prime Minister Indira Gandhi said on 6 June, 1967, 'I do not wish to utter harsh words or use strong language. But on the basis of information available, there can be no doubt that Israel has escalated the situation into an armed conflict which has now acquired the proportions of a full-scale war.'[16]

Indira Gandhi, under whose leadership NAM emerged as a stronger and larger platform of the countries in the Third World, strengthened India's support for the Palestinian cause, while cultivating strong ties with the Arab world. During the 1973 Yom Kippur War, which was triggered by a joint attack by Egypt and Syria on the Israeli forces in the occupied Sinai Peninsula and Golan Heights, India blamed Israel for the war. According to Indira Gandhi, India would 'stand by its friends in the time of their travail'. She said Israel's continued occupation of the Arab lands captured in 1967 and its refusal to honour UN resolutions led to the war.[17]

Until the 1973 war, India's Palestine policy was shaped largely by its relationship with Arab countries. But Palestine nationalism had emerged stronger in the 1960s with the formation of the Palestine Liberation Organization (PLO). Yasser Arafat, the PLO chairman, became an embodiment of the Palestinian resistance, and he cultivated strong ties with most leaders in the Third World, including Indira Gandhi. India was ready to recognize the Palestinian nationalism championed by the PLO and pushed for the PLO's international recognition, especially in platforms such as NAM, where India wielded considerable influence.

NAM repeatedly issued statements expressing support for the Palestine cause. The Algiers declaration of NAM in 1973 was a case in point. It stated that durable peace in West Asia could be achieved only on the basis of 'two indispensable fundamental prerequisites; restoration of the Palestine people's national rights, the foremost among which is the right to return to self determination—and *ensuring global recognition of the PLO* as the legitimate and the sole representative of the Palestinian people.' (Emphasis is the author's)[18]

A year later, India became the first non-Arab state to recognize the PLO 'as the sole and legitimate representative of the Palestinian people'. In 1988, India became one of the first countries to recognize the Palestinian State. And in 1996, India opened its Representative Office in Gaza, which was later shifted to Ramallah in 2003.[19]

New Regional Reality

Even when India remained a steadfast supporter of Palestine, it maintained diplomatic engagements as well as backchannel defence relations with Israel, which was very keen on developing ties with New Delhi. In 1962, when India was attacked by China, Nehru reached out to world leaders, including Israel's David Ben-Gurion, for help. It was the time of the Cuban Missile Crisis and major world powers were preoccupied with the crisis. When much of the world turned away, Israel offered to send weapons to New Delhi. '[I]t is incumbent upon us to do all in our power. All states, big or small, must be guaranteed of their sovereignty. We believe that every possible support should be lent to every measure contributing toward easing of tensions on your borders so that

India will once again be able to devote its undivided energies under your distinguished leadership to construction and development,' Ben-Gurion wrote back to Nehru.[20]

Nehru thanked the Israeli leader and requested him to send weapons in ships that did not carry Israeli flags. But Ben-Gurion rejected the request. India, pushed back by the Chinese from the border, went ahead with the plan to buy Israeli arms. It would later pause the arms purchase after Egyptian leader Nasser registered his objections with Prime Minister Nehru. But India and Israel continued their defence cooperation secretively. India bought Israeli weapons during the 1965 and 1971 wars with Pakistan. In 1965, Israel supplied M-58 160 mm mortar ammunition to India.[21] P.N. Haskar, the Principal Secretary to Prime Minister Indira Gandhi during the 1971 Bangladesh liberation war, described arms shipments from Israel as 'a surprising minor success'. Then Israel Prime Minister Golda Meir had supplied mortars and ammunition and facilitated even instructors.[22] India found it convenient to maintain backroom defence and political ties with Israel, while at the same time remaining a champion of the Palestine cause. It was not ready to establish full diplomatic relations with the Jewish state.

India's position would change in 1992. By that time, both the global order and regional dynamics were undergoing massive changes. The Soviet-led communist bloc collapsed in 1989 and the Soviet Union itself disintegrated in 1991. The United States emerged as the world's sole superpower. Post-Soviet Union, India opted for stronger ties with the West and deeper integration with the global economy. The non-alignment movement lost its Cold War-era charm. In the Arab world, Egypt, which under Nasser was a close partner of India and a strong advocate of the Palestine cause, had already signed a peace treaty with Israel and switched to the

US side. Other Arab countries, including Jordan, had established back-channel links with Israel. And in 1991, the Israelis and the Palestinians participated in the Madrid Conference that sought a diplomatic solution to the Palestine question. Israel, which had termed the PLO a terrorist entity, and the PLO, which had vowed to 'liberate' the whole of Palestine, 'from the river to the sea', were warming up to the idea of direct talks. India found it as a historical moment to formalize the back-channel ties and it established full diplomatic relations with the Jewish state in 1992.

In the following years, India's ties with Israel would transform into a vibrant bilateral partnership. The Oslo Agreements, signed in 1993 and 1995, and Israel's growing acceptability in the Arab world, particularly after the formation of the Palestinian Authority in the occupied territories and the Jordan–Israel peace treaty of 1994, meant that India found it relatively easier to balance between its ties with the Jewish state and its commitment for the Palestinian cause. But even after the collapse of the Oslo process and a spike in Israel–Palestine tensions during the Second Intifada that broke out in 2000, India–Israel partnership would stay on track and continue to flourish. For Israel, which was isolated in the region and was facing criticism internationally for the continuing occupation of the Palestinian territories, relations with India, a democracy and a rising power, was placed high on its foreign policy agenda. Israel was one of the few countries that chose to not condemn India's nuclear tests in Pokhran in 1998. And it continued to sell arms to India even after that latter was placed under international sanctions following the nuclear test. During the Kargil war of 1999, Israel supplied Unmanned Aerial Vehicle (UAV) 'Searcher', surveillance systems, Laser Guided Bombs and 160-mm mortar ammunition to India.[23]

The subsequent years witnessed a boom in India–Israel defence ties, especially in surveillance and intelligence-related equipment. The rise of the right-wing Bharatiya Janata Party (BJP) to power in India, first in 1998, also gave a new fillip to relations with Israel. The BJP, free of the Congress's foreign policy legacy, made it a priority to improve ties with Israel. The party's rank and file watched Israel's tough security model with admiration. The majoritarian character of Zionism in Israel–Palestine and the majoritarian ideology of Hindutva of the BJP saw ideological resonance in each other. All these factors expedited India's gradual tilt towards Israel. The fact that Arab nations themselves, especially the rich and powerful Gulf Arabs, had established indirect ties with Israel made it easier for India in expanding its partnership with Israel without letting it affect its multifaceted relationship with the Arab world.

The result? India emerged as the largest purchaser of Israeli weapons in the last decade, providing the Israeli defence industrial base, which faced opposition from the US to sell arms to China, a sizeable and stable market. Between 2001 and 2021, India's defence purchases from Israel totalled some $4.2 billion, according to the Stockholm International Peace Research Institute's arms transfer database.[24] Overall bilateral trade has also seen a major jump since the establishment of full diplomatic relations. If merchandise trade between the two countries, comprising primarily diamonds, stood at $200 million in 1992, it hit $10.7 billion (excluding defence) in 2022–23, with Indian exports valued at around $8.4 billion.[25] In recent years, India and Israel also became more ambitious in building a stronger geopolitical partnership, particularly after the United Arab Emirates normalized ties with Israel in 2020 as part of the Abraham Accords. India, Israel, the UAE and the United

States are now part of a new grouping called I2U2, which is also called 'the Middle East Quad'.[26] This grouping, according to the US Department of State, 'identifies bankable projects and initiatives to tackle some of the greatest challenges confronting our world, with a particular focus on joint investments and new initiatives in water, energy, transportation, space, health, food security, and technology'.[27] In September 2023, on the sidelines of the G-20 summit in New Delhi, world leaders unveiled an ambitious economic corridor involving India, Israel and Gulf countries. Termed the India–Middle East–Europe Economic Corridor (IMEEC), the project seeks to connect India's western coast with Israel through the Gulf and Arab countries such as the UAE, Saudi Arabia and Jordan and then with Europe across the Mediterranean Sea.[28] For the IMEEC to be a reality, peace between Israel and Saudi Arabia was necessary. The project was announced at a time when the Israelis and the Saudis were making rapid progress in talks aimed at reaching a normalization agreement.

But then came the 7 October attack.

The Modi Factor

I was in Ramallah when Prime Minister Modi visited the West Bank in February 2018. The previous year, he had travelled to Israel—the first visit to the Jewish nation by an Indian Prime Minister. Modi's ascent to power in 2014 had triggered speculations that India's traditional position on Palestine would change. Modi, the first Prime Minister who had an absolute majority in Parliament since Rajiv Gandhi, enjoyed a warm personal chemistry with the Israeli Prime Minister, Benjamin Nentanyahu. His admiration for the Israeli security model was also not a secret.[29] In May 2015, External

Affairs Minister Sushma Swaraj stated that the Prime Minister would travel to Israel, without announcing any date.[30] But India also maintained that pursuing stronger ties with Israel did not mean that India was abandoning its traditional Palestine policy.

In November 2015, the Palestine ambassador in India, Adnan Abu Alhaijaa, told me Modi 'will visit Palestine' as well. I met the ambassador at his large office in the Palestine Embassy in Delhi. Large photos of Yasser Arafat, the late Palestine leader and Palestine authority President Mahmoud Abbas were hanging on the wall behind him.

He said President Abbas had already sent an official invitation to Prime Minister Modi. 'At a book launch at the Prime Minister's residence recently, Mr Modi said he would visit both Israel and Palestine. I asked him while I shook hands with him, Prime Minister, will you come to Palestine? He said, "I am coming to both of you. For sure, I will visit both of you," Ambassador Alhaijaa said, with great enthusiasm. I asked him about India's growing ties with Israel. His response was quick and crisp. 'Till now, India's position has not changed. We're looking up to India for political support. We want India to play a bigger role in the Middle East, and in the peace process between Israel and Palestine,' he said. 'India has strong ties with the Palestinian people. It also has friendship with the Israelis. So it's in a position to play a constructive role in the peace process.'

Contrary to the ambassador's wish, India has historically been reluctant to play any role in the peace process. But Mr Modi kept his word on visiting both countries. He carried out the visits as two stand-alone trips, though.

In February 2018, on a chilly afternoon, the helicopter carrying Modi touched down on the helipad of Muqataa, the administrative headquarters of the Palestinian Authority in Ramallah. He was offered a red carpet welcome by Prime Minister Rami Hamdallah. Later, President Abbas joined to greet Modi. While Abbas and Modi were walking to the administrative building after the guard of honour, someone from a group journalists assembled to cover the summit asked aloud if the Prime Minister would take questions from the media. Modi, wearing a grey suit, his white beard trimmed neat, continued to wave his hands at the crowd with a broad smile and walked away, while Palestinian officials said the Prime Minister and the President would meet the press after their meeting. During the visit, Modi was conferred the Grand Collar of the State of Palestine by President Abbas, the highest order given to foreign dignitaries, recognizing his contribution to promote relations between India and Palestine.

In the evening, the leaders met reporters at the news conference hall of Muqataa, but they did not take questions. Palestinian officials told us that it was at the insistence of the Indian side. Both leaders read out their respective statements. 'I am here, in Ramallah, because India's support for Palestine is unbroken and unwavering,' said Modi, with Abbas, in his trademark blue suit, standing beside him. 'Friendship between India and Palestine has stood the test of time. The people of Palestine have shown remarkable courage in the face of several challenges. India will always support Palestine's development journey,' Modi said. 'You have shown steely resolve to overcome [challenges] and advance despite instability and insecurity that threaten hard-fought gains,' he told the Palestinians. 'We hope for peace and stability in Palestine. We believe a permanent solution is possible with dialogue.' In his remark, Abbas thanked India for 'the noble and dignified positions it has taken towards the Palestinians'.[31]

The next day, I took a taxi from East Jerusalem, which came to Ramallah to pick me up and drop me off at the Tel Aviv airport (cabs in Ramallah are not allowed to go to Tel Aviv and cabs from Israel proper can't come to Ramallah). On the Turkish Airlines flight to Istanbul, I was seated next to a young Indian diplomat who was in Ramallah to help the mission there to organize the Prime Ministerial visit. During the roughly five-hour flight, we started discussing foreign policy and international affairs. The diplomat told me India had taken realistic readjustments in its policy towards Israel–Palestine given the changes in the regional and global circumstances, but the essence of the policy hadn't changed. 'Then why was there no reference to the border and Jerusalem in Modi's comments in Ramallah?' I asked him. There was short silence on the other side.

Traditionally, Indian statements of support for Palestine have said that New Delhi backed an independent, sovereign state of Palestine within the 1967 borders and East Jerusalem as its capital. When then President Pranab Mukherjee visited Jordan, Israel and Palestine in October 2015, he said, 'I reiterated India's principled support to the Palestinian cause and called for a negotiated solution resulting in a sovereign, independent, viable and united State of Palestine, with East Jerusalem as its capital, living within secure and recognized borders, side by side at peace with Israel as endorsed in the Quartet Roadmap and relevant UNSC Resolutions.'[32] The Quartet Roadmap Mukherjee referred to is the two-state plan suggested by the United States, the European Union, Russia and the United Nations to resolve the Israeli–Palestine conflict. In November 2013, Prime Minister Manmohan Singh issued a statement on the occasion of the International Solidarity Day with the Palestinian People, reiterating India's position. It read: 'India supports a negotiated resolution, resulting in a sovereign, independent, viable and united state of Palestine with East Jerusalem as its capital, living within secure and recognised borders side by side and at peace with Israel...'[33]

However, in the statement issued by Prime Minister Modi after the India visit of Palestine President Abbas in May 2017, there was no reference to Jerusalem. '[W]e hope to see the realization of a sovereign, independent, united and viable Palestine, coexisting peacefully with Israel. I have reaffirmed our position on this to President Abbas during our conversation today,' the Prime Minister said on May 16, 2017.[34] On 10 February 2018, in Ramallah, Modi reiterated this line, with no direct reference either to the borders or to Jerusalem. The Prime Minister said India hoped to see an independent sovereign Palestine living in a peaceful environment, whereas President Abbas, in his statement, stressed on achieving the national goals of Palestine 'according to the two-state solution on the 1967 borders and the resolutions of international legitimacy. And Israel in peace and security, with East Jerusalem as the capital of a Palestinian state'.[35]

The diplomat on the flight told me this was a tweak that was long overdue. 'We are not a party to the conflict. This is about the Israelis and the Palestinians. There are questions about borders, refugees, settlers and the status of Jerusalem. And both sides will have to make concessions and compromises to arrive at a final solution. Who are we to tell them which border belongs to which side? Let them sort it out,' he said, adding, 'our position is clear. We have a vibrant bilateral relationship with Israel. We also support an independent, sovereign future Palestine state. We shouldn't allow one position to hurt the other. We support finding a solution to this issue through dialogue.'

After 7 October

On 26 October 2023, barely three weeks after the 7 October Hamas attack in Israel, India abstained from a vote at the United Nations General Assembly that called for an 'immediate, durable and sustainable humanitarian truce' in Gaza. India explained its standby saying that there was no explicit condemnation of the 7 October 'terror attack in the resolution'.[36] The abstention, which came close on the heels of Prime Minister Modi's tweet declaring solidarity with Israel after the attack, had ruffled some diplomatic feathers in Delhi. In December, a retired Indian diplomat told me, 'When it comes to Israel, the MEA is always under pressure from the PMO.' When I pressed him further to talk about India's Israel–Palestine policy, he said, 'See, the MEA wants to maintain the traditional balance. But Israel is a hot topic in the PMO. So, there would be a lot of balancing act before taking positions.'

When the war continued in Gaza with heavy civilian casualties and Israel's growing international isolation, India moved back to its traditional balancing act. But India offered neither a strong moral critique, like Brazil or South Africa did, of Israel, nor unquestionable support, like the United States or the United Kingdom did in the early stage of the war. A few days after Mr Modi's tweet declaring solidarity with Israel over the 'terror attack', the MEA stated that India backed 'a sovereign, independent viable state of Palestine'. After its first abstention, there were at least four votes at the UNGA on Israel. On 12 November 2023, India voted in favour of a resolution that condemned Israeli settlements 'in the occupied Palestinian territories, including East Jerusalem and the occupied Syrian Golan'. Two weeks later, New Delhi voted in favour of another resolution that expressed 'deep concern' over Israel's continuing occupation of Syria's Golan Heights. On 12 December, India supported a resolution that called for 'an immediate humanitarian ceasefire'. And on 19 December, it voted for the Palestinian right to self-determination.[37]

To be sure, the voting record is consistent with the Palestine policy India has taken over the years. One cannot have a two-state solution if Israeli settlements continue in Palestinian territories. And the only path towards a solution is diplomacy, not war, as there is no balance of power between Israel, the mightiest military in West Asia, and the Palestinian militants. So, in essence, if one supports the two state-solution, they should call for an immediate end to violence, support dialogue, condemn settlements and, in principle, back Palestinian right to self-determination. India did all this, unlike, say, the United States, which claims to be supporting the two-state solution while voting against all resolutions that are critical of the state of Israel at the United Nations.

The 7 October attack and Israel's retaliatory war have also turned the strategic clock in the region back. Before 7 October, India was gearing up to work in the post-Abraham Accords strategic reality through its cooperation with the Arabs, Israelis and Americans. Both I2U2 and IMEEC offered India new avenues of engagement in the region. But further Arab–Israel reconciliation is now on hold. The United States' reputation stands as tarnished as that of Israel. If Saudi–Israel normalization is not taking place, the IMEEC project will have to wait. If the crisis persists and Houthis continue to target vessels in the Red Sea, which connects the Arabian Sea with the Mediterranean Sea through Bab el-Mandeb and Suez Canal, it would create lasting economic pains for India. A prolonged war in Gaza would also enhance risks of a wider conflict in the region, involving Iran, Israel and the United States, who are all India's partners. An immediate end to the war, restoration of order and stability in West Asia and a permanent fix to the Palestine question are as much in India's interests as anybody else's in West Asia.

When the war ground on, India became more vocal about the way Israel was conducting its offensive. External Affairs Minister S. Jaishankar said at the Munich Security Conference in February 2024 that Israel 'should be and should have been mindful of the civilian casualties in Gaza', a rare public criticism.[38] In March, Jaishankar was blunter. 'The fact is whatever the rights and wrongs of the issue, there is an underlying issue of the rights of the Palestinians and the fact that they have been denied of their homeland,' he said during an interaction in Malaysia.[39] He added, 'How different pulls and pressures can be. On one hand, what happened on 7 October was terrorism. On the other hand, nobody would countenance the death of innocent civilians. Countries may be justified in their own minds in responding, but you cannot have a response that... every response must take into account something called international humanitarian law.'

Back in the Ministry of Foreign Affairs in April 2024, I asked the senior Israeli diplomat about Jaishankar's repeated comments critical of the way Israel is conducting the war. The diplomat played down his remarks. 'Jaishankar is a good friend of Israel. We don't see his comments as a problem. Sometimes you have to say things for the interests of your country,' he said.

'I don't think the position India has taken since the 7 October terror attack has diminished our partnership,' he added.

Conclusion:
The Revenge of Old West Asia

'THERE was no such thing as Palestinians,' Golda Meir, the then Labour Prime Minister of Israel, told *The Sunday Times* on 15 June 1969, on the second anniversary of the Six-Day War.[1] It was during the 1967 war, Israel brought the whole of historical Palestine under its control. In the 1948–49 first Arab–Israeli war, Israel had captured 23 per cent more territories, including West Jerusalem, than what the 1947 United Nations Partition Plan for Palestine had proposed. In 1967, it seized the West Bank and East Jerusalem from Jordan and the Gaza Strip and Sinai Peninsula from Egypt, and the Golan Heights from Syria. Ever since, Palestinian territories have remained under Israel's military occupation and control (it pulled back both troops and Jewish settlers from Gaza in 2005 after the second intifada, but has laid siege to the enclave since 2007).

After Hamas's brutal 7 October Sabbath attack on Israel, killing at least 1,200 people, mostly civilians, Israel launched a devastating invasion of Gaza. Over 42,000 Palestinians were killed until late-October, a vast majority of them women and children. Almost all of Gaza's 2.3 million people have been displaced, some of them several times. Around 100,000 Palestinians were wounded, and the enclave, which doesn't have a functional, effective healthcare system, is on the verge of epidemic outbreaks, according to the UN. Most Gazans are hungry as the local economy was totally destroyed and Israel is controlling all entry and exit points of Gaza, rationing the flow of international aid. Israel's narrative is that it has the right to respond to Hamas's terror attack. Most of Israel's allies in the West, mainly the United States led by President Joe Biden, back this narrative.

The use of disproportionate force against the enemy, deliberately targeting civilians, is a well-known Israeli method (the Dahiya doctrine). General Gadi Eisenkot, a former Israeli chief of General Staff, once said about the Israel defence forces' bombing of Dahiya, Lebanon, 'We will apply disproportionate force on it and cause great damage and destruction there. From our standpoint, these are not civilian villages, they are military bases.'[2] Gen. Eisenkot was a minister without portfolio in the unity government formed after the 7 October attack. Israel's President Isaac Herzog echoed Gen. Eisenkot when he said on 14 October 2023 (after Israel ordered over a million people in northern Gaza to evacuate), that there are no innocent civilians in Gaza. 'It's an entire nation out there that's responsible,' Herzog, a centre-left leader, said in a press conference.[3]

Between what Golda Meir said in 1969 and Herzog claimed on 13 October 2023 lies the reality of the Palestinians—either they do not exist as a national category, or they are all culpable and punishable. What Israel wanted to do to Gaza was laid bare by its leaders and celebrities post-7 October. Heritage Minister Amichai Eliyahu wanted Israel to consider dropping a nuclear bomb on the territory.[4] Agriculture Minister Avi Dichter declared that Israel was now carrying out a *nakba*, a word, meant catastrophe, used to refer to the expulsion of over 700,000 Palestinians from their homes, villages and towns in 1948–49 during and after the state of Israel was created.[5] For Knesset member and former Public Diplomacy Minister Galit Distal Atbaryan, the IDF must invest all their energy 'in one thing: erasing all of Gaza from the face of the Earth'.[6] Finance Minister Bezalel Smotrich wanted Gazans to 'voluntarily emigrate to countries around the world'.[7] These views were echoed by the country's celebrities and even media practitioners. Eyal Golan, one of the most popular singers in Israel, appeared along with Netanyahu on Channel 14, declaring, 'Wipe Gaza out, leave no one there.'[8] Pop star Kobi Peretz danced with Israeli soldiers singing 'Let their villages burn.'[9] Television broadcaster Yinon Magal was seen shouting in a video with soldiers, 'I will eradicate the seed of Amalek,' referring to the Biblical enemy of the Israelites.[10] There were many more.

Israel says its heavy response is necessitated by its circumstances. It is living in a hostile regional environment faced with Islamist terrorism. There is a history of wars with the Arab world. Hamas is a Palestinian terrorist organisation with which political dialogue is impossible. Hamas and Hezbollah are directly supported by a Holocaust-denying Iran. So, this argument goes, Israel has to stay tough for its own survival. And being tough means continuing the occupation of the Palestinian territories endlessly and responding with massive force and collective punishment to violence by Palestinians. For them, 7 October marked a watershed moment. In the past Palestinian violence was limited to the occupied territories. But on 7 October 2023, Israel proper was invaded for the first time since 1948. Israel doesn't want that to happen again. And it wants to push that message down the throat of Palestinian nationalism.

Let us look at these arguments one by one. Hamas, 'the key impediment to peace', was created in 1987, twenty years after Israel started the direct military occupation of the Palestinian territories. In the 1970s and the early 1980s, the Islamic Centre, a Muslim Brotherhood offshoot and a precursor to Hamas, had Israel's recognition as a charity which allowed the group to raise funds for their activities. Israel then saw Fatah, Yasser Arafat's secular nationalist guerrilla movement, and the Palestine Liberation Organisation (PLO), the coalition Arafat had built, as its main rivals. The PLO had used violence against Israelis, and Israel launched two wars (1978 and 1982) in Lebanon to fight the PLO, which was termed a terrorist outfit by Israel's leadership. But during the Oslo talks, the PLO, which for long denied Israel's right to exist and advocated for the liberation of the whole of Palestine ('from the river to the sea'), made a major compromise. Arafat recognised the state of Israel and accepted the formation of an independent Palestine state within the 1967 borders, which is just 22 per cent of historical Palestine.

It was the collapse of Oslo in the subsequent years and continuing Israeli occupation of the Palestinian territories that led to the strengthening of Hamas, which had always opposed the Oslo process. By the time the second intifada broke out in 2000, Hamas was already in the driving seat and the PLO's non-violent campaign for statehood was seen as toothless by most Palestinians. So, from a historical perspective, it is not the Palestinian radicalism that prevented peace. Rather, it is the absence of peace and the continuing occupation of the Palestinian territories that strengthened Islamist radicalism in Palestine.

Second, it is a fact that Iran remains a major rival of Israel in West Asia. Iran also backs Hamas and the Palestinian Islamic Jihad, which jointly carried out the 7 October attack. Thus, the crisis has a clear geopolitical angle. But is Iran the central factor of the Israel–Palestine crisis? Iran became a hostile nation to Israel only in 1979, after the revolution and the subsequent birth of the Islamic Republic. Before the revolution, the Iranian monarchy was so close to Israel that both nations had agreed in 1977 to build a military co-production complex inside Iran to make ballistic missiles. Even after the Mullahs seized power in Tehran, Israel supplied the Islamic revolutionary regime in the 1980s with weapons, under US supervision, during the 1980–88 Iran–Iraq war.

Iran did not have much of an influence among the Palestinians during the Oslo process. It was after the Oslo talks collapsed and Hamas began rising as a key pillar of the Palestinian resistance and Arabs started slowly shifting their focus away from Palestine to their bilateral ties with Israel that the Islamic Republic became a major player through its support for Palestinian non-state militias. The lack of peace, the inability of Palestinian secular nationalist forces to push for independence and the de facto Arab–Israel reconciliation left vacuums both within Palestine and in the larger West Asian region. While Hamas filled the vacuum in Palestine, Iran tried to do it within the region.

Lastly, defenders of Israel's disproportionate aggression always argue that Israel's existence is at stake in a hostile neighbourhood and hence it has no choice but to be tough. True, neighbouring Arab countries attacked Israel immediately after the new state was declared in May 1948. After that, it was Israel which launched the 1956 and 1967 wars. The last time an Arab country attacked Israeli troops was in 1973 when Egypt, along with Syria, launched the Yom Kippur war. Since then, six Arab countries have normalized ties with Israel—namely Egypt, Jordan, the United Arab Emirates,

Bahrain, Sudan and Morocco. And it is hardly a secret that Saudi Arabia and Israel have very good backroom ties, though they have not officially established diplomatic relations. Israel is now an undeclared nuclear power, the only nuclear-armed state in West Asia, with massive air power, ballistic missiles and other weapons. It is also unconditionally supported—militarily, politically and financially—by the United States, the world's most powerful country. Israel is no longer the David; it is the Goliath of West Asia.

But Israel's regional hegemony and deterrence against and reconciliation with Arab countries have not brought peace for the Israelis. Why? Because the Palestine question remains unaddressed. The Palestine question may no longer be an Arab–Israel problem, but it continues to remain an Israel-Palestine problem. Ever since its forced withdrawal from Gaza in 2005, Israel's approach has been to ignore the question of occupation, as Golda Meir articulated in 1969: treat Palestinians as a security nuisance and move on with Arab peace plans, shaping 'the new Middle East', with the blessings of Washington.[11] But Hamas's 7 October attacks shattered the foundations of the 'new Middle East'. Hamas's indiscriminate attacks and Israel's collective punishment of Gazans suggest that the Palestine question remains the source of all maladies in the region. It is the revenge of old West Asia.

Israel seems to be unperturbed as of now. It is ready to live by the sword. Yet, after twelve months of war, there were signs of uneasiness and war–weariness even among the soldiers, while Israel's regional challenges multiplied since 7 October. When Israel declared its war on Gaza on 7 October 2023, Prime Minister Netanyahu said his forces would 'crush' Hamas.¹² Since then, Israeli leaders have said, several times, that 'eliminating' Hamas is the top objective of the war. The war has destroyed much of Gaza. But did this destruction help Israel meet its objective? On 19 June, after 256 days of fighting, Rear Admiral Daniel Hagari, a spokesperson of the IDF, said Hamas cannot be eliminated. 'Hamas is an idea, Hamas is a party. It's rooted in the hearts of the people—anyone who thinks we can eliminate Hamas [read Netanyahu] is wrong,' he said.¹³

Israel wanted a quick and decisive victory against Hamas. It wanted to destroy Hamas's governing structures, defeat its highly trained brigades, destroy its vast tunnel networks and kill its top leadership. Israel also wanted to free the over 240 hostages in Hamas custody, and bolster its deterrence that was weakened by the Hamas attack. Israel has killed most of Hamas's top leadership, including Ismail Haniyeh, the political chief of the group who was killed in Tehran on 31 July 2024, Mohammed Deif, the military chief of Hamas, who was killed in an Israeli strike on Khan Yunis on 13 July, and Yahya Sinwar, the Hamas leader in Gaza and a key architect of the 7 October attack, in an operation in Rafah on 16 October. But the group has survived twelve months of heavy bombardment and ground operations in a besieged enclave, prompting even the IDF to question the achievability of the objectives set by Netanyahu. Hamas resurfaced in areas which the IDF initially declared were clear of the militants, mainly in northern Gaza. But that is not the only bad news Israel is dealing with.

When Israel attacked Gaza, Hezbollah, Lebanon's powerful Iran-backed Shia militia, launched controlled attacks from southern Lebanon to Israel's Upper Galilee region on the northern border. Hezbollah's rocket attacks and shelling have displaced some 60,000 Israelis. Israel carried out dozens of strikes in Lebanon targeting

Hezbollah. On 31 July, the same day Ismail Haniyeh was killed in Tehran, Israel bombed Beirut, killing Fuad Shukr, a senior Hezbollah commander.

Israel faced a dilemma in the north. The controlled aggression did little in deterring Hezbollah. The displaced Israelis cannot return to their homes unless there is a ceasefire. And Hezbollah chief Hassan Nasrallah made it clear that it would not cease fire unless there was a ceasefire in Gaza. Israel doesn't want to stop fighting in Gaza without meeting its objectives. If Israel agrees to stop fighting in Gaza, Hamas would survive. A ceasefire will also have political implications for Netanyahu as his far-right coalition partners have threatened to pull their support for his government if the IDF reached a ceasefire deal with Hamas. The other option Israel had was to invade Lebanon to push Hezbollah away from the border region.

That's what Israel did in September. On 27 September, an Israeli air strike killed Hassan Nasrallah, the Hezbollah chief. On 1 October, it launched its four invasion of Lebanon. In the initial weeks, Israel has carried out waves of bombing of Beirut's suburbs as well as southern Lebanon, killing thousands of Lebanese. Many of Hezbollah's top commanders were killed. But the incapacitation of the leadership did little in degrading Hezbollah's military capabilities. The Shia militant group has stepped up rocket attacks into Israel after the Israeli invasion began, firing dozens of rockets almost every day. If Netanyahu went to Lebanon to push Hezbollah away from the border region and return the displaced Israelis back home, he is now facing the threat of more displacement in the north.

The second problem is Iran. Israel had adopted a two-pronged military approach when it launched the Gaza war. The first was to pound Gaza, while the second was to attack Hamas's allies across the region. Besides Hezbollah, Israel carried out airstrikes targeting Iranian military officers in Syria. But Israel miscalculated Iran's response when it attacked the Iranian embassy complex in Damascus on 1 April, killing senior generals. Iran launched an unprecedented barrage of missiles and drones on 14 April. In the past, Israel had carried out attacks inside Iran, and the latter typically responded through its proxies. But by carrying out its first major direct attack on Israel, Iran was sending an unambiguous message—future Israeli attacks would invite direct response from Tehran, setting the stage for a one-on-one game of chicken. The Iranian attack, however, did not stop Israel from killing Ismail Haniyeh, the Hamas leader, in Tehran, where he was a state guest to attend the inauguration of President Masoud Pezeshkian. On 1 October, Iran launched another direct attack at Israel with close to 200 ballistic missiles, in retaliation for the killings of Haniyeh and Nasrallah. Israel has vowed to retaliate, but Iran has threatened to counter-retaliate if Israel retaliates. So if one of the key objectives of Netanyahu's war on Gaza was to bolster Israel's deterrence against non-state actors, one of its outcomes was to weaken even Israel's conventional deterrence, which had been solid at least since 1973. At this point nobody is deterring anybody in West Asia. Israel's military might did not prevent Hamas from launching the 7 October attack. It did not stop Hezbollah and Houthis from attacking Israel either. Iran's conventional might and proxy power did not stop Israel from taking the war to the Israeli Republic by bombing its embassy complex in Damascus. Israel's nuclear weapons did not deter Iran from directly attacking Israel, not once, but twice.

Moreover, Iran has signalled that it has been dramatically expanding its nuclear programme, with higher production of highly enriched uranium at two of its facilities—Fordow and Natanz.

Conclusion

Israel has always seen Iran's nuclear programme as its number one security threat. Over the years, it has carried out a number of subversive operations aimed at weakening the Iranian nuclear programme, including the assassination of Mohsen Fakhrizadeh, the father of Iranian nuclear programme, in the outskirts of Tehran in November 2020. But none of this slowed down the Iranian nuclear programme. World powers reached a deal with Iran in 2015 aimed at scuttling the Iranian nuclear programme, but the United States, under President Donald Trump, unilaterally withdrew from the deal despite Iran's total compliance, sabotaging the agreement. Iran revived its nuclear programme thereafter.

Iran says its nuclear programme is for civilian purposes and that it doesn't want to make a bomb. But Iran is enriching uranium to higher purity and in larger quantities than what's required for nuclear power. And Israel's nuclear monopoly in West Asia and its repeated attacks inside Iran could act as a stronger strategic incentive for Tehran to push for nuclear threshold status. Israel, on the other side, is back in Gaza, a Palestinian territory which it left behind in 2005, and is stuck in Lebanon, which it left in 2000 after 18 years of bloody occupation, while rivalry with a more aggressive Iran is escalating at a regional level.

The third problem is the setback to the Arab normalisation process. Before the October 7 attack, Israel was set to expand its regional cooperation with the Arab world in the framework of the Abraham Accords, which was reached in 2020 with the United Arab Emirates, Bahrain, Morocco and Sudan. The Biden administration was keen on expanding the Abraham Accords, by bringing Saudi Arabia, arguably the most influential Arab country today, into it. In September 2023, when India was hosting the G20 summit in Delhi, Mohammed bin Salman, the Saudi Crown Prince and Prime

Minister, said both countries were in a very advanced stage of the normalisation talks.[14] If Saudi Arabia, a champion of the Arab Peace initiative which offered recognition to Israel in return for a two-state solution based on the 1967 border, reached a normalisation deal with Israel when the occupation was on, it would have been a coup of sorts for Israel and the makers of 'the new Middle East'. But today, the Saudi normalisation plan has been shelved. Riyadh says there will not be peace with Israel unless there is a clear path towards the creation of a Palestinian state 'based on the 1967 border with East Jerusalem as its capital'.[15] In the words of Saudi Ambassador to Britain, Prince Khalid bin Bandar, 'we can't live with Israel without a Palestinian state.'[16]

Fourth, Israel is facing global isolation for its conduct of the war. There have been two United Nations Security Council resolutions, as of August, that called for a ceasefire in Gaza—which Israel has ignored. There is a genocide case against Israel at the International Court of Justice (ICJ). The ICJ, which in January ordered Israel to take steps 'to prevent a genocide in Gaza', asked the Jewish state, in May, to stop its offensive in Rafah.[17] This was also ignored. A prosecutor at The International Criminal Court (ICC) has sought arrest warrants against the top leadership of Israel and Hamas. The war has also triggered student protests across universities in the West. The Internet is flooded with images of the suffering of Palestinian children at the hands of the IDF. Even Donald Trump, a highly pro-Israel US politician, admits that the war has been a public relations disaster for Israel.[18] According to Israel's *Zman* magazine, which analysed data from the Population and Immigration Authority, nearly 5,00,000 Israelis have left the country since 7 October.[19]

Finally, Israel has always wanted to keep its occupation of Palestine as a non-issue when it deals with the rest of the world—

occupation without consequences. A key message of the 2020 Abraham Accords was that the Palestine question had become immaterial even for Arab countries when it comes to engagement with Israel. But Hamas's attack on 7 October and Israel's subsequent war on Gaza have brought the Palestine question back to the centre of West Asia's geopolitics. If Israel wanted to localise the Palestine question, Hamas has re-regionalised it, at a great human cost.

This doesn't mean that there would be a solution to the Palestine question once the war is over. The two state-solution looks as unreachable as the one-state/federal state solution today. Israel's right wing, which dominates its domestic polity, now publicly states that they would not accept an independent Palestine state. They want Israel to continue the occupation at any cost. The unconditional support it enjoys from the United States puts Israel in a special position in the region with the freedom to use disproportionate violence against Palestinians without facing any major international opprobrium or actions such as sanctions which other rogue states would have faced. And Israel, the only nuclear power in West Asia, has enormous fire power. It thought it could manage the situations in Gaza and the West Bank without letting it explode. This model, which I call occupation without consequences, was proved a myth on October 7.

The Palestinian anger did not just explode on 7 October, but it snowballed into a regional crisis, encompassing Israel, Hamas, the Islamic Jihad, Hezbollah, Houthis, Hashad al Shabi and the Islamic Republic of Iran. Whatever happened over the past twelve months in the region underscores the centrality of the Palestine question in West Asia's geopolitics.

Israel is a great survivor. It was born in a hostile region and it has successfully neutralised Arab countries over the years. But Israel is also a country that hasn't seen peace. Israel today controls the whole of historical Palestine and only those living in Israel proper (Green line Israel, based on the 1967 border) and the Jewish settlers living in the West Bank enjoy civil and voting rights. Millions of Palestinians living in the West Bank, East Jerusalem and Gaza, territories directly controlled by Israel, are denied even basic rights. This dichotomy poses a moral question to the very idea of Israel, even if Israel's leadership continues to play down criticisms of apartheid. Israel's response to the violent resistance to the occupation has been militarism. And its militarism continued to spawn more enemies. Arab states are now replaced by Arab militias, which are backed by Israel's key geopolitical rival, Iran.

Today's Israel, internally divided and externally isolated (sans the US support), wants to destroy Hamas, weaken Hezbollah and roll back Iran, while continuing the occupation of the Palestinian territories. It is ready to continue to live by the sword, but that is also because it doesn't see any practical path towards peace. This is a moral, geopolitical and historical trap. The cost of occupation, moral, human and strategic, is rising fast. But the state of Israel, which Theodore Herzle dreamed as 'an outpost of civilisation as opposed to barbarism', is in a chimera.[20]

Notes

Introduction

1   Rachel Shabi, 'Israel's apartheid road,' *The Guardian*, 17 May 2010, accessed 3 August 2024, https://www.theguardian.com/commentisfree/2010/may/17/israel-palestine-highway-443-segregation.
2   Stanly Johny, 'On Israel's border with Gaza, an uneasy calm amid worries of the next spark', *The Hindu*, 19 November 2022, accessed 10 July 2024, https://www.thehindu.com/news/international/on-israels-border-with-gaza-an-uneasy-calm-amid-worries-of-the-next-spark/article66155114.ece.
3   Stanly, Johny, 'On Israel's border with Gaza, an uneasy calm amid worries of the next spark,' *The Hindu*, 19 November 2022, accessed on 7 September 2024, https://www.thehindu.com/news/international/on-israels-border-with-gaza-an-uneasy-calm-amid-worries-of-the-next-spark/article66155114.ece.
4   Stanly Johny, 'On Israel's border with Gaza, an uneasy calm amid worries of the next spark,' *The Hindu*, 19 November 2022, accessed 10 July 2024, https://www.thehindu.com/news/international/on-israels-border-with-gaza-an-uneasy-calm-amid-worries-of-the-next-spark/article66155114.ece.

5   Yaacov Bar-Siman-Tov, 'The United States and Israel since 1948: A "Special Relationship"?' *Diplomatic History* 22, no. 2 (1998), 231–62.

1. In Search of a Homeland

1   Theodor Herzl, *The Complete Diaries of Theodor Herzl*, Internet Archive, accessed 20 January 2024, https://archive.org/details/TheCompleteDiariesOfTheodorHerzl_201606/TheCompleteDiariesOfTheodorHerzlEngVolume1_OCR/.
2   'Herzl meets the German Kaiser', *World Zionist Organization: The Central Zionist Archives*, accessed 12 February 2024, http://www.zionistarchives.org.il/en/datelist/Pages/ZionistDelegation.aspx.
3   Theodor Herzl, 'The Jewish State', *Jewish Virtual Library*, accessed 2 January 2024, https://www.jewishvirtuallibrary.org/quot-the-jewish-state-quot-theodor-herzl.
4   Moses Hess, '*Rome and Jerusalem: A Study in Jewish Nationalism*, translated from the German with introduction and notes by Meyer Waxman', *Marxists.org*, accessed 10 January 2024, https://www.marxists.org/subject/jewish/rome-jerusalem.pdf.
5   Leon Pinsker, 'Auto-Emancipation', *Jewish Virtual Library*, accessed 10 January 2024, https://www.jewishvirtuallibrary.org/quot-auto-emancipation-quot-leon-pinsker.
6   Herzl, 'The Jewish State'.
7   David B. Green, 'This Day in Jewish History: May Laws Punish Russia's Jews', *Haaretz*, 15 May 2014, accessed 18 December 2024, https://www.haaretz.com/jewish/2014-05-15/ty-article/.premium/this-day-may-laws-punish-russias-jews/0000017f-e87f-dc91-a17f-fcff17b60000.
8   'Zionist Congress in Basel: The Delegates Adopt Dr. Herzl's Programme for Re-establishing the Jews in Palestine, *The New York Times*, 31 August 1897, accessed 12 December 2024, https://www.nytimes.com/1897/08/31/archives/zionist-congress-in-basel-the-delegates-adopt-dr-herzls-programme.html.
9   Shlomo Avineri and Haim Watzman, *Herzl's Vision, Theodore Herzl and the Foundation of the Jewish State* (London: Blue Bridge, 2014), 202.

10 Adam Rovner, *In the Shadow of Zion: Promised Lands Before Israel* (New York: New York University Press, 2014), 51–52.
11 Herzl, *The Complete Diaries of Theodor Herzl.*
12 Michael Cliansmith, 'The Uganda Offer, 1902-1905: A study of settlement concessions in British East Africa'. *Ufahamu: A Journal of African Studies*, 5 no. 1 (1974), 71–96, accessed 12 February 2024, https://escholarship.org/uc/item/91x5k9wm.
13 'Aliens Bill', *UK Parliament*, 2 May 1905, accessed 12 January 2024, https://api.parliament.uk/historic-hansard/commons/1905/may/02/aliens-bill-1.
14 'A storm is brewing which, if it is allowed to burst, will have deplorable results,' Conservative politician, Major William Evans-Gordon said in 1904, calling for restrictions on Jewish immigration. David Rosenberg, 'Immigration,' *Channel 4*, accessed 10 January 2024, https://web.archive.org/web/20070514215717/http://www.channel4.com/culture/microsites/O/origination/immigration.html.
15 Chaim Weizmann, *Trial and Error, The Autobiography of Chaim Weizmann*, (Philadelphia: Jewish Publication Society of America, 1949), 111.
16 James de Rothschild, son of Baron Edmond de Rothschild, told Weizmann in a meeting in November 1914 that Zionists should demand not just colonization of Palestine through settlements but the creation of a Jewish state in Palestine. Danny Gutwein, 'The Politics of the Balfour Declaration: Nationalism, Imperialism and the Limits of Zionist-British Cooperation', *Journal of Israeli History*, 35 no. 2 (2016), 117–152.
17 Walter Reid, *Empire of Sand: How Britain Made the Middle East*, (Edinburgh: Birlinn, 2011), 115.
18 'Mr Scott, who has, I believe, given the whole problem a very careful and sympathetic attention, was good enough to promise that he would talk to Mr. Lloyd George on the subject ... As it happened, Mr. Lloyd George, having several engagements for the week suggested that I should see Mr. Herbert Samuel, and an interview took place at his office.' Chaim Weizmann, *The Letters and Papers of Chaim*

Weizmann: August 1898–July 1931 (New Jersey: Transaction Publishers, 1983), 122.
19 Ibid, 301.
20 Ibid, 122.
21 Colin Shindler, *A History of Modern Israel*. (Cambridge: Cambridge University Press, 2008) 39.
22 Herbert Samuel, 'The Future of Palestine', *United Nations*, January 1915, accessed 8 September 2024, https://www.un.org/unispal/document/future-of-palestine-by-herbert-samuel-government-of-united-kingdom-memorandum/.
23 'As soon as I became Prime Minister, I talked the whole matter over with Mr. Balfour, who was then Foreign Secretary. As a scientist, he was immensely interested when I told him of Dr. Weizmann's achievement. We were anxious at that time to gather Jewish support in neutral countries, notably in America. Dr. Weizmann was brought into direct contact with the Foreign Secretary. This was the beginning of an association, the outcome of which, after long examination, was the famous Balfour Declaration.' David Lloyd George, *War Memoirs of David Lloyd George: 1915–1916, vol. II* (New York: AMS Press, 1933), 50.
24 Shlomo Avineri, 'Britain's True Motivation Behind the Balfour Declaration', *Haaretz*, 2 November 2017, accessed 3 January 2024, https://www.haaretz.com/opinion/2017-11-02/ty-article/.premium/britains-true-motivation-behind-the-balfour-declaration/0000017f-dc3d-d3ff-a7ff-fdbdc5ed0000.
25 'Correspondence between Sir Henry McMahon and the Sharif Hussein of Mecca, July 1915-March 1916', *His Majesty's Stationary Office*, accessed 12 February 2024, https://upload.wikimedia.org/wikipedia/commons/7/75/Correspondence_between_Sir_Henry_McMahon_and_the_Sherif_Hussein_of_Mecca_Cmd_5957.pdf.
26 The Arabs came to know about the Sykes Picot agreement only after it was published in late 1917. See, David Fromkin, *A Peace to End All Peace: The Fall of the Ottoman Empire and the Creation of the Modern*

Middle East (New York: Owl, 1989), 286. Also see: Robin Wright, 'How the curse of Sykes Picot still haunts the Middle East', *The New Yorker*, 30 April 206, accessed 22 January 2024, https://www.newyorker.com/news/news-desk/how-the-curse-of-sykes-picot-still-haunts-the-middle-east.

27 Kamal Salibi, *The Modern History of Jordan* (London: I B Tauris, 1998), 93.

28 'The Palestine Mandate', *The Yale Law School: Lillian Goldman Law Library*, accessed 3 January 2024, https://avalon.law.yale.edu/20th_century/palmanda.asp.

29 '1922 Census of Palestine', *The Economic Cooperation Foundation*, https://ecf.org.il/issues/issue/1087#:~:text=Population%20figures%20in%20the%20census,%25)%20Christians%20and%209%2C474%20others.

30 Sabri Jiryis, 'Ben Gurion Looks at Israel's History', *Journal of Palestine Studies*, 1(1) (Autumn 1971), 116–121.

31 'Zionism: Ahdut ha-Avodah', *Jewish Virtual Library*, accessed 9 January 2024, https://www.jewishvirtuallibrary.org/a-dut-ha-avodah.

32 In 1939, the British government issued a policy paper, which came to be known as the White Paper. It introduced several measures to better the colonial governance of Palestine amid growing violence between Arabs and Jews. It introduced quotas for Jews migrating to Palestine, imposed restrictions on settlements and land sales to Jews, and called for the establishment of a Jewish national home in an independent Palestine state in ten years. Lauren Elise, 'Disorderly decolonization: The White Paper of 1939 and the end of British Rule in Palestine' (PhD Dissertation, The University of Texas, 2008), accessed 12 January 2024, https://repositories.lib.utexas.edu/server/api/core/bitstreams/d0d43d62-55e8-4a17-bc6d-c7183ac572f8/content; For the full text of the White Paper, see: 'British White Paper of 1939', *Yale Law School, Lillian Goldman Law Library*, accessed 10 January 2024, https://avalon.law.yale.edu/20th_century/brwh1939.asp.

33 'Jewish and non-Jewish population of Israel/Palestine (1517–Present)', *Jewish Virtual Library*, accessed 29 January 2024, https://

www.jewishvirtuallibrary.org/jewish-and-non-jewish-population-of-israel-palestine-1517-present.

2. War and Un-peace

1. 'The Irgun: Bombing of the King David Hotel', *Jewish Virtual Library*, accessed on 28 February 2024, https://www.jewishvirtuallibrary.org/bombing-of-the-king-david-hotel.
2. William Roger Louis, *The British Empire in the Middle East, 1945–1951: Arab Nationalism, the United States, and Postwar Imperialism* (New York: Oxford University Press, 1986), 430; also see: Thurston Clarke, *Blood & Fire July 22, 1946: The Attack on the King David Hotel* (New York: GP Putnam's Sons, 1981).
3. 'UN Background Paper No. 47', *United Nations*, accessed 12 December 2023, https://unispal.un.org/UNISPAL.NSF/0/2248AF9A92B498718525694B007239C6.
4. 'Declaration of Establishment of State of Israel', *Israeli Ministry of Foreign Affairs*, 14 May 1948, accessed 15 December 2022, http://www.mfa.gov.il/mfa/foreignpolicy/peace/guide/pages/declaration%20of%20establishment%20of%20state%20of%20israel.aspx.
5. David Remnick, 'The Spirit Level: Amos Oz writes the story of Israel', *The New Yorker*, 8 November 2004, accessed 20 July 2023, https://www.newyorker.com/magazine/2004/11/08/the-spirit-level.
6. For a detailed account of *Nakba*, read Ilan Pappe, *A History of Modern Palestine* (Cambridge University Press, London, 2022.
7. Nur Masalha, *Expulsion of the Palestinians: The Concept of "Transfer" in Zionist Political Thought, 1882-1948* (Beirut: Institute for Palestine Studies, 1992), 66.
8. *Ibid*, 17.
9. Ami Gluska, *The Israeli Military and the Origins of the 1967 War: Government, Armed Forces and Defence Policy 1963–67* (London: Routledge, 2007), 152.
10. Simon Dunstan, *The Six Day War 1967: Jordan and Syria* (New York: Bloomsbury, 2013*)*.

11 Adam Shatz, 'Indecision as Strategy', *London Review of Books*, 34 (19) (October 11, 2012), accessed 12 January 2024, https://www.lrb.co.uk/the-paper/v34/n19/adam-shatz/indecision-as-strategy.
12 Serge Schmemann, 'A Symbol on a Hill', *The New York Times*, 8 December 1996, accessed 18 December 2018, https://archive.nytimes.com/www.nytimes.com/books/97/05/18/nnp/20511.html.
13 'The Legal Status of Jerusalem', *Norwegian Refugee Council*, December 2013, accessed 23 January 2024, https://www.nrc.no/globalassets/pdf/reports/the-legal-status-of-east-jerusalem.pdf.
14 Shatz, 'Indecision as Strategy'.
15 For the full text of the resolution, see: 'The Khartoum Resolutions; September 1, 1967', *The Avalon Project, Yale Law School*, accessed 22 January 2024, https://avalon.law.yale.edu/20th_century/khartoum.asp.
16 Chaim Herzog, *War of Atonement: The Inside Story of the Yom Kippur War, 1973* (London: Greenhill Books, 1998), Kindle.
17 Summarizing his approach towards the Palestinians, Jimmy Carter wrote: 'Since I had made our nation's commitment to human rights a central tenet of our foreign policy, it was impossible for me to ignore the various problems on the West Bank. In my opinion it was imperative that the United States work to obtain for these people the right to vote, the right to assemble, and to debate issues that affected their lives, the right to own property without fear of it's confiscated, and the right to be free of military rule. To deny these rights was an indefensible position for a free and democratic society.' Jimmy Carter, *Keeping Faith* (Toronto: Bantam Books, 1982), 284.
18 'Likud Party: Original Party Platform', *Jewish Virtual Library*, accessed 25 January 2024, https://www.jewishvirtuallibrary.org/original-party-platform-of-the-likud-party.
19 Nathan Thrall, *The Only Language They Understand: Forcing Compromise in Israel and Palestine* (New York: Metropolitan Books, 2017).
20 Thrall, *The Only Language*.

21 Adam M. Howard, ed. *Foreign Relations of the United States, 1977-80, Volume VIII: Arab-Israeli Dispute, January 1977-August 1978* (Washington: US Government Printing Office, 2013), 881.
22 Henry Tanner, 'Sadat vows to back a Palestine state and Israeli pullout', *The New York Times*, 28 December 1977, accessed 30 January 2024, https://www.nytimes.com/1977/12/28/archives/sadat-vows-to-back-a-palestinian-state-and-israeli-pullout-he-tells.html.
23 'Palestine National Charter of 1964', *Permanent Observer Mission of Palestine to the UN*, accessed 14 January 2024, https://web.archive.org/web/20101130144018/http://www.un.int/wcm/content/site/palestine/pid/12363.
24 Paul Hofmann, 'Dramatic Session', *The New York Times*, 14 November 1974, accessed 30 January 2024, https://www.nytimes.com/1974/11/14/archives/dramatic-session-plo-head-says-he-bears-olive-branch-and-guerrilla.html.
25 David McDowall, *Palestine and Israel: The Uprising and Beyond* (London: IB Tauris, 1989), 1.
26 King Hussein, 'Address to the Nation', 31 July 1988, accessed 20 December 2023, http://www.kinghussein.gov.jo/88_july31.html.
27 Dan Cohn-Sherbok, *The Palestinian State: A Jewish Justification* (London: Impress Books, 2012), 105.
28 'The Historic Compromise: The Palestinian Declaration of Independence and the Twenty-year struggle for a two-state solution', *The PLO Negotiations Affairs Department*, accessed 22 December 2023, https://web.archive.org/web/20120426022554/http://www.carim.org/public/polsoctexts/PS2PAL005_EN.pdf.
29 Avi Shlaim, *The Iron Wall: Israel and the Arab World* (New York: Norton, 2001), 483.
30 'Israel-PLO Recognition: Exchange of Letters between PM Rabin and Chairman Arafat', *United Nations*, 9 September 1993, accessed 12 January 2024, https://www.un.org/unispal/document/auto-insert-205528/.
31 Yitzhak Rabin, *The Rabin Memoirs, Expanded Edition with Recent Speeches, New Photographs, and an Afterword*, (California: University of California Press 1996), 401.

32 (1) The five-year transitional period will begin upon the withdrawal from the Gaza Strip and Jericho area. (2) Permanent status negotiations will commence as soon as possible, but not later than the beginning of the third year of the interim period, between the Government of Israel and the Palestinian people's representatives. (3) It is understood that these negotiations shall cover remaining issues, including: Jerusalem, refugees, settlements, security arrangements, borders, relations and cooperation with other neighbours, and other issues of common interest. (4) The two parties agree that the outcome of the permanent status negotiations should not be prejudiced or pre-empted by agreements reached for the interim period. 'Declaration of Principles on Interim Self-Government Arrangements,' *Knesset*, 13 September 1993, accessed 22 December 2023, https://web.archive.org/web/20021115183950/http://knesset.gov.il/process/docs/oslo_eng.htm.
33 '1995 Oslo Interim Agreement', *ProCon.org*, 24 April 2008, accessed 12 December 2023, https://israelipalestinian.procon.org/view.background-resource.php?resourceID=000921.
34 Avi Shlaim, 'It's now clear: the Oslo peace accords were wrecked by Netanyahu's bad faith,' *The Guardian*, 12 September 2013, accessed 8 September 2024, https://www.theguardian.com/commentisfree/2013/sep/12/oslo-israel-reneged-colonial-palestine.
35 Jeremy Pressman, 'Visions in Collision: What Happened at Camp David and Taba?' *International Security* 28 no. 2 (Fall 2003), 15-19.
36 'An Engineered Tragedy: Statistical Analysis of Fatalities', *Casualties Project*, 3 July 2007, accessed 28 November 2023, https://web.archive.org/web/20070703195937/http://212.150.54.123/casualties_project/stats_page.cfm.
37 *Ibid.*
38 'Address by PM Ariel Sharon at the Fourth Herzliya Conference', *Israeli Ministry of Foreign Affairs*, 18 December 2003, accessed 26 November 2023, http://www.mfa.gov.il/MFA/PressRoom/2003/Pages/Address%20by%20PM%20Ariel%20Sharon%20at%20the%20Fourth%20Herzliya.aspx.

39 Jefferson Morley, 'Israeli Withdrawal From Gaza Explained', *The Washington Post*, 10 August 2005, accessed 22 December 2023, http://www.washingtonpost.com/wp-dyn/content/article/2005/08/10/AR2005081000713.html.
40 Hanne Cuyckens, 'Is Israel Still an Occupying Power in Gaza?' *Netherlands International Law Review* 63 no. 3 (2016), 275–295, accessed 17 December 2023, https://link.springer.com/article/10.1007%2Fs40802-016-0070-1.
41 Roald Høvring, 'Gaza: The world's largest open-air prison', *NRC*, 26 April 2018, accessed 23 January 2024, https://www.nrc.no/news/2018/april/gaza-the-worlds-largest-open-air-prison/.
42 Barak Ravid, 'U.S. Ambassador: Israel Has Legal Double Standard in West Bank', *Haaretz*, 18 January 2016, accessed 10 January 2024, https://www.haaretz.com/israel-news/.premium-u-s-envoy-israel-has-legal-double-standard-in-west-bank-1.5392371.
43 Peter Beaumont and Jennifer Rankin, 'EU adopts resolution criticising Israeli settlement activity', *The Guardian*, 18 January 2016, accessed 18 December 2023, https://www.theguardian.com/world/2016/jan/18/eu-adopts-resolution-criticising-israeli-settlement-activity-occupied-palestinian-territories.
44 'Secretary-General's remarks to the Security Council on the Situation in the Middle East', *UN Secretary General*, 26 January 2016, accessed 26 December 2023, https://www.un.org/sg/en/content/sg/statement/2016-01-26/secretary-generals-remarks-security-council-situation-middle-east.
45 The UNGA resolution states that 'refugees wishing to return to their homes and live at peace with their neighbours should be permitted to do so at the earliest practicable date, and that compensation should be paid for the property of those choosing not to return and for loss of or damage to property which, under principles of international law or equity, should be made good by the Governments or authorities responsible'. 'Resolution 194', *UNGA*, accessed 24 December 2023, https://www.unrwa.org/content/resolution-194; For details on the Arab Peace Initiative, see Scott MacLeod, 'Time to Test the Arab

Peace Offer', *TIME*, 8 January 2009, accessed 9 December 2023, https://web.archive.org/web/20090117001303/http://mideast.blogs.time.com/2009/01/08/time-to-test-the-arab-peace-offer/.
46 'Statement of the Middle East Quartet', 20 December 2002, accessed 19 December 2023, https://unispal.un.org/DPA/DPR/UNISPAL.NSF/0/1217FD6D7731896385256C9B004CEC90.
47 Ben Birnbaum and Amir Tibon, 'Israel-Palestine Peace Plan—and Watched It Crumble', *The Atlantic*, 21 July 2014, accessed 15 December 2023, https://newrepublic.com/article/118751/how-israel-palestine-peace-deal-died.
48 'Number of Settlers by Year', *Peace Now*, accessed 15 January 2024, https://peacenow.org.il/en/settlements-watch/settlements-data/population.
49 'Netanyahu: No Palestinian state on my watch', *Associated Press*, 16 February 2024, accessed 19 December 2018, https://www.timesofisrael.com/netanyahu-no-palestinian-state-under-my-watch/.
50 Lara Friedman, 'Israel's Unsung Protector: Obama', *The New York Times*, 10 April 2016, accessed 9 December 2023, https://www.nytimes.com/2016/04/12/opinion/international/israels-unsung-protector-obama.html.

3. A Passage to the West Bank

1 Juliana Ochs, *Security and Suspicion: An Ethnography of Everyday Life in Israel* (University of Pennsylvania Press), 147.
2 Additionally, eighty obstacles, including twenty-eight constantly staffed check-points, segregate part of the Israeli-controlled area of Hebron (H2) from the remainder of the city; many check-points are fortified with metal detectors, surveillance cameras and face recognition technology, and with facilities for detention and interrogation. Combined, there are 645 physical obstacles, an increase of about 8 per cent compared with the 593 obstacles recorded in the previous OCHA closure survey in January-February 2020. See, Factsheet: Movement and Access in the West Bank, OCHA,

August 2023, accessed 23 February 2024, file:///C:/Users/10354/ Downloads/Factsheet_Movement_and_Access_Aug2023.pdf..
3   *Ibid.*
4   '"Do we have the right to struggle for freedom?", Interview with Mustafa Barghouti', *CNN*, accessed 12 January 2024, https://edition.cnn.com/videos/world/2023/10/08/gps-1008-mustafa-barghouti-on-israels-war-on-hamas.cnn.
5   'Israel's Practices against Palestinian Economy Exacerbating Dire Living Conditions in Occupied Territory, Syrian Golan', *Senior Official Tells Second Committee, UN*, 17 October 2022, accessed 12 February 2024, https://press.un.org/en/2022/gaef3574.doc.htm.
6   'The Economic Costs of the Israeli Occupation for the Palestinian People: The cost of restrictions in Area C viewed from above', *UNCTAD*, 13 December 2022, accessed 12 February 2024, https://unctad.org/publication/economic-costs-israeli-occupation-palestinian-people-cost-restrictions-area-c-viewed.
7   Sonikka Loganathan and Vignesh Radhakrishnan, 'Israel has an iron grip over Gaza and West Bank's economy', *The Hindu*, 30 October 2023, accessed 29 February 2024, https://www.thehindu.com/data/israel-has-an-iron-grip-over-gaza-and-west-banks-economy-data/article67467169.ece#:~:text=Israel's%20control%20over%20Palestine's%20economy,all%20exports%20went%20to%20Israel.
8   Yasmine Salam, 'Palestinian support for "armed struggle" is rising as Gaza death estimate tops 20,000', *NBC News*, 22 December 2023, accessed 23 January 2024, https://www.nbcnews.com/investigations/palestinian-support-armed-struggle-rising-gaza-death-estimate-tops-200-rcna130516.
9   'Operation Defensive Shield, Zionism and Israel', *Encyclopedic Dictionary*, accessed 14 January 2024, https://zionism-israel.com/dic/Defensive_Shield.htm.
10 Serge Schmemann, 'Arafat Remains Defiant Amid Rubble of His Compound', *The New York Times*, 22 September 2022, accessed 23 January 2024, https://www.nytimes.com/2002/09/22/world/arafat-remains-defiant-amid-rubble-of-his-compound.html.

11 On 11 September 2003, the Israeli Security Cabinet decided to 'remove' Arafat. 'Recent days' events have proven again that Yasser Arafat is a complete obstacle to any process of reconciliation ... Israel will act to remove this obstacle in the manner, at the time, and in the ways that will be decided on separately,' it said. Excerpts: 'Israeli security cabinet statement', *BBC*, 11 September 2003, accessed 12 January 2024, http://news.bbc.co.uk/2/hi/middle_east/3102154.stm.

12 Nathan Thrall, 'Mismanaging the Conflict in Jerusalem', *The New York Times*, 18 October 2015, accessed 20 January 2014, https://www.nytimes.com/2015/10/19/opinion/mismanaging-the-conflict-in-jerusalem.html.

13 Stanly Johny, 'Israel systematically killing Palestinians: Mahmoud Abbas', *The Hindu*, 6 December 2015, accessed 1 March 2024, https://www.thehindu.com/opinion/interview/full-text-of-the-interview-with-palestine-president-mahmoud-abbas/article61450868.ece.

14 'Building inscription commemorating the rebuilding of the walls of Jerusalem', imj.org, accessed 13 January 2024, https://www.imj.org.il/en/collections/374383-0.

15 Dov Lieber, 'Amid Temple Mount tumult, the who, what and why of its Waqf rulers,' *The Times of Israel*, 20 July 2017, accessed 14 January 2024. https://www.timesofisrael.com/amid-temple-mount-tumult-the-who-what-and-why-of-its-waqf-rulers/.

16 James E. Lancaster, 'The Church and the ladder: Frozen in time', *CoastDailyLight*, July 1996, accessed 15 February 2024, https://coastdaylight.com/ladder.html.

17 Responding to a request from the United Nations General Assembly, the International Court of Justice said the Assembly and the Security Council should consider what steps to take 'to bring to an end the illegal situation resulting from the construction of the wall and the associated régime, taking due account of the present Advisory Opinion.' See, 'International Court of Justice finds Israeli barrier in Palestinian territory is illegal', *United Nations*, 9 July 2004, accessed 5 January 2024, https://news.un.org/en/story/2004/07/108912.

18 The hotel was temporarily shuttered in December 2023 following Israel's war on Gaza, which was launched after Hamas's 7 October attack. See, Elaine Velie, 'Banksy Hotel in Occupied West Bank hutters', *Hyperallergic*, 21 December 2023, accessed 15 January 2024, https://hyperallergic.com/863486/banksy-hotel-in-occupied-west-bank-shutters/.

19 Matt Rees/Bethlehem, 'The Saga of the siege', *TIME*, 20 May 2022, accessed 22 January 2024, https://content.time.com/time/subscriber/article/0,33009,1002452,00.html.

20 'CCP working paper on the holy places (1949)', *ECF*, 8 April 1949, accessed 15 January 2024, https://ecf.org.il/issues/issue/1420#:~:text=A%20working%20paper%20prepared%20by,the%20status%20quo%20governing%20them.

21 'Mosque of Omar: Bethlehem, Palestinian Territories, Middle East', *Lonely Planet*, accessed 10 January 2024, https://www.lonelyplanet.com/israel-and-the-palestinian-territories/the-west-bank-and-gaza-strip/bethlehem/attractions/mosque-of-omar/a/poi-sig/451497/361063.

4. Axis of Resistance

1 Stanly Johny, *The ISIS Caliphate: From Syria to the Doorsteps of India* (New Delhi: Bloomsbury, 2018).

2 Olmo Gölz, 'Khomeini's Face is in the Moon: Limitations of Sacredness and the Origins of Sovereignty', January 2017, accessed 25 August 2024, https://www.researchgate.net/publication/334836849_Khomeini's_Face_is_in_the_Moon_Limitations_of_Sacredness_and_the_Origins_of_Sovereignty.

3 'Israel's prime minister explains his new approach to Iran', *The Economist*, 8 June 2022, accessed 10 March 2024, https://www.economist.com/middle-east-and-africa/2022/06/08/israels-prime-minister-explains-his-new-approach-to-iran.

4 Stanly Johny, 'What does the killing of nuclear scientist Fakhrizadeh mean for Iran?', *The Hindu*, 28 November 2020, accessed 10 March 2024, https://www.thehindu.com/news/international/what-

does-the-killing-of-nuclear-scientist-fakhrizadeh-mean-for-iran/article33198985.ece.

5   Ewen MacAskill and Chris McGreal, 'Israel should be wiped off map, says Iran's president', *The Guardian*, October 2005, accessed 2 March 2024, https://www.theguardian.com/world/2005/oct/27/israel.iran.

6   'Israel's Netanyahu says will not allow Iran to obtain nuclear weapons', *Reuters*, 12 April 2021, accessed 12 March 2024, https://www.reuters.com/article/idUSKBN2BZ1GK/.

7   Ronen Bergman, *The Secret War with Iran: The 30-Year Clandestine Struggle Against the World's Most Dangerous Terrorist Power* (New York: Free Press, 2011), Kindle.

8   'Saudi Arabia Defense Market Size, Trends, Budget Allocation, Regulations, Acquisitions, Competitive Landscape and Forecast to 2028', *Global Data*, 6 May 2023, accessed 7 March 2024, https://www.globaldata.com/store/report/saudi-arabia-defense-market-analysis/#:~:text=Saudi%20Arabian%20defense%20expenditure%20increased,year%2C%20valued%20at%20%2469.1%20billion.

9   Alex Vatanka, 'Soleimani Ascendant: The Origins of Iran's "Forward Defense" Strategy', *New America*, 1 January 2021, 11–19.

10 James F. Clarity, 'Begin says nobody should preach to us on attacks or siege', *The New York Times*, 5 August 1982, accessed 11 March 2024, https://www.nytimes.com/1982/08/05/world/begin-says-nobody-should-preach-to-us-on-attacks-or-siege.html.

11 Clyde G. Hess, Jr. and Herbert L. Bodman, Jr., 'Confessionalism and Feudality in Lebanese Politics', *Middle East Journal* 8(1), (Winter 1985), 10–26.

12 James F. Clarity, 'Begin says nobody should preach to us ...' *The New York Times*.

13 'The Hizballah programme: An open letter', *The Jerusalem Quarterly*, 1 January 1988, accessed 2 March 2024, https://www.ict.org.il/UserFiles/The%20Hizballah%20Program%20-%20An%20Open%20Letter.pdf.

14 Adam Shatz, 'In Search of Hezbollah', *The New York Review of Books*, 29 April 2004, accessed 12 February 2024, https://www.nybooks.com/articles/2004/04/29/in-search-of-hezbollah/.
15 Aurélie Daher, *Hezbollah: Mobilisation and Power*, translated from French by H.W. Randolph (New York: Oxford University Press, 2019), 127–150.
16 Hussain Abdul-Hussain, 'Hezbollah: A State Within a State', Hudson Institute, 21 May 2009, accessed 20 February 2024, https://www.hudson.org/national-security-defense/hezbollah-a-state-within-a-state.
17 Majorie Miller, John Daniszewski and Tracy Wilkinson, 'Israel Leaves South Lebanon After 22 Years', *Los Angeles Times*, 24 May 2000, accessed 10 February 2024, https://www.latimes.com/archives/la-xpm-2000-may-24-mn-33497-story.html.
18 'Nasrallah: Arab nation must free Jerusalem from Israeli occupation', *Ibcgrouptv*, 4 March 2012, accessed 1- March 2024, https://lbcgroup.tv/news/d/lebanon-news/22736/nasrallah-arab-nation-must-free-jerusalem-from-isr/en.
19 'Nasrallah wins the war', *The Economist*, 17 August 2006, https://www.economist.com/leaders/2006/08/17/nasrallah-wins-the-war.
20 Ziad Abu-Amr, 'Hamas: A Historical and Political Background', *Journal of Palestine Studies*, 22(4), (Summer 1993), 5–15.
21 Olmo Gölz, '"Khomeini"s Face is in the Moon: Limitations of Sacredness and the Origins of Sovereignty,"' January 2017, accessed 25 August 2024, https://www.researchgate.net/publication/334836849_Khomeini's_Face_is_in_the_Moon_Limitations_of_Sacredness_and_the_Origins_of_Sovereignty.
22 'Iran's nNetworks of Influence in the Middle East', IISS, November 2019, 20 accessed February 20, 2024, https://www.iiss.org/en/publications/strategic-dossiers/iran-dossier/.
23 Ziad Abu-Amr, 'Hamas: A Historical and Political Background', *Journal of Palestine Studies*, 22(4), (Summer 1993), 5–15.
24 Muhammad Maqdsi, 'Charter of the Islamic Resistance Movement (Hamas) of Palestine', *Journal of Palestine Studies*, 22(4), (Summer 1993): 122–134.

25 Mehdi Hasan & Dina Sayedahmed, 'Blowback: How Israel went from helping create Hamas to bombing it', *The Intercept*, 19 February 2018, accessed 20 January 2024, https://theintercept.com/2018/02/19/hamas-israel-palestine-conflict/. Also see, Andrew Higgins, 'How Israel Helped to Spawn Hamas', *The Wall Street Journal*, 324 January 2009, accessed 20 January 2024, https://www.wsj.com/articles/SB123275572295011847.

26 'The Covenant of the Islamic Resistance Movement,' Yale Law School, Lillian Goldman Law Library, 18 August 1988, accessed 19 January 2024, https://avalon.law.yale.edu/20th_century/hamas.asp.

27 Quoted in Baraa Nizar Rayan, 'Palestine and the illusion of Islamization of the conflict', (translated from Arabic), *Al Jazeera*, 18 December 2017, accessed 2 February 2024, https://www.aljazeera.net/amp/blogs/2017/12/18/%D9%81%D9%84%D8%B3%D8%B7%D9%8A%D9%86-%D9%88%D9%88%D9%87%D9%85-%D8%A3%D8%B3%D9%84%D9%85%D8%A9-%D8%A7%D9%84%D8%B5%D8%B1%D8%A7%D8%B9.

28 Serge Schmemann, 'Sheik Vows to Continue the Hamas Holy War Against Israel', *The New York Times*, 23 October 1997, accessed 20 February 2014, https://www.nytimes.com/1997/10/23/world/sheik-vows-to-continue-the-hamas-holy-war-against-israel.html.

29 Quoted in 'Hamas Ceasefire Proposal: Peace or Pause?', *The Washington Institute for Near East Policy*, 16 March 2004, accessed 10 February 2024, https://www.washingtoninstitute.org/policy-analysis/hamas-ceasefire-proposal-peace-or-pause.

30 James Bennet, 'Leader of Hamas killed by missile in Israeli strike', *The New York Times*, 22 March 2004, accessed 10 March 2024, https://www.nytimes.com/2004/03/22/world/leader-of-hamas-killed-by-missile-in-israeli-strike.html.

31 Steven Erlanger and Greg Myre, 'Hamas wins clear majority', *The New York Times*, 26 January 2006, accessed 20 January 2024, https://www.nytimes.com/2006/01/26/world/africa/26iht-web.0126vote.html.

32 'Hamas in 2017: The document in full', *Middle East Eye*, 2 May 2017, accessed 11 February 2024, https://www.middleeasteye.net/news/hamas-2017-document-full.
33 'Soleimani, "living martyr" who rose above Iran rifts', *Agence France-Presse*, 7 January 2020, accessed 10 January 2024, https://www.rfi.fr/en/wires/20200107-soleimani-living-martyr-who-rose-above-iran-rifts.
34 Tim Arango, Ronen Bergman and Ben Hubbard, 'Qassim Suleimani, master of Iran's intrigue, built a shiite axis of power in Mideast', *The New York Times*, 3 January 2020, accessed 5 January 2024, https://www.nytimes.com/2020/01/03/obituaries/qassem-soleimani-dead.html.
35 Stanly Johny, 'The importance of Qasem Soleimani', *The Hindu*, 3 January 2020, accessed 5 January 2024, https://www.thehindu.com/news/international/analysis-the-importance-of-qasem-soleimani/article61649189.ece#:~:text=Soleimani%20was%20rewarded%20for%20his,faced%20in%20a%20hostile%20region.
36 Dexter Filkins, 'The shadow commander', *The New Yorker*, 23 September 2013, accessed 10 March 2024, https://www.newyorker.com/magazine/2013/09/30/the-shadow-commander.
37 'Iran's Soleimani claims he and Nasrallah barely escaped Israeli air raid in 2006', *Times of Israel*, 1 October 2019, accessed 28 February 2024, https://www.timesofisrael.com/irans-soleimani-claims-israeli-uav-targeted-him-nasrallah-mughniyeh-in-2006/#:~:text=Late%20one%20night%2C%20Soleimani%20said,two%20Israeli%20bombardments%20hit%20nearby.
38 'Palestinians in Gaza mourn Iran's Soleimani', *Reuters*, 4 January 2020, accessed 10 January 2024, https://www.reuters.com/article/idUSKBN1Z30E6/.
39 Arash Azizi, 'Can Qasem Soleimani's young daughter continue his path?', *Atlantic Council*, 14 April 2020, accessed 15 February 2024, https://www.atlanticcouncil.org/blogs/iransource/can-qasem-soleimanis-young-daughter-continue-his-path/.

5. The Partisan Superpower

1. Ben Quinn, 'UK will consider recognising Palestinian state, says David Cameron', *The Guardian*, 30 January 2024, accessed 20 March 2024, https://www.theguardian.com/world/2024/jan/30/uk-will-consider-recognising-palestinian-state-says-david-cameron#:~:text=UK%20will%20consider%20recognising%20Palestinian%20state%2C%20says%20David%20Cameron,-This%20article%20is&text=Britain%20will%20consider%20recognising%20a,%2C%20David%20Cameron%2C%20has%20said.
2. Andrew McDonald, 'No change in UK policy on recognizing Palestinian state, Sunak insists', *Politico*, 5 February 2024, accessed 11 March 2024, https://www.politico.eu/article/no-change-uk-policy-recognize-palestine-state-rishi-sunak-israel-war/.
3. Sam Sokol, 'Knesset votes resoundingly against unilateral Palestinian state recognition', *Times of Israel*, 22 February 2024, accessed 10 March 2024, https://www.timesofisrael.com/knesset-votes-resoundingly-against-unilateral-palestinian-state-recognition/#:~:text=The%20Knesset%20voted%20on%20Wednesday,to%20the%20decades%2Dlong%20conflict.
4. Selig Adler, 'The Palestine Question in the Wilson era', *Jewish Social Studies*, 10 no. 4 (October 1948): 303–334.
5. *Ibid.*
6. 'U.S.-Israel relations: Roots of the U.S.-Israel relationship', *Jewish Virtual Library*, accessed 14 March 2024, https://www.jewishvirtuallibrary.org/roots-of-the-u-s-israel-relationship.
7. Khaled Elgindy, 'The 1922 US Congressional debate on the Balfour declaration', *Journal of Palestine Studies*, 47 no. 1 (Autumn 2017), 98-106.
8. In 1947, Ralph Bunche travelled to Palestine and met Zionist leaders, including Menachem Begin, the future Prime Minister, whose Irgun underground was considered a terrorist organization. Bunche told Begin, 'I can understand you. I am also a member of a persecuted minority.' Richard Crossman of Britain asked Bunche if his exposure to the Jews had made him anti-Semitic 'yet'. Bunche replied: 'That

would be impossible ... I know the flavour of racial prejudice and racial persecution. A wise Negro can never be an anti-Semite.' Cited in 'U.S.-Israel relations: Roots of the U.S.-Israel relationship', *Jewish Virtual Library*, accessed 10 March 2024, https://www.jewishvirtuallibrary.org/roots-of-the-u-s-israel-relationship.

9   'Eliahu Epstein to Harry S. Truman with attachments re: recognition of Israel, May 14, 1948', *National Archives: Harry S. Truman Library*, 15 accessed March 2024, https://www.trumanlibrary.gov/library/research-files/eliahu-epstein-harry-s-truman-attatchments-re-recognition-israel.

10 'Press release announcing U.S. recognition of Israel (1948)', *National Archives: Milestone Documents*, accessed 15 March 2024, https://archives.gov/milestone-documents/press-release-announcing-us-recognition-of-israel.

11 'The Suez Crisis, 1956, Office of the historian', *US Department of State*, accessed 12 March 2024, https://history.state.gov/milestones/1953-1960/suez#:~:text=On%20July%2026%2C%201956%2C%20Egyptian,since%20its%20construction%20in%201869.

12 Avi Shlaim, 'The protocol of Sèvres,1956: Anatomy of a War Plot', *International Affairs*, 73 no. 3 (1997), 509–530.

13 *Ibid*.

14 Avi Shlaim, *The Iron Wall: Israel and the Arab World* (London: Penguin Books, 2014), 191–192.

15 O.M. Smolansky, 'Moscow and the Suez crisis, 1956: A Reappraisal', *Political Science Quarterly*, 80 no. 4 (December 1965), 581–605.

16 'Conversation with Israel Foreign Minister Meir', *Office of the Historian, US Department of State*, 27 December 1962, accessed 20 March 2024, https://history.state.gov/historicaldocuments/frus1961-63v18/d121.

17 Abraham Rabinovich, 'Moshé Dayan's Yom Kippur War', *The Jerusalem Post*, 6 October 2013, accessed 10 March 2024, https://www.jpost.com/opinion/op-ed-contributors/moshe-dayans-yom-kippur-war-328029.

18 On 15 March 1976, CIA officials confirmed, during a non-classified briefing, what was until then remained an open secret. 'Israel is estimated to have 10 to 20 nuclear weapons ready and available for use,' the officials said. Arthur Kranish, 'CIA: Israel has 10-20 A-weapons', *The Washington Post*, 15 March 1976, accessed 10 March 2024, https://www.cia.gov/readingroom/docs/CIA-RDP88-01315R000300100014-6.pdf.
19 Seymour Hersh, *The Samson Option: Israel's Nuclear Arsenal and American Foreign Policy* (New York: Random House, 1991), 225.
20 'Foreign Relations of the United States, Diplomatic Papers, Volume 25, United States Department of State', *United States Government Printing Office*, Washington, 2011, 112.
21 'Memorandum of Conversation, Foreign Relations of the United States, 1969-1979, Volume XXV, Arab Israeli Crisis and war, 1973', *Office of the Historian, US Department of State*, 10 October 1973, accessed 11 March 2014, https://history.state.gov/historicaldocuments/frus1969-76v25/d143.
22 Walter J. Boyne, 'Nickel Grass', *Airforce-Magazine*, December 1998, accessed archived link 18 March 2024, https://web.archive.org/web/20120331195111/http://www.airforce-magazine.com/MagazineArchive/Pages/1998/December%201998/1298nickel.aspx.
23 'U.S. Foreign Aid to Israel', *Congressional Research Service*, 1 March 2023, 20 accessed March 2024, https://sgp.fas.org/crs/mideast/RL33222.pdf.
24 'House okays $17 billion in military aid for Israel under major spending package', *Times of Israel*, 20 April 2024, accessed 28 April 2024, https://www.timesofisrael.com/house-approves-26-billion-in-aid-for-israel-and-gaza-under-major-spending-package/#:~:text=This%20included%20%2417%20billion%20in,billion%20would%20go%20to%20Gaza.
25 'US Relations With Israel: Fact sheet', *Office of the Spokesperson, US Department of State*, 30 January 2023, accessed 12 March 2024, https://www.state.gov/u-s-relations-with-israel-

2/#:~:text=ECONOMIC%20TIES,)%2C%20solidify%20 bilateral%20economic%20relations.
26. Pieter D. Wezeman, Alexandra Kuimova and Siemon T. Sezeman, 'Trends in International Arms Transfers, 2021', *Stockholm International Peace Research Institute*, March 2022, accessed 10 March 2024, https://www.sipri.org/sites/default/files/2022-03/fs_2203_at_2021.pdf.
27. The United States and its allies pulled back the MNF after they came under attacks by the Islamic Resistance (Hezbollah). See Chapter 4.
28. The Jerusalem Embassy Act of 1995 declares it to be US policy that: (1) Jerusalem remain an undivided city in which the rights of every ethnic religious group are protected; (2) Jerusalem be recognized as the capital of the State of Israel; and (3) the US Embassy in Israel be established in Jerusalem no later than 31 May 1999. 'S.1322 - Jerusalem Embassy Act of 1995, 104th Congress (1995-1996)', *Congress.gov*, accessed, 10 March 2024, https://www.congress.gov/bill/104th-congress/senate-bill/1322.
29. 'Statement by Former President Trump on Jerusalem, US Embassy in Israel', 7 December 2020, accessed 9 February 2024, https://il.usembassy.gov/statement-by-president-trump-on-jerusalem/.
30. 'The State of Israel took control of the Golan Heights in 1967 to safeguard its security from external threats. Today, aggressive acts by Iran and terrorist groups, including Hizballah, in southern Syria continue to make the Golan Heights a potential launching ground for attacks on Israel. Any possible future peace agreement in the region must account for Israel's need to protect itself from Syria and other regional threats. Based on these unique circumstances, it is therefore appropriate to recognize Israeli sovereignty over the Golan Heights,' stated the Trump White House. 'Proclamation on Recognizing the Golan Heights as Part of the State of Israel', *Trump White House Archives*, 25 March 2019, accessed 11 March 2024, https://trumpwhitehouse.archives.gov/presidential-actions/proclamation-recognizing-golan-heights-part-state-israel/.
31. White House Spokesperson Ari Fleischer said Ariel Sharon's comments were unacceptable. 'The president believes that these

remarks are unacceptable. Israel could have no better or stronger friend that the United States and no better friend that President Bush,' he said. Suzanne Goldenberg and Julian Borger, 'Furious Bush hits back at Sharon', *The Guardian*, 6 October 2022, accessed 2 March 2024, https://www.theguardian.com/world/2001/oct/06/israel.

32 Daniel Dombey, 'Leading Republican lambasts Bush', *Financial Times*, 14 October 2004, accessed 8 March 2024, https://www.ft.com/content/7f1575fa-1d62-11d9-abbf-00000e2511c8.

33 John Mearsheimer: 'Israel is choosing "apartheid" or "ethnic cleansing"', *The Bottom Line*, YouTube, 16 December 2023, accessed 15 January 2024, https://www.youtube.com/watch?v=rc0mws9NT-0.

34 Walter Russel Mead, *The Arc of Covenant: The United States, Israel and the Fate of the Jewish People* (New York: Knopf, 2022), Kindle.

35 'History of the US-Israel relationship with Walter Russell Mead', *Middle East Forum*, YouTube, 22 October 2022, accessed 19 March 2024, https://www.youtube.com/watch?v=haHqedmZOdE.

36 John Mearsheimer and Stephen Walt, 'The Israel Lobby', *London Review of Books*, 28 no. 6 (23 March 2006), accessed 20 March 2024, https://www.lrb.co.uk/the-paper/v28/n06/john-mearsheimer/the-israel-lobby; also see John Mearsheimer and Stephen Walt, *The Israel Lobby and US Foreign Policy* (New York: Penguin Books, 2008).

37 'Pro-Israel Top Contributors,' *Open Secrets*, accessed 1 March 2024, https://www.opensecrets.org/industries/contrib?cycle=2020&ind=Q05.

38 'Let's Talk About: Israel and Palestine: Understanding the history and different facets of the conflict', *Newslaundry*, 28 February 2024, accessed 15 March 2024, https://www.newslaundry.com/2024/02/28/lets-talk-about-israel-and-palestine?login_success=true.

6. A Troubled Brotherhood

1 'Jordan is home to the world's largest Palestinian diaspora, communities forged by decades of war', *The New York Times*, 20 December 2023, accessed on 13 April 2024, https://www.nytimes.

com/interactive/2023/12/20/magazine/jordan-palestinian-refugees.html.
2   Bruce Masters, *The Arabs of the Ottoman Empire, 1516–1918: A Social and Cultural History* (Cambridge: Cambridge University Press, 2013), 177-182.
3   Eliezer Tauber, *The Formation of Modern Iraq and Syria*, (London: Routledge, 1994), 30.
4   Edward W. Said and Christopher Hitchens, *Blaming the Victims: Spurious Scholarship and the Palestinian Question* (London: Verso, 2001), 197.
5   Edward Said and Christopher Hitchens, *Blaming the Victims* 198.
6   Check Balfour Declaration, Chapter 1.
7   Check Sykes-Picot Agreement, Chapter 1.
8   George Antonius (1938) The Arab Awakening. The Story of The Arab National Movement (London: Hamish Hamilton, 1945), 316.
9   Edward Said and Christopher Hitchens, *Blaming the Victims*, 198.
10 'Further, His Majesty's Government have been entrusted with the Mandate for "Palestine". If they wish to assert their claim to Transjordan and to avoid raising with other Powers the legal status of that area, they can only do so by proceeding upon the assumption that Transjordan forms part of the area covered by the Palestine Mandate. [Memorandum drawn up in London by Middle East Department Prior to Palestine Conference]. Report on Middle East Conference held in Cairo and Jerusalem, The National Archives, June 1921, accessed 12 June 2024, https://discovery.nationalarchives.gov.uk/details/r/C8916116.
11 Kamal S. Salibi, *The Modern History of Jordan* (London: I B Tauris, 1998), 93.
12 For the full text of the memorandum, see 'Transjordan Memorandum, *The Economic Cooperation Foundation*, 9 September 1922, accessed 12 June 2024, https://ecf.org.il/issues/issue/233.
13 Edward Said and Christopher Hitchens, *Blaming the Victims*, 198.
14 T.E. Lawrence, *Seven Pillars of Wisdom* (London: Penguin Classics, 2000), 276.

15 Mary Christina Wilson, *King Abdullah, Britain and the Making of Jordan* (Cambridge: Cambridge University Press, 1990), 120.

16 The term 'West Bank' was first used by the British Foreign Office and by the Jordanians towards the second half of 1949. See Ilan Pappe, *Britain and the Arab-Israeli Conflict, 1948-51* (London: Palgrave Macmillan, 1988), 77.

17 'Abdullah Proclaims Himself "King of Palestine" in "Coronation" Ceremony in Jerusalem,' *Jewish Telegraphic Agency*, 16 November 1948, accessed 12 March 2024, https://www.jta.org/archive/abdullah-proclaims-himself-king-of-palestine-in-coronation-ceremony-in-jerusalem.

18 Six resolutions were proposed at the Jericho Conference but four were adopted: 1. Palestine Arabs desire unity between Transjordan and Arab Palestine and therefore make known their wish that Arab Palestine be annexed immediately to Transjordan. They also recognise Abdullah as their King and request him proclaim himself King of new territory; 2. Palestine Arabs express gratitude to Arab states for their efforts in behalf of liberation of Palestine; 3. Expression of thanks to Arab states for their generous assistance and support to Palestine Arab refugees; and 4. Resolve that purport of first resolution be conveyed to King at once. 'The Jericho Conference on Palestine–Jordan Unity', *Jewish Virtual Library*, accessed 10 June 2024, https://www.jewishvirtuallibrary.org/the-jericho-conference-on-palestine-jordan-unity. Also see, 'Foreign relations of the United States, 1948. The Near East, South Asia, and Africa, Vol V, Part 2,' *Office of the Historian*, 4 December 1948, accessed 17 June 2024, https://history.state.gov/historicaldocuments/frus1948v05p2/d809.

19 'Foreign Relations of the United States, The Near East, South Asia and Africa, Volume V,' *Office of the Historian*, 13 April 1950, accessed 12 June 2024, https://history.state.gov/historicaldocuments/frus1950v05/pg_856/.

20 Yehuda Z. Blum, *Will "Justice" Bring Peace?: International Law - Selected Articles and Legal Opinions*, (Leiden: Martinus Nijhoff, 2016), 230–231.

21 In a meeting in Cairo, the Egyptian Ambassador to the U.S. told the American Secretary of State on May 23, 1950, "With regard to Palestine, [Foreign Minister] Salaheddin Bey observed that all the Arab states except Jordan had recognised the All-Palestine government headed by the great leader, Ahmed Hilmy Pasha. Even though present circumstances prevent that government from exercising authority in Palestine, the object of its recognition by Egypt and the Arab states is to place on record their insistence on the Arab character of Palestine until such time as a final Palestinian settlement is made on the basis of right and justice." See, "Foreign Relations of the United States, 1950, Near East, South Asia, and Africa, Volume V", *Office of the Historian*, May 23, 1950, accessed June 14, 2024, https://history.state.gov/historicaldocuments/frus1950v05/d477.

22 Yitzhak Ben Gad, *Politics, Lies, and Videotape: 3,000 Questions and Answers on the Mideast Crisis* (New York: Sapolsky Publishers, 1991), 113.

23 All quotes in the paragraph and the one below are from, Michael Sharnoff, 'Does Jordan Want the West Bank?', *Middle East Quarterly*, 27(4), Fall 2020, 1–11.

24 Avi Shlaim, *Lion of Jordan: The Life of King Hussein in War and Peace* (New York: Vintage Books, 2008), 318.

25 Charles River, *Black September: The History and Legacy of the Conflict Between the Palestinians and Jordan in 1970*, (California: CreateSpace Independent Publishing, 2017), 66.

26 Avi Shlaim, *Lion of Jordan: The Life of King Hussein in War and Peace* (New York: Vintage Books, 2008), 312–321.

27 Conservative estimates put Palestinian losses at 2,000. Judith Miller, 'Yasir Arafat, Palestinian Leader and Mideast Provocateur, Is Dead at 75,' *The New York Times*, 12 November 2014, accessed 24 June 2024, https://www.nytimes.com/2004/11/12/obituaries/world/yasir-arafat-palestinian-leader-and-mideast-provocateur-is.html?pagewanted=3.

28 Some Palestinians radicalized by the Jordanian military operation formed a militant group called the Black September Organisation

(BSO). BSO militants were responsible for the assassination of Jordanian Prime Minister Wasfi Tal, and the Munich massacre, in which eleven Israeli athletes and officials were kidnapped and killed. John B. Wolf, 'Black September: Militant Palestinianism', *Current History*, 64(377), January 1973, 5–8.
29 Avi Shlaim, *Lion of Jordan*, 43.
30 Michael Sharnoff, 'Does Jordan Want the West Bank?', 1–11.
31 For the full text of the resolution, see, 'PLO sole legitimate representative of the Palestinian people–resolution Seventh Arab League Summit Conference,' *United Nations*, 28 October 1974, accessed on 8 June 2014, https://www.un.org/unispal/document/auto-insert-194621/.
32 'Twelfth Arab Summit Conference/Fez Declaration,' *United Nations*, 15 December 1982, accessed 12 June 2024, https://www.un.org/unispal/document/auto-insert-176666/.
33 'King Hussein bin Talal, Address to the Nation,' *King Hussein*, 31 July 1988, accessed 10 June 2024, http://www.kinghussein.gov.jo/88_july31.html. Also see John Kifner, 'Hussein Surrenders Claims on West Bank to the PLO; US Peace Plan in Jeopardy,' *The New York Times*, 1 August 1988, accessed 2 July 2024, https://www.nytimes.com/1988/08/01/world/hussein-surrenders-claims-west-bank-plo-us-peace-plan-jeopardy-internal-tensions.html.
34 While the Resolution 242 calls for Israel's withdrawal from all territories it captured from its neighbours in 1967, Resolution 338, passed in the aftermath of the 1973 Yom Kippur War, called for a ceasefire between all parties and the implementation of Resolution 242. See, 'UN Security Council Resolution 242', 22 November 1967, accessed June 10, 2024, https://www.securitycouncilreport.org/un-documents/document/ip-s-res-242.php; 'UN Security Council Resolution 338,' 10 October 1973, accessed 10 June 2024, https://peacemaker.un.org/middleeast-resolution338.
35 Shimon Peres, *Battling for Peace: A Memoir* (London: Orion Books, 1995), 423.

36 Clyde Haberman, "Palestinian Says His Delegation Will Assert P.L.O. Ties at Talks," *The New York Times*, October 22, 1991, accessed June 9, 2024, https://www.nytimes.com/1991/10/22/world/palestinian-says-his-delegation-will-assert-plo-ties-at-talks.html.

37 Douglas Jehl, "Mideast Accord: Jordan and Israel join in pact aimed at broad Mideast Peace," *The New York Times*, July 26, 1994, accessed June 20, 2014, https://www.nytimes.com/1994/07/26/world/mideast-accord-overview-jordan-israel-join-pact-aimed-broad-mideast-peace.html; For the full text of the Declaration, see: "The Washington Declaration: Israel-Jordan-The United States," *Yale Law School, Lillian Goldman Law Library*, July 25, 1994, accessed June 20, 2024, https://avalon.law.yale.edu/20th_century/pal06.asp.

38 For the full text of the Jordan-Israel treaty, see, 'Treaty of Peace: Between The Hashemite Kingdom of Jordan And The State of Israel', *King Hussein*, 26 October 1994, accessed 23 June 2024, http://www.kinghussein.gov.jo/peacetreaty.html.

39 Clyde Haberman, 'Israel and Jordan Sign a Peace Accord,' *The New York Times*, 27 October 1994, accessed 17 June 2024, https://www.nytimes.com/1994/10/27/world/the-jordan-israel-accord-the-overview-israel-and-jordan-sign-a-peace-accord.html.

40 *Ibid.*

41 Raphel Ahren and Adam Rasgon, 'Colder than ever: 25 years on, Israel and Jordan ignore peace treaty anniversary,' *Times of Israel*, 25 October 2019, accessed 3 June 2024, https://www.timesofisrael.com/colder-than-ever-25-years-on-israel-and-jordan-ignore-peace-treaty-anniversary/.

42 Nicola Lombardozzi, 'Interview with His Majesty King Abdullah II,' *La Repubblica*, 19 October 2009, accessed 12 June 2024, https://kingabdullah.jo/en/interviews/interview-his-majesty-king-abdullah-ii-34.

43 Joel Greenberg, 'Sharon Touches a Nerve, and Jerusalem Explodes,' *The New York Times*, 29 September 2000, accessed 20 June 2024, https://www.nytimes.com/2000/09/29/world/sharon-touches-a-nerve-and-jerusalem-explodes.html.

44 For the full text of the resolution, see, 'Khartoum Resolution,' *United Nations*, 1 September 1967, accessed 14 June 2024, https://www.un.org/unispal/document/auto-insert-193039/#:~:text=LAS%20Khartoum%20Resolution%2C%201%20September%201967&text=2., 3.

45 The United States is Jordan's single largest provider of bilateral assistance. The US Government has provided Jordan with more than $17.3 billion in foreign aid since 1946. In 2021, the US provided more than $1.65 billion, including over $1.197 billion appropriated by the US Congress to Jordan through USAID in the 2021 fiscal year budget, and $425 million State Department Foreign Military Financing funds. 'U.S. Relations With Jordan,' *US Department of State*, 27 April 2022, accessed 12 June 2024, https://www.state.gov/u-s-relations-with-jordan/.

46 Felicia Schwartz and Summer Said, 'Israel's Netanyahu, Saudi Crown Prince Hold First Known Meeting,' *The Wall Street Journal*, 23 November 2024, accessed 16 June 2024, https://www.wsj.com/articles/israels-netanyahu-meets-saudi-crown-prince-hebrew-media-says-11606120497.

47 Nadeen Ebrahim, 'Saudi crown prince says normalization deal with Israel gets 'closer' every day', *CNN*, 21 September 2023, accessed 7 September 2024, https://www.cnn.com/2023/09/21/middleeast/saudi-arabia-mbs-interview-fox-intl/index.html.

7. 7 October 2023

1 Kevin Sieff, 'A kidnapped Israeli activist and two sons grappling with a war in her name,' *The Washington Post*, November 7, 2023, accessed June 20, 2024, https://www.washingtonpost.com/world/2023/11/07/israel-war-peace-activist-sons/.

2 David Sheen and Raphael Ahren, 'The Year's 10 Most Influential Anglo Immigrants,' *Haaretz*, 28 September 2011, accessed 22 June 2024, https://www.haaretz.com/2011-09-28/ty-article/the-years-10-most-influential-anglo-immigrants/0000017f-dbb9-d3a5-af7f-fbbf25310000.

3 'Israeli survivors recount terror at music festival, where Hamas militants killed at least 260,' *Associated Press*, 10 October 2023, accessed 20 June 2024, https://apnews.com/article/israel-palestinians-gaza-hamas-music-festival-6a55aae2375944f10ecc4c52d05f2ffe.
4 Emmanuel Fabian and Gianluca Pacchlian, 'IDF estimates 3,000 Hamas terrorists invaded Israel in Oct. 7 onslaught,' *The Times of Israel*, 1 November 2023, accessed 2 June 2024, https://www.timesofisrael.com/idf-estimates-3000-hamas-terrorists-invaded-israel-in-oct-7-onslaught/.
5 "Today, the People Claim their Revolution": This is What Al-Qassam Commander Said in His Speech,' *Palestine Chronicle*, 7 October 2023, accessed 10 June 2024, https://www.palestinechronicle.com/today-the-people-claim-their-revolution-this-is-what-al-qassam-commander-said-in-his-speech/.
6 Sudarsan Raghavan, 'Mohammed Deif, the shadowy figure who heads Hamas's military wing,' *The Washington Post*, 2 August 2014, accessed 13 June 2024, https://www.washingtonpost.com/world/middle_east/mohammed-deif-the-shadowy-figure-who-heads-hamass-military-wing/2014/08/02/ed68c46e-1a85-11e4-85b6-c1451e622637_story.html.
7 'Today, the People Claim their Revolution...,' *Palestine Chronicle*, 7 October 2023, accessed on 8 September 2024, https://www.palestinechronicle.com/today-the-people-claim-their-revolution-this-is-what-al-qassam-commander-said-in-his-speech/.
8 'Netanyahu, Gallant say all Hamas members, even outside Gaza, are 'dead men',' *Times of Israel*, 18 November 2023, accessed 19 June 2024, https://www.timesofisrael.com/liveblog_entry/netanyahu-gallant-say-all-hamas-members-even-outside-gaza-are-dead-men/.
9 'A brief history of Gaza's 75 years of woe,' *Reuters*, 11 October 2023, accessed 12 June 2024, https://www.reuters.com/world/middle-east/brief-history-gazas-75-years-woe-2023-10-10/.
10 'Gaza: Israel's "Open-Air Prison" at 15,' *Human Rights Watch*, 14 June 2022, accessed 10 June 2024, https://www.hrw.org/news/2022/06/14/gaza-israels-open-air-prison-15.

11 'Gaza unemployment since start of Israel's war soars to nearly 80 per cent: ILO,' *Al Jazeera*, 7 June 2024, accessed 13 June 2024, https://www.aljazeera.com/economy/2024/6/7/gaza-unemployment-since-start-of-israels-war-soars-to-nearly-80-ilo#:~:text=Unemployment%20in%20the%20Gaza%20Strip,the%20United%20Nations%20labour%20agency.

12 Stanly Johny, 'On Israel's border with Gaza, an uneasy calm amid worries of the next spark,' *The Hindu*, 9 November 2022, accessed 20 June 2024, https://www.thehindu.com/news/international/on-israels-border-with-gaza-an-uneasy-calm-amid-worries-of-the-next-spark/article66155114.ece.

13 David S. CloudFollow, Anat PeledFollow and Dov Lieber, 'Hamas Militants Had Detailed Maps of Israeli Towns, Military Bases and Infiltration Routes,' *The Wall Street Journal*, 12 October 2023, accessed 20 June 2024, https://www.wsj.com/world/middle-east/hamas-militants-had-detailed-maps-of-israeli-towns-military-bases-and-infiltration-routes-7fa62b05.

14 Ronen Bergman and Adam Goldman, 'Israel Knew Hamas's Attack Plan More Than a Year Ago,' *The New York Times*, 30 November 2023, accessed 25 June 2024, https://www.nytimes.com/2023/11/30/world/middleeast/israel-hamas-attack-intelligence.html?campaign_id=307&emc=edit_igwb_20231201&instance_id=109019&nl=israel-hamas-war-briefing&regi_id=64680187&segment_id=151409&te=1&user_id=1e9c9142246ac5796beabc2f49486341.

15 'Israel Officially Declares War on Hamas After Surprise Attack,' *Voice of America*, 8 October 2023, accessed 20 June 2024, https://www.voanews.com/a/israel-officially-declares-war-on-hamas-after-surprise-attack-/7301836.html.

16 Matt Spetalnick, Jeff Mason, Steve Holland and Patricia Zengerle, "'I am a Zionist': How Joe Biden's lifelong bond with Israel shapes war policy,' *Reuters*, 21 October 2023, accessed 12 June 2024, https://www.reuters.com/world/us/i-am-zionist-how-joe-bidens-lifelong-bond-with-israel-shapes-war-policy-2023-10-21/.

17 'Israel orders 1.1 million northern Gaza residents to evacuate south within 24 hours,' *Le Monde*, 13 October 2023, accessed 16 June 2024,

https://www.lemonde.fr/en/international/article/2023/10/13/israel-hamas-war-death-toll-in-gaza-climbs-to-1-537-with-over-423-000-people-displaced_6168911_4.html.
18 'Israel warns Hezbollah war would invite destruction,' *Reuters*, 3 October 2008, accessed 19 June 2024, https://www.reuters.com/article/economy/israel-warns-hezbollah-war-would-invite-destruction-idUSL3251393/.
19 'The Likud Party's 1977 manifesto says 'between the Sea and the Jordan there will only be Israeli sovereignty. The Right of the Jewish People to the Land of Israel (Eretz Israel),' *Jewish Virtual Library*, accessed 10 June 2024, https://www.jewishvirtuallibrary.org/original-party-platform-of-the-likud-party.
20 'Lebanon front is 'pressuring Israel', Hezbollah chief Nasrallah says,' *Al Jazeera*, 31 May 2024, accessed 20 June 2014, https://www.aljazeera.com/news/2024/5/31/lebanon-front-is-pressuring-israel-hezbollah-chief-nasrallah-says

8. The View from India

1 'Transcript of Weekly Media Briefing by the Official Spokesperson,' *Ministry of External Affairs, Government of India*, 19 October 2023, accessed 12 July 2024, https://www.mea.gov.in/media-briefings.htm?dtl/37199/Transcript_of_Weekly_Media_Briefing_by_the_Official_Spokesperson_October_19_2023.
2 'Netanyahu: No Palestinian state on my watch,' *The Times of Israel*, March 15, 2015, accessed July 10, 2024, https://www.timesofisrael.com/netanyahu-no-palestinian-state-under-my-watch/.
3 Harriet Sherwood, 'Naftali Bennett interview: 'There won't be a Palestinian state within Israel',' *The Guardian*, 7 January 2013, https://www.theguardian.com/world/2013/jan/07/naftali-bennett-interview-jewish-home.
4 'Israel's Knesset votes to reject Palestinian statehood,' *Al Jazeera*, 18 July 2024, accessed 20 July 2024, https://www.aljazeera.com/news/2024/7/18/israels-knesset-votes-to-reject-palestinian-

statehood#:~:text=Israel's%20parliament%20has%20passed%20a, against%20it%20early%20on%20Thursday.
5 There are the thirteen countries that voted against the resolution: Afghanistan, India, Iran, Iraq, Lebanon, Pakistan, Saudi Arabia, Syria, Yemen, Greece, Turkey, Egypt and Cuba. 'Origins and Evolution of the Palestine Problem,' *United Nations*, accessed July 10, 2024, https://www.un.org/unispal/history2/origins-and-evolution-of-the-palestine-problem/.
6 Jawaharlal Nehru, *Eighteen Months In India 1936-1937* (Delhi: Kitabistan), 142.
7 M.K. Gandhi, 'The Jews In Palestine' (published in the *Harijan* on 26 November 1938), reproduced in *Countercurrents*, accessed July 10, 2024, https://www.countercurrents.org/pa-gandhi170903.htm.
8 'Speech of MOS(ST) on the occasion of 'International Day of Solidarity with the Palestinian People',' *Ministry of External Affairs, Government of India*, 2 December 2009, accessed 12 July 2024, https://www.mea.gov.in/Speeches-Statements.htm?dtl/1399/Speech_of_MOSST_on_the_occasion_of_International_Day_of_Solidarity_with_the_Palestinian_People.
9 'The Question of Palestine/Majority plan (Partition), Minority plan (Federal State), UN Special Committee on Palestine (UNSCOP) Report,' *The United Nations*, 1947, accessed 1 July 2024, https://www.un.org/unispal/document/auto-insert-179435/
10 'The Origins and Evolution of the Palestine Problem: Part II (1947-1977),' *United Nations*, accessed 10 July 2024, https://www.un.org/unispal/history2/origins-and-evolution-of-the-palestine-problem/part-ii-1947-1977/.
11 Mridula Mukherjee, 'Nehru's Word: Zionist aggression against Palestinians is wrong,' *National Herald*, 13 June 2021, accessed 7 September 2024, https://www.nationalheraldindia.com/india/nehrus-word-zionist-aggression-against-palestinians-is-wrong.
12 Sasmita Tripathy, 'India's Policy Towards Palestine: A Historical Perspective,' *The Indian Journal of Political Science*, 74(1) (January-March 2013), 159–172.

13 Pinak Ranjan Chakravarty, 'When Einstein tried to convince Nehru to support Israel... but failed,' *ORF*, 13 February 2017, accessed July 21, 2024, https://www.orfonline.org/research/30081.
14 Prithvi Ram Mudiam, *India and the Middle East* (London: British Academic Press, 1994), 20.
15 Swapna Kona Nayudu, 'Nehru's India & the Suez Canal Crisis of 1956,' *Centre for Advanced Study of India: University of Pennsylvania*, 7 November 2016, accessed 10 July 2024, https://casi.sas.upenn.edu/iit/swapnakonanayudu2016.
16 'Parliament Digital Library, General Discussion,' accessed 12 July 2024, https://eparlib.nic.in/bitstream/123456789/808936/1/pms_04_02_06-06-1967.pdf.
17 Krishan Gopal and Kokila Krishan Gopal, *West Asia and North Africa: A Documentary Study of Major Crises*. V.I Publications, (New Delhi, 1981), 153–154.
18 '4th Summit Conference of Heads of State or Government of the Non-Aligned Movement,' 5–9 September 1973, accessed 18 July 2024, http://cns.miis.edu/nam/documents/Official_Document/4th_Summit_FD_Algiers_Declaration_1973_Whole.pdf.
19 'India-Palestine Relations,' *Representative Office of India in Ramallah*, accessed July 24, 2024, https://roiramallah.gov.in/pages.php?id=32#:~:text=In%201974%2C%20India%20became%20the,to%20recognize%20the%20Palestinian%20State.
20 Nehru, *Eighteen Months in India*, 143.
21 Hasrh V. Pant. and Ambuj Sahu, 'Israel's Arms Sales to India: Bedrock of a Strategic Partnership,' *ORF Issue Brief*: 311, September 2019, accessed 3 July 2024, https://www.orfonline.org/wp-content/uploads/2019/09/ORF_Issue_Brief_311_India-Israel.pdf.
22 Gary Bass, *The Blood Telegram: Nixon, Kissinger and a Forgotten Genocide* (New York: Vintage, 2014), Kindle.
23 Pant and Sahu, *ORF Issue brief*.
24 'SIPRI Arms Transfers Database,' *SIPRI*, accessed 20 July 2024, https://www.sipri.org/databases/armstransfers; also see Sameer Patil, 'The deepening of India–Israel defence ties,' ORF, 7 June 2022.

https://www.orfonline.org/expert-speak/the-deepening-of-india-israel-defence-ties.

25 'India, Israel Bilateral Relations,' *Ministry of External Affairs, Government of India*, accessed 20 July 2024, https://www.mea.gov.in/Portal/ForeignRelation/EOI_TELAVIV_BILATERAL_BRIEF2.pdf.

26 Rajeswari Pillai Rajagopalan, 'A Second Quad in the Making in the Middle East?,' *ORF*, 1 June 2023, accessed 3 July 2024, https://www.orfonline.org/research/a-second-quad-in-the-making-in-the-middle-east.

27 The group has already announced to set up a hybrid renewable energy project in Gujarat. 'I2U2: India, Israel, United Arab Emirates, United States,' *the US Department of State*, accessed 6 July 2024, https://www.state.gov/i2u2/#:~:text=Clean%20Energy%3A%20The%20I2U2%20Group,feasibility%20study%20for%20the%20project.

28 Huma Siddiqui, 'World leaders launch India-Middle East-Europe Economic Corridor seen as counter to China's BRI,' *Financial Express*, 10 September 2023, accessed 12 July 2024, https://www.financialexpress.com/business/defence-world-leaders-launch-india-middle-east-europe-economic-corridor-seen-as-counter-to-chinas-bri-3238862/.

29 Speaking at a public event in Himachal Pradesh on October 18, 2016 Modi said, 'Our Army's valour is being discussed across the country these days. We used to hear earlier that Israel has done this. The nation has seen that the Indian Army is no less than anybody.' Stanly Johny, 'Myths about Israel's security model,' *The Hindu*, 21 October 2016, accessed 20 July 2024, https://www.thehindu.com/opinion/columns/Myths-about-Israel%E2%80%99s-security-model/article15629219.ece.

30 'So far as the Prime Minister is concerned, he will also be visiting [West Asia]. Israel will also be visited. No dates have been fixed. When we arrive at mutually convenient dates, that too will be finalised,' Sushma Swaraj told reporters in Delhi. P.R. Kumaraswamy, 'Modi's stand-alone visit to Israel?' *IDSA*, 2 January

2017, accessed 12 July 2024, https://idsa.in/idsacomments/modi-stand-alone-visit-to-israel_prkumaraswamy_020117.

31. All quotes are from this report by the author from Ramallah: Stanly Johny, 'Modi reiterates support for Palestine,' *The Hindu*, 10 February 2018, accessed 10 July 2024, https://www.thehindu.com/news/national/modi-reiterates-support-for-palestine/article61483932.ece.

32. 'Media statement by the President of India upon the conclusion of his state visit to Jordan, Palestine and Israel,' *Representative Office of India in Ramallah*, 16 October 2015, accessed 17 July 2024, https://roiramallah.gov.in/press.php?id=54.

33. 'International Day of Solidarity with Palestinian People, Special Bulletin,' *United Nations*, accessed 18 July 2024, https://www.un.org/unispal/document/auto-insert-202133/#:~:text=%E2%80%9CFor%20decades%2C%20we%20have%20expressed,capital%2C%20and%20to%20reach%20a.

34. 'PM's Press Statement during the State Visit of President of Palestine to India,' *PM India*, 16 May 2017, accessed 19 July 2024, https://www.pmindia.gov.in/en/news_updates/pms-press-statement-during-the-state-visit-of-president-of-palestine-to-india/.

35. Stanly Johny, 'Modi omits Jerusalem in Ramallah,' *The Hindu*, 11 February 2018, accessed 12 July 2024, https://www.thehindu.com/news/national/modi-omits-jerusalem-in-ramallah/article22716281.ece.

36. Suhasini Haidar, 'Why did India abstain from the call for truce?,' *The Hindu*, 5 November 2023, accessed 7 July 2024, https://www.thehindu.com/news/national/why-did-india-abstain-from-the-call-for-truce-explained/article67498732.ece.

37. For India's post-7 October voting record, see, Stanly Johny, 'Change and continuity in India's Palestine policy,' *The Hindu*, 2 March 2024, accessed 3 July 2024, https://www.thehindu.com/opinion/lead/change-and-continuity-in-indias-palestine-policy/article67904383.ece.

38. Sriram Lakshman, 'India wants Israel to be mindful of Gaza civilian deaths,' *The Hindu*, 18 February 2024, accessed 10 July 2024, https://

www.thehindu.com/news/national/israel-should-have-been-very-mindful-of-civilian-casualties-jaishankar-at-munich-security-conference-eam-also-calls-out-hamas-terror/article67857429.ece.

39 'Fact is that Palestinians have been denied of their homeland: EAM Jaishankar,' *The Times of India*, 28 March 2024, accessed 22 July 2024, https://timesofindia.indiatimes.com/india/fact-is-that-palestinians-have-been-denied-their-homeland-eam-jaishankar-on-israel-palestine-conflict/articleshow/108838069.cms.

Conclusion

1 In this 1972 interview with *The New York Times*, Golda Meir was asked about her 1969 comment that 'There was no such thing as Palestinians'. The Israeli Prime Minister said she was referring to Palestinian nation. 'A talk with Golda Meir', *The New York Times*, 27 August 1972, accessed 7 September 2024, https://www.nytimes.com/1972/08/27/archives/a-talk-with-golda-meir.html.

2 'Israel warns Hezbollah war would invite destruction,' *Reuters*, 3 October 2008, accessed 7 September 2024, https://www.reuters.com/article/economy/israel-warns-hezbollah-war-would-invite-destruction-idUSL3251393/.

3 Paul Blumenthal, 'Israeli President Suggests That Civilians In Gaza Are Legitimate Targets', *Huffpost*, 13 October 2023, accessed 7 September 2024, https://www.huffpost.com/entry/israel-gaza-isaac-herzog_n_65295ee8e4b03ea0c004e2a8.

4 Michael Bachner, 'Far-right minister says nuking Gaza an option, PM suspends him from cabinet meetings', *Times of Israel*, 5 November 2023, accessed 7 September 2024, https://www.timesofisrael.com/far-right-minister-says-nuking-gaza-an-option-pm-suspends-him-from-cabinet-meetings/.

5 Michael Hauser Tov, "We're Rolling Out Nakba 2023,' Israeli Minister Says on Northern Gaza Strip Evacuation', *Haaretz*, 12 November 2023, accessed 7 September 2024, https://www.haaretz.com/israel-news/2023-11-12/ty-article/israeli-security-cabinet-member-calls-

north-gaza-evacuation-nakba-2023/0000018b-c2be-dea2-a9bf-d2be7b670000.

6   Israel-Palestine war: Likud MP calls for Gaza to be 'erased from the face of the earth', *Middle East Eye*, 1 November 2023, accessed 7 September 2024, https://www.middleeasteye.net/news/israel-palestine-war-likud-mp-calls-gaza-erased-face-earth.

7   Israeli minister supports 'voluntary migration' of Palestinians in Gaza, *AlJazeera*, 14 November 2023, accessed 7 September 2024, https://www.aljazeera.com/news/2023/11/14/israeli-minister-supports-voluntary-migration-of-palestinians-in-gaza.

8   Rachel Fink, '"Wipe Out Gaza": State Prosecutor Advises Against Probing Israeli Megastar Eyal Golan Over Incitement', *Haaretz*, 19 August 2024, accessed 7 September 2024, https://www.haaretz.com/israel-news/2024-08-19/ty-article/.premium/state-prosecutor-mulls-probe-of-israeli-megastar-eyal-golan-for-calling-to-wipe-gaza-out/00000191-6a82-dda8-af9b-6fe244840000.

9   'South Africa includes Eyal Golan lyrics as evidence against Israel at ICJ', *i24News*, 4 January 2024, accessed 7 September 2024, https://www.i24news.tv/en/news/international/1704376559-south-africa-includes-eyal-golan-lyrics-as-evidence-against-israel-at-icj.

10 Alex Demas, 'Fact Checking Claims About Israeli Soldiers and the "Seed of Amalek"', *The Dispatch*, 14 December 2023, accessed 7 September 2024, https://thedispatch.com/article/fact-checking-claims-about-israeli-soldiers-and-the-seed-of-amalek/.

11 Jake Sullivan, the National Security Advisor in the Biden administration, said in September 2023, a week before the Hamas attack, that the Middle East was calmer because of the initiatives taken by the Biden administration. Gal Beckerman, 'The Middle East Region Is Quieter Today Than It Has Been in Two Decades', *The Atlantic*, 7 October 2023, accessed 7 September 2024, https://www.theatlantic.com/international/archive/2023/10/israel-war-middle-east-jake-sullivan/675580/.

12 Agence France-Presse, 'We will crush Hamas as world destroyed Daesh': Israel PM ahead of Blinken visit,' *India Today*, 12 October 2023, accessed 7 September 2024, https://www.indiatoday.in/

world/story/israel-hamas-war-benjamin-netanyahu-pledges-to-eliminate-hamas-palestinian-group-dead-man-2447781-2023-10-12.

13 'IDF spokesman says Hamas can't be destroyed, drawing retort from PM: "That's war's goal"', *Times of Israel*, 20 June 2024, accessed 7 September 2024, https://www.timesofisrael.com/idf-spokesman-says-hamas-cant-be-eliminated-will-remain-in-gaza-if-no-alternative/.

14 Nadeen Ebrahim, 'Saudi crown prince says normalization deal with Israel gets 'closer' every day', *CNN*, 21 September 2023, accessed 7 September 2024, https://www.cnn.com/2023/09/21/middleeast/saudi-arabia-mbs-interview-fox-intl/index.html.

15 'Saudi Arabia: no Israel ties without recognition of Palestinian state', *Reuters*, 7 February 2024, accessed 7 September 2024, https://www.reuters.com/world/middle-east/saudi-arabia-says-there-will-be-no-diplomatic-relations-with-israel-without-an-2024-02-07/.

16 Dale Gavlak, 'Saudi Arabia: Normalized Ties With Israel Come Only With Palestinian State', *Voice of America*, 11 January 2024, accessed 7 September 2024, https://www.voanews.com/a/saudi-arabia-normalized-ties-with-israel-come-only-with-palestinian-state/7436230.html.

17 'ICJ orders Israel to halt its offensive on Rafah, Gaza in new ruling', *AlJazeera*, 24 May 2024, accessed 7 September 2024, https://www.aljazeera.com/news/2024/5/24/icj-orders-israel-to-halt-its-offensive-on-rafah-gaza-in-new-ruling.

18 Jill Colvin, 'Trump says Israel has to get war in Gaza over "fast" and warns it is "losing the PR war"', *Associated Press*, 5 April 2024, accessed 7 November 2024, https://apnews.com/article/trump-biden-israel-pr-hugh-hewitt-21faee332d95fec99652c112fbdcd35d.

19 'Nearly 0.5m Israelis left Israel after 7 October', *Middle East Monitor*, 7 December 2023, accessed 7 September 2024, https://www.middleeastmonitor.com/20231207-report-nearly-0-5m-israelis-left-israel-after-7-october/.

20 Theodore Herzl, 'The Jewish State,' Jewish Virtual Library, accessed 7 September 2024, https://www.jewishvirtuallibrary.org/quot-the-jewish-state-quot-theodor-herzl.

About the Author

STANLY Johny is the International Affairs editor with *The Hindu*. He has a PhD in international studies from the Centre for West Asian Studies, JNU, New Delhi. He has been writing on geopolitics and Indian foreign policy for over a decade and has reported from different parts of the world. He is a visiting professor at KREA University, Sri City, Andhra Pradesh; an adjunct faculty member at Asian College of Journalism, Chennai; and a visiting fellow at Kerala University, Thiruvananthapuram. He is the author of *The ISIS Caliphate: From Syria to the Doorsteps of India* (2018), and co-author of *The Comrades and the Mullahs: China, Afghanistan and the New Asian Geopolitics* (2022).

HarperCollins *Publishers* India

At HarperCollins India, we believe in telling the best stories and finding the widest readership for our books in every format possible. We started publishing in 1992; a great deal has changed since then, but what has remained constant is the passion with which our authors write their books, the love with which readers receive them, and the sheer joy and excitement that we as publishers feel in being a part of the publishing process.

Over the years, we've had the pleasure of publishing some of the finest writing from the subcontinent and around the world, including several award-winning titles and some of the biggest bestsellers in India's publishing history. But nothing has meant more to us than the fact that millions of people have read the books we published, and that somewhere, a book of ours might have made a difference.

As we look to the future, we go back to that one word— a word which has been a driving force for us all these years.

Read.

Harper Collins | 4th | HARPER FICTION | HARPER NON-FICTION | HARPER BUSINESS | HCCB HARPERCOLLINS CHILDREN'S BOOKS

HARPER DESIGN | Harper Sport | HARPER PERENNIAL | HARPER VANTAGE | हार्पर हिन्दी